BUILDINGS & LANDSCAPES

JOURNAL OF THE VERNACULAR ARCHITECTURE FORUM

VOLUME 16 | NUMBER 1 | SPRING 2009

Buildings & Landscapes (ISSN 1936-0886) is published biannually in the fall and spring by the University of Minnesota Press, 111 Third Avenue South, Suite 290, Minneapolis, MN 55401-2520. http://www.upress.umn.edu

Published in cooperation with the Vernacular Architecture Forum (VAF). Members of the VAF receive the journal as one of the benefits of membership. For further information about membership contact Gabrielle Lanier, VAF Secretary, Vernacular Architecture Forum, P. O. Box 1511, Harrisonburg, VA, 22803-1511, or visit us on the Web at http://www.vernaculararchitectureforum.org.

Postmaster: Send address changes to *Buildings & Landscapes,* University of Minnesota Press, 111 Third Avenue South, Suite 290, Minneapolis, MN 55401-2520.

Manuscript submissions should be prepared to conform to the Chicago Manual of Style. Contributors agree that manuscripts submitted to *Buildings & Landscapes* will not be submitted for publication elsewhere while under review by the journal. Two hard copies of the manuscript and photocopied reproductions of the illustrations should be sent directly to each of the two editors. Please feel free to direct any inquiries to either editor via e-mail: Howard Davis, Professor of Architecture, School of Architecture and Allied Arts, 1206 University of Oregon, Eugene, OR 97403-1206, hdavis@uoregon.edu; Louis P. Nelson, Associate Professor of Architectural History, School of Architecture, Campbell Hall, University of Virginia, Charlottesville, VA 22904-4122, Lnelson@virginia.edu.

Address subscription orders, changes of address, and business correspondence (including requests for permission and advertising orders) to *Buildings & Landscapes,* University of Minnesota Press, 111 Third Avenue South, Suite 290, Minneapolis, MN 55401-2520.

Subscriptions: Regular rates, U.S.A.: individuals, 1 year, $30; libraries, 1 year, $65. Other countries add $5 for each year's subscription. Checks should be made payable to the University of Minnesota Press. For back issues contact the Vernacular Architecture Forum. *Buildings & Landscapes* is a benefit of membership in the Vernacular Architecture Forum.

Buildings & Landscapes is available online through *Project* MUSE, http://muse.jhu.edu, and JSTOR, http://jstor.org.

THE VERNACULAR ARCHITECTURE FORUM
is the premier organization in the United States studying ordinary buildings and landscapes. Established in 1979–80 to promote the appreciation of and scholarship on vernacular structures, it is an interdisciplinary organization composed of scholars from many fields, including history, architectural history, geography, anthropology, sociology, landscape history, preservation, and material culture studies. Since its founding, the VAF has played a major role in the academic study and preservation of common buildings. The VAF holds an annual meeting, publishes a newsletter and a journal, and maintains a Web site.

BUILDINGS & LANDSCAPES

JOURNAL OF THE VERNACULAR ARCHITECTURE FORUM
VOLUME 16 | NUMBER 1 | SPRING 2009

HOWARD DAVIS AND LOUIS P. NELSON

Editors' Introduction

Welcome to the first of the biannual editions of *Buildings & Landscapes*. With this edition, we begin to pick up the pace of publication, doubling the number of articles that will appear in print each year. The Vernacular Architecture Forum has long been committed to the publication of excellent scholarship in the study of everyday, ordinary, and vernacular architecture, and with biannual editions we will do so with even greater frequency. We are encouraged by the positive feedback we continue to receive from readers about the material in the new journal, and we hope that more articles each year will augment conversation and debate about the significance of recording, preserving, and interpreting vernacular architecture.

We open this volume with a *Viewpoint* essay that offers a new perspective on an icon of American vernacular studies: the balloon frame. Iain Bruce joins his voice to the many who have complicated Sigfried Gideon's attribution of the balloon frame to George Snow, or any single author for that matter. But Bruce does so in an entirely new way: by finding evidence for balloon frame technologies in Scotland. His viewpoint on this historically American debate is international. In many ways, he parallels the arguments of Fred Peterson, whose excellent essay on the balloon frame in *Perspectives in Vernacular Architecture* 8 (2000) blurred the boundary between braced frame and balloon frame construction through a careful analysis of surviving examples in the Midwest. Similarly, Bruce's essay emerges from observations made in the field. Yet by locating examples far removed from middle America, Bruce questions the association of those discrete technological advances with the peculiarities of place.

If Bruce asks us to consider new perspectives on vernacular architecture, the same can be said of the four articles that follow. In her article on the Pennsylvania barn, Sally McMurry offers a challenge to the interpretive tradition that sees this much-studied building type as evidence in the narratives of ethnic continuity and change, and as a signal of the functional and structural hybridity that marks so much of the early American landscape. In the tradition of Bernie Herman and *The Stolen House*, McMurry turned to court records, and there she found evidence of a tradition of tenancy that complicates the vision of the independent Yeoman farmer and his barn. Then turning to examples in the field, the documentary evidence casts the physical evidence of these barns in an entirely new light. Rather than asking questions about where they came from and how they developed and proliferated, she asks how they functioned.

Moving to the towns of the early nineteenth-century West—specifically Ohio—Whitney Martinko examines the ways Ohioans appropriated earthworks of the long-disappeared Adena and Hopewell peoples into the making of new towns. Rather than entirely wiping away the evidence of earlier settlements, town planners selectively incorporated earthworks into their places and, Martinko argues, into their own histories of place. Like McMurry, Martinko turns to the documentary record to illumine the meanings of architectural choices. Using both travel narratives and local accounts, Martinko finds that the physical appropriation of these sites paralleled a narrative appropriation that enlisted these venerated American antiquities into the making of Ohio's place in the new nation.

As yet another hurricane slams into the Gulf Coast—the mayor of Galveston today called for continued evacuations in the aftermath of Ike—Jay Edwards's article defending the New Orleans shotgun house seems all the more timely. Framing this distinctive building type in the context of the larger debates over the preservation, restoration, and reconstruction efforts in New Orleans, Edwards revisits John Vlach's now canonical and much-debated essay on the origins of the shotgun house. Edwards argues that in this case, architectural history has the capacity to fundamentally reframe the implications of race in the effort to revitalize the city so devastated by Katrina. If the shotgun is associated with early black life and identity in New Orleans, as Edwards argues it does, then the persistent drive to extensively revamp the "shotgun crescent" simply exacerbates the racial inequity that hovers over so much of the recovery effort.

Our final essay takes us westward to Colorado. Eric Sandeen uses the 1960s and 1970s photography of Robert Adams to explore the evocative power and the conceptual boundaries of the vernacular. In those years, Adams worked on two books of traditional vernacular subjects—one entitled *White Churches of the Plains* and the other *The Architecture and Art of early Hispanic Colorado*—while also capturing the emerging suburbs of Colorado Springs for a volume entitled *The New West*. If Frances Benjamin Johnson before him was entranced by the formal qualities of vernacular architecture, Sandeen argues that Adams finds the power of these places manifest in their relationships. Sandeen addresses Adams's images in *White Churches* as powerfully vernacular because they are the culmination of vernacular processes; he describes them as locally generated. Sandeen finds in the images of *Hispanic Colorado* vernacular places that find their power in their connection to belief, faith, and tradition. But in the end, Sandeen questions these constructs by echoing Richard Harris's *Viewpoint* essay in Volume 15 as he offers tract housing and suburban sprawl as equally vernacular spaces. Sandeen's work centers not on real vernacular spaces but on the practice of representing vernaculars. And by focusing on representations of vernaculars rather than reality, he contributes to the continued conversations about the bounds of the term.

Considered together, these essays intersect in some very interesting ways. They demonstrate a wide breadth of methods to be used in vernacu-

lar architecture studies. If Bruce's observations and Edwards's arguments emerge from extensive work in the field, McMurry's and Martinko's demonstrate the value of the careful investigation of documentary sources. While we remain committed to fieldwork in its traditional sense, these essays remind us of the potential of closely reading buildings together with texts and to avoid the trap of fetishizing the object for its own sake. And Sandeen's article on the photography of Adams also reminds us of the value of reaching beyond our traditional scope of inquiry to find new ways to interrogate the vernacular.

But possibly the most important lesson in these articles is their commentary on the capacity of historic preservation to selectively shape vernacular landscapes and, by extension, the material histories that survive the present generation. Whitney Martinko's Ohioan town planners preserved surviving earthworks of the ancient past, but only when it suited their particular agendas. Those that fell in the path of proposed development were quickly leveled with little concern for the stories they might have told. The same fate awaits thousands of shotgun houses in New Orleans. As the debates over the recovery effort continue, planners need to heed the call to preserve one of the most significant markers of black identity in nineteenth-century America. And lastly, the evocative photography of Robert Adams was equally selective. His photographs are being used in Historic Structures Reports that become the foundation for (often) highly selective preservation efforts. Sites that were evocative enough to capture Adams's eye were more likely to be saved through preservation efforts. Each of these essays challenges us to question why we preserve the buildings we do and what is lost when we choose not to preserve others.

IAIN BRUCE

Viewpoint: The Balloon Frame, George Snow, Augustine Taylor, and All That

A View from Abroad

It is common currency among architectural historians that Scotland's high style and vernacular building is characterised by stone-and-lime technology with timber very much confined to the margins. As a result of the field work and the unexpected evidence of balloon frame construction in Scotland, this perception now requires reevaluation. The strong similarities between posthole, braced, stud, and post-and-rail frames that the study revealed provided sufficient material to offer this contribution to the debate on the origins of the balloon frame.

The study is based on a taxonomic methodology using a comparative analysis in which frame typologies and their characteristics are examined with a selection of case studies. Prompted by a professional inquisitiveness about the concentration of timber buildings in both Deeside and Speyside, two of Highland Scotland's significant river valleys, initial assumptions were based on the association of timber construction and the history of timber extraction in the respective river systems. Predominately but not exclusively of late Victorian vintage, the buildings in the survey range from the esoteric Swiss Cottage of 1837 at Fochabers on Speyside to a former aircraft hangar near Aberdeen built one hundred years later.

Apart from the unexpected extent of timber-framed buildings, diversity is a feature of the fieldwork: diversity of frame type and size, and of both history and geography. There are railway buildings, sports buildings, commercial buildings, as well as dwellings, a range that encompasses single-chamber bothies—with remarkable similarities to slave quarters in Virginia—family houses, and the imposing Edwardian Forest Lodge in the depths of the Abernethy forest. Although the cladding of these buildings varies from timber board and batten to corrugated iron and roughcast cement render, the common denominator is that they are *all* framed buildings in which a timber structure is the means of transmitting both dead and superimposed loads to the foundations.

As there is no body of literature on the subject, the study attempted to bring into focus the disparate elements by comparing and contrasting the varying approaches to building timber frames on both sides of the Atlantic. Figure 1, which was constructed from the variety of sources,[1] places these differing forms of construction on the same page for the first time. In addition, the study seeks to demonstrate Sigfried Gideon's idea that "History is not simply the repository of unchanging facts, but a process, a pattern of living and changing attitudes and interpretations."[2] In so doing, the study simultaneously contradicts Gideon's assertion that George Snow was the inventor of the balloon frame.

As American economic development spread west in the early nineteenth century, successive waves of emigrants from the northeast of Scotland were in the vanguard and consequently had access to the continuing development and refinement of American frame techniques, culminating in Chicago in 1834. Individuals of particular note are George "Chicago" Smith and Alexander White. With this background of two-way connections between the communities in Scotland's northeast and the development of American frame technology, the study was able to demonstrate that the apparent lack of a timber frame

post hole construction

great or English frame

brazed frame

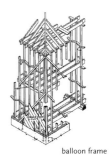

balloon frame

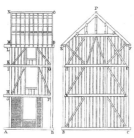

stud frame

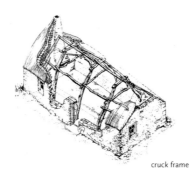

cruck frame

post and rail frame

Figure 1. Comparative illustration of frame types in Scotland and America. This composite drawing compares the development of American frame systems from the posthole and great frame methods of the original settlers through to the balloon frame. In the lower section, the frame systems used in Scotland are illustrated beginning with the stud frame, with its Saxon antecedents as used in urban centres and in contrast to the archaic form of the cruck frame used in rural areas. The post-and-rail frame, with its possible palisade connections, completes the collection. Based on an illustration compiled by author as part of a fieldwork study for a PhD thesis submitted to the Robert Gordon University.

tradition in Scotland was not founded on lack of knowledge.

Smith first set foot in Chicago in 1834, returning home to rural Aberdeenshire three years later, having made his first fortune as a land speculator and lumber merchant.[3] Unable to settle, he returned in 1839 to found the Illinois Investment Company, which was a prelude to his much more successful Wisconsin Marine and Fire Insurance Company. According to the *American Dictionary of Biography,* "During the troublesome days of wildcat money, the credit of George Smith & Company was as good as the Government's and better than that of most States.'"[4]

He was a cousin to Sir Alexander Anderson, Aberdeen's pre-eminent Victorian entrepreneur as promoter of the North of Scotland Bank and the Great North of Scotland Railway Company among other ventures. The close association between these two cousins in the Aberdeen North American Investment Company and the North of Scotland North America Investment Company was initially considered to have been

the conduit for the knowledge for timber frame techniques being developed contemporaneously in America, however no evidence was found to substantiate this.

Alexander White was born in Elgin, Morayshire, and reached Chicago in 1837, starting his career as a painter of wagons before making his fortune as a property developer, which was a prelude to becoming one of the greatest collectors of art in nineteenth-century America. He, like Smith, would undoubtedly have been knowledgeable of balloon frame technology through the early development of his property interests and in particular his retail and wholesale premises in the frenetic development of early Chicago.[5]

A question that arose early for the Scottish study was, if the balloon frame was indeed invented in Chicago, did these individuals contribute to its introduction in their native northeast Scotland?

In the debate on Sigfried Gideon's assertion that "the balloon frame was invented in Chicago in 1834 by George Snow in his construction of St Mary's Church,"[6] it is difficult to accept that a single-storey church can be credited as the threshold between the medieval heritage of timber construction and its modern lineage. For his evidence Gideon relied on the report by John Mills van Odsel, who in 1883 wrote, "Mr. Snow was the inventor of the balloon frame method of constructing wooden buildings which in Chicago completely superseded the old style of framing with posts, girts, beams, and braces."[7] Subsequent work by Paul E. Sprague and Walker Field debated whether it was Snow or Augustine Taylor and whether it was the Saint Mary's Church or a warehouse near Lakeshore. In more recent work, Cavanagh uses an etymological basis to examine the origins of the system, claiming that "if balloon was a popular term that already identified a distinct way of building, then perhaps it was an Anglicised version of a term in use in the French settlements along the Mississippi River" and proceeds to provide several possibilities.[8]

The fieldwork evidence from the Scottish study amply demonstrates that such is the commonality of elements described as studs, sill plates, and head plates in posthole, braced frame, and balloon frame construction as to make the distinction between the stud and balloon frames somewhat artificial. The case is

well illustrated by the esoteric Swiss cottage (Figure 2). Sited not far from the banks of the River Spey and built in 1837 in the Swiss style prevalent in the pattern books of the time, this was a two-storey family home. The 1841 census records the occupant as Jean Ansermet, a Swiss national whose occupation was park keeper and servant to the Marquis of Huntly.

The frame consists of 5" x 2" studs continuous over two storeys at 18" centres and spans 17'6" from ground to eaves. This elegant structure is clad in checked weatherboarding, and close inspection at the first floor reveals no ledger plate, with the joists nailed to the cheeks of the studs. This compares with the railway shed at Blacksboat (Figure 3) further upstream on the River Spey and deep in the heart of malt whisky country. More properly described as a braced frame, the studs are $6^{3}/_{4}$" x 3" at 2'9" centres and spanning 14'6" to the eaves.

In contrast, the classic balloon frame was found in a private house in Braemar, twelve miles from Balmoral castle in rural Aberdeenshire. The house, Downfield Cottage (Figure 4), was built by the great-grandfather of the present

Figure 2. Swiss Cottage near Fochabers. Photograph by author.

Figure 3. Former goods shed at Blacksboat upper Speyside. Photograph by author.

conventional lapped weatherboarding on all the other elevations. The substantial central chimney is particularly unusual in the Braemar collection of timber houses, where gable flues predominate. Such are the similarities to the style of the Cape Cod cottage that it suggests that the design was imported to the area despite obvious limitations of communications of the period.

The former Elgin station signal box, built circa 1890, is a two-storey rectangular 31' x 10' 9" plan with projecting entrance porch and toilet to the west at first-floor level. It is a standard design, large Great North Railway signal box with typical rectangular, slated gable roof. The balloon frame consists of 6" x 3" studs at 3' centres on a 6" x 4^1/$_4$" bottom plate with 7^3/$_8$" x 7^1/$_2$" corner posts and 6^1/$_4$" x 2^1/$_2$" ledger board along the long elevations. Floor joists of 6^1/$_2$" x 2^1/$_2$" at variable 18^1/$_2$" centres span between the frame and the intermediate longitudinal 10^3/$_4$" x 7^3/$_4$" summer beam, which in turn is attached to 9" x 3" end beams fixed to the corner posts. This substantial structure is clearly secondary to the envelope and appears to be in support of the signaling apparatus.

If the description "balloon" is taken as a term of disparagement or as designating something ephemeral in nature, then the post-and-rail frame with considerably more space between the principal elements could be described as more "balloon" than the balloon frame.

This is a frame type not recorded in nineteenth-century construction textbooks. Despite its prevalence in different building types and throughout the survey area, there appears to be no reference to this form of construction in either the American literature or in British construction manuals dating from Peter Nicholson's *The Carpenter's New Guide,* published in 1792, to the twentieth century.

Figure 5 illustrates the Fishermens' Store, built in the 1880s to serve the expanding fishing fleet at what was then the recently opened Cluny harbor in Buckie. It is one of three interlinked gabled buildings. The 7" x 2^1/$_2$" posts but at 6'6" centres and make for a significantly different frame from that of the stud. The horizontal rails spanning the posts in the style of purlins are generally at equal intervals between the sill plate and eaves. This creates a distinctly horizontal rect-

owners some fifteen years prior to Queen Victoria's love affair with Deeside. In search of work he had walked through the hills from Dundee to take up employment as a joiner in the village in the early 1830s. The history of the house is well documented and contemporaneous photographs show the various stages in its development. Studs, 6" x 2" in this example, are at 18" centres and fixed to the sill plate laid directly on the ground, there are 6" x 6" corner posts. The 4" x 2" ledger plate fully checked to the studs supports the first-floor joists. On the north elevation the original tongued and grooved boarding had a layer of lathing between the inside face of the board and the outside face of the stud, compared with the

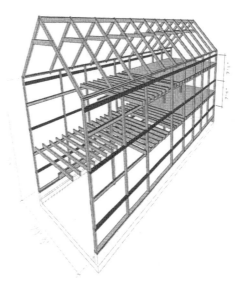

Figure 4. Dowanfield Cottage Braemar. Photograph by author.

Figure 5. Illustration of a post-and-rail frame. Drawing by Stuart J. Anderson.

angular form in contrast to the verticality of the stud frame. In the case of the unlined industrial sheds, which represent the definitive examples of this type of frame, it appears that an irregular number of bays is a distinguishing feature. Post sizes vary from 6" x 5" at 9' centers, 6" x 6" at 10'10" centres, to the more generally 7" x 2$^{1}/_{2}$" at 6'6" centres (see Figure 6).

The similarity to medieval defensive palisade construction (Figure 7) is striking, with the earth-fast posts and the horizontal rails providing support for the pales nailed vertically to them.

Despite the lack of a written record, this frame type was used by at least three generations of joiners and wrights in northeast Scotland in a variety of buildings from 1843 to 1937. Clad in both board and batten and corrugated iron sheeting, the survey evidence is of a more diverse geographical and typological distribution than the other frame types.

Carson, Barka, et al., in their study "Impermanent Architecture in the Southern American Colonies," noted, "To be told that the seventeenth-century civilisation of England's largest and most populous American dominion, the Chesapeake colonies of Virginia and Maryland, has vanished almost without trace above ground, challenges credulity."[9] With its horizontal rails,

presenting the logical means of fixing vertical boarding, it is similarly inconceivable that this frame was not known to Andrew Jackson Downing in his deliberations on the "stick built" aesthetic and who considered board-and-batten siding as symbolic or expressive of the timber frame that it covered.[10]

As the literature deals in discrete elements such as the great or English frame or the balloon frame, the value of the Scottish field study

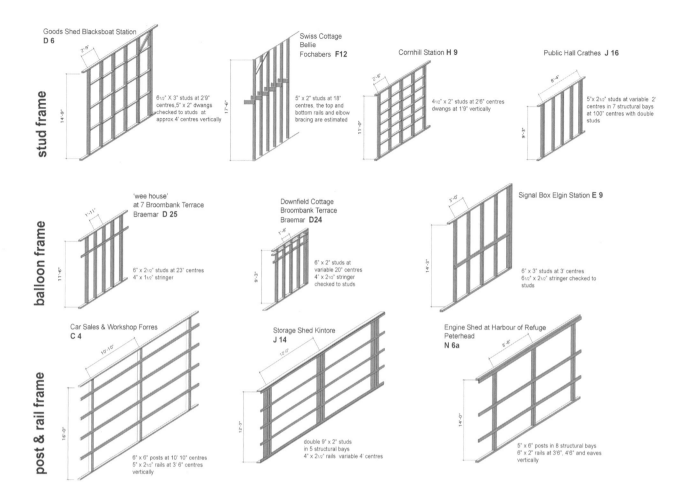

stud frame

Goods Shed Blacksboat Station **D 6**

14'-9"

2'-9"

6½" X 3" studs at 2'9" centres,5" x 2" dwangs checked to studs at approx 4' centres vertically

Swiss Cottage Bellie Fochabers **F12**

17'-6"

5" x 2" studs at 18" centres, the top and bottom rails and elbow bracing are estimated

Cornhill Station **H 9**

11'-0"

2'-6"

4½" x 2" studs at 2'6" centres dwangs at 1'9" vertically

Public Hall Crathes **J 16**

9'-3"

8'-4"

5"x 2½" studs at variable 2' centres in 7 structural bays at 100" centres with double studs

balloon frame

'wee house' at 7 Broombank Terrace Braemar **D 25**

11'-6"

1'-11"

6" x 2½" studs at 23" centres
4" x 1½" stringer

Downfield Cottage Broombank Terrace Braemar **D24**

9'-3"

1'-8"

6" x 2" studs at variable 20" centres
4" x 2½" stringer checked to studs

Signal Box Elgin Station **E 9**

14'-3"

3'-0"

6" x 3" studs at 3' centres
6½" x 2½" stringer checked to studs

post & rail frame

Car Sales & Workshop Forres **C 4**

16'-0"

10'-10"

6" x 6" posts at 10' 10" centres
5" x 2½" rails at 3' 6" centres vertically

Storage Shed Kintore **J 14**

12'-3"

12'-0"

double 9" x 2" studs in 5 structural bays
4" x 2½" rails variable 4' centres

Engine Shed at Harbour of Refuge Peterhead **N 6a**

14'-0"

6'-6"

5" x 6" posts in 8 structural bays
6" x 2" rails at 3'6", 4'6" and eaves vertically

Figure 6. Comparative illustration of frame types found in field study. Illustration by author for a PhD thesis submitted to the Robert Gordon University.

can only be appreciated within the context of the generality of timber frame buildings. By bringing together the detailed knowledge available on the American side of the Atlantic with the much more fragmented information on timber construction in Scotland, the study postulates that, far from being invented, the balloon frame emerged merely in the continuum of the development and refinement of construction techniques.

In greater consideration of Gideon's source material, subsurface drainage conditions were particularly difficult in embryonic Chicago. A. T. Andreas describes the soil as

a black loam soil, varying in depth from 1–2 ft.; underneath was a bed of quick sand 3–4 ft. resting on a stratum of blue clay which was almost impervious to water. In wet seasons it was almost impossible to dig trenches for foundations, as the water

would fill such excavations to the surface; drainage was out of the question owing to the low and level surface of the ground and owing to the watertight stratum of the blue clay, already mentioned. The only recourse was to wait until the ground became dry and firm by the slow process of evaporation. In consequence of these difficulties, buildings were sunk into the ground and resting on the hard clay, which under the circumstances furnished the best foundations to be had.[11]

As a consequence, "many of the earlier framed buildings of Chicago were built on posts"[12] in the manner of block construction.

Such clear evidence of responsive modification to meet particular foundation conditions might suggest that the ledger plate of the balloon frame was a simple modification to the stud frame to meet particular load conditions.

Perhaps however William Hoskins, Esq., a contributor to the seventh edition of *Encyclopedia Britannica*, published in Edinburgh in 1832, may have the last word with his description of historical construction methods:

Having built up the walls as far as he can conveniently from the ground and from a scaffold on tressels perhaps, he plants a row of poles which vary in height from thirty, to forty and even fifty feet, parallel to and at a distance of about four feet six inches from the walls and from twelve to fourteen feet apart. To these, which are called standards, are attached by means of ropes other poles called ledgers, horizontally and on the inside, with their upper surface on a level with the highest course of the wall yet laid; and on the ledgers and wall, short transverse poles called putlogs or putlocks are laid as joists to carry the floor of scaffold boards. These putlocks are placed about six or seven feet apart according to the length and strength of the scaffold boards; and the ends which rest on the walls are carefully laid on the middle of a stretcher, so as to occupy the place of a header brick which is inserted when the scaffolds are struck after the work is finished.[13]

Some one hundred and sixty years later, the *Penguin Dictionary of Building* (1995 edition) defines *ledger* as "a horizontal framing member, either a ribbon board or a tube in a scaffold to carry putlogs." A ribbon board in turn is defined as "a horizontal beam fixed to a wall or housed into studs to carry the ends of floor joists."

Is it not possible, therefore, that, far from the balloon frame being "invented" in Chicago on a specific site in a specific year by either George Snow or Augustine Taylor, the balloon frame was merely an expedient adaptation of the scaffolding techniques used for the construction of masonry buildings of the period?

Figure 7. Replica palisade fence at Fort George near Inverness Scotland. Photograph by author.

NOTES

1. The sources are as follows. Posthole construction: drawing by Cary Carsen and Ching Hoang, reproduced from *Winterthur Portfolio* 16, nos. 2/3 (Summer/Autumn 1981). Great or English frame: reproduced from Abbot Lowell Cummings, *The Frame House of Massachusetts Bay, 1625–1725* (Cambridge, Mass.: Harvard University Press, 1979). Braced frame: reproduced from Paul E. Buchanan, "The Eighteenth-century Frame Houses of Tidewater Virginia," in *Building Early America: Contributions towards the History of a Great Industry*, ed. Charles E. Petersen, 54–73 (Radnor, Penn.: The Carpenters' Company of the City and County of Philadelphia, 1976). Balloon frame: reproduced from Raymond P. Jones and John E. Ball, *Framing, Sheathing, and Insulation* (Albany, N.Y.: Delmar Publishing, 1970). Stud frame: reproduced from Peter Nicholson, *Mechanical Exercises of the Elements and Practices of Carpentry, Joinery, Bricklaying, Masonry* (London: J. Taylor, 1812). Cruck frame: Cruck-framed cottage, Torthowald, Dumfriesshire, by Geoffrey Stell (Crown copyright, RCAHMS). Post-and-rail frame: from unpublished drawing by Stuart Anderson.

2. Sigfried Gideon, *Space, Time, and Architecture* (Cambridge, Mass.: n.p., 1941), 260.

3. There are a number of land parcels attributed to a George Smith entered or patented between 1828 and 1836 on the plan attached to the *Book of Original Entry* for Chicago.

4. Entry for George Smith, February 10, 1806–October 1899, *Dictionary of American Biography*, ed. by Allen Johnson (New York: Charles Scribner's Sons, 1955–1964).

5. Entry for Alexander White, *Dictionary of American Biography*.

6. Sigfried Gideon, *Space, Time, and Architecture*, 83.

7. Ibid.

8. See Paul E. Sprague, "The Origin of Balloon Framing," *Journal of the Society of Architectural Historians* 40, no. 4 (1981); Walker Field, "A Re-examination into the Invention of the Balloon Frame," *The Journal of the Society of Architectural Historians* 2, no. 4 (1942): 3–29; Ted Cavanagh, "Balloon Houses: The Original Aspects of Wood Frame Construction Re-examined," *Journal of Architectural Education* 51, no. 1 (September 1977): 5–115.

9. Cary Carson, Norman F. Barka, William M. Kelso, Gary Wheeler Stone, and Dell Upton, "Impermanent Architecture in the Southern American Colonies," *Winterthur Portfolio* 16, no. 25 (Summer/ Autumn 1981): 138.

10. See Vincent Scully Jr., "Romantic Rationalism and the Expression of Structure in Wood: Downing, Wheeler, Gardner and the 'Stick Style,' 1841–1876," *Art Bulletin* 35 (June 1953): 121–42.

11. A. T. Andreas, *History of Chicago* (Chicago: n.p., 1884), 505.

12. Ibid.

13. William Hoskins, "Treatises on Architecture and Building," *The Encyclopedia Britannica*, 7th ed. (Edinburgh: Adam Black, 1832), 77.

SALLY MCMURRY

The Pennsylvania Barn as a Collective Resource, 1830–1900

In the predawn hours of a September morning in 1873, a large bank barn belonging to Daniel Durst, located in the rich Penns Valley of Centre County, Pennsylvania, burned to the ground. Soon after the fire, it became apparent that someone had torched Durst's barn deliberately. An item in the local newspaper reported: "Tracks of a person who wore rubber shoes, were detected in the dust leading from the Old Fort hotel to the barn and from the barn back again to the hotel pavement, and on Friday evening Sheriff Shaffer arrested Jacob Durst, a nephew of the owner of the barn, near Centre Hill, on suspicions, as he wore rubber shoes, and lodged him in jail for further examination." Jacob Durst was eventually convicted of arson and sentenced to serve time in the Western Penitentiary.[1]

What moved Jacob Durst to his incendiary act? Tax records show that he was tenant on this property at least from 1859 through 1866, working on shares for his father, Peter Durst Jr., who owned the property at the time. As longtime tenant and son, Jacob must have harbored some hopes of inheriting the property. But in 1872, after Peter Durst Jr. had died, Jacob received a nasty shock: his uncle Daniel (Peter's brother) had managed to purchase the land from the estate. Perhaps Jacob, already forty-four years old and still not a landowner, was making a violent statement about his frustrations when he set his uncle's barn aflame.[2]

The case of the Durst arson illustrates some aspects of the Pennsylvania barn that have been hidden from historians' view. This essay will set out the case for viewing the Pennsylvania barn not only as a productive space but as a collective resource linking farming households together through ties of kinship, marriage, or tenancy. In

both its form and its daily uses, the Pennsylvania barn was shaped in a rural society where farming households seldom operated independently but, rather, were intricately intertwined.

Historical understandings of the classic "Pennsylvania barn" are most nuanced in the realms of historical geography, formal analysis, and description of construction materials and techniques. Robert Ensminger and others have analyzed the Pennsylvania barn's distinguishing architectural characteristics. The Pennsylvania barn was built into a bank, usually with its longitudinal side along the bank. This gave it a vertical multilevel organization, with basement stables that accommodated horses, cattle, and other livestock. From the lower level, divided doors led out to the barnyard. An upper level, accessible from the bankside, permitted storage for hay, straw,

Figure 1. Stitzer barn, Berks County, circa 1820. Note the divided stable door giving ingress and egress to the barnyard, and the cantilevered overhang or "forebay." Photograph by the author.

fodder, and grains, and also facilitated thresh-ing. Most had a granary somewhere on the upper level. The forebay (sometimes called an overshot or overshoot) was the most important feature setting apart the Pennsylvania barn as a specific type. This eave-side overhang, often eight to ten feet wide and sometimes even wider, projected out above the basement stable, on the opposite side from the bank entrance. The forebay served to shelter stock and machinery, and to extend the working floor on the upper level. Scholars have identified numerous subtypes of the Pennsylvania barn, but all have these basic features.[3]

The classic Pennsylvania barn originated with antecedents in the Prätigau region of Switzer-land, where barns with similar characteristics can be found. German-speaking settlers to Penn-sylvania brought with them the basic principles and design ideas, but specific circumstances in the late eighteenth century allowed it to take root and spread. Colonial agriculture in the region had been quite diversified, but cleared acreages were small, and the principal cash-generating crops were grains, which were exchanged locally and exported to Atlantic and Caribbean markets. Around the turn of the nineteenth century, a fundamental shift in production took place, to a grain-and-livestock system. Horses (rather than oxen) became the draft animals of choice. Clear-ing proceeded at a steady pace. The rise of inland towns, improved transport, and the growth of metropolitan areas such as Philadelphia and Bal-timore supplied new, domestic markets. Now, the possibilities were hugely expanded, since farm producers no longer had to think exclusively in terms of products that could be shipped a long way. An intensive stall-feeding industry devel-oped, for example. Young cattle were acquired from herds driven on the hoof along newly opened transport routes from the Ohio Valley and other westward points, and fattened for sale on the East Coast.[4]

About the same time, the transition from bound to free labor was completed. In addition to the usual complement of family members, hired hands working for wages supplanted bound labor-ers. By 1838, for example, a tally in Berks County counted over six thousand farmhands (or more than three for each farm) "steadily employed" at 9 dollars per month.[5]

These developments, experienced simulta-neously, stimulated people to build new and improved Pennsylvania barns. By the end of the eighteenth century, it has been estimated, Pennsylvania barns represented about twenty percent of barns in the state.[6] The Pennsylvania barn appeared at this moment because it suited the grain-and-livestock system and because it was very flexible and efficient. The Pennsylvania barn fit well with the grain-and-livestock sys-tem because it brought together all the needed elements: animals, feed, bedding, and farming implements. On the upper level, hay was kept for winter fodder. Straw was also put in mows, and this was very important to a self-sustaining system because it was used for animal bedding, then returned to the fields mixed with manure. Grain was stored in the granary and machin-ery on the threshing floor. The lower level was divided into stalls for horses, milk cows, steers, and sometimes other livestock. Agriculturalists everywhere were seeking more flexible designs, and the new Pennsylvania barn was one exam-ple. The Pennsylvania barn's flexibility recom-mended it to builders. The basic layout could be shaped into many combinations. On the upper level, for example, there might be just one threshing floor and a single mow, but floors and mows could be combined into various con-figurations. The pattern of mow/floor/mow was common. Pennsylvania barns were also flexible in that they could be executed in any available building material: stone, log, frame, brick, or a combination. They could range from diminutive two-bay structures to barns eighty and ninety feet long. Pennsylvania barns were efficient mainly because they conserved labor. Everything was in one central location. Workers used grav-ity to throw grain, hay, or straw down into the stables from the upper level. Stored grain could also be offloaded to wagons from bankside gra-naries. In some barns, cisterns supplied water to the stables. Often, drive-through corncribs were integrated into barn design. In the age of free wage labor, every time- or labor-saving fea-ture counted.

RES. OF JOSEPH STROCK MECHANICSBURG.

RESIDENCE OF J.N.STROCK AND J.C.REESER, PROPERTY OF JOSEPH STROCK.
TRINDLE SPRING STA, MONROE TWP, CUMBERLAND CO, PENN.

Figure 2. Image from Conway Wing, *History of Cumberland County, Pennsylvania* (Philadelphia, 1879), 221. This shows Joseph Strock's town residence and his tenant farm, which seems to have been occupied by at least two families. Census records show that Joseph Strock, who built a brickend barn in 1865, lived in 1870 as a "retired farmer" with his son Jacob, 28, a landless farmer. Reproduced with the permission of Rare Books and Manuscripts, Special Collections Library, the Pennsylvania State University Libraries.

By the mid- to late nineteenth century, the population expanded, farming began to mechanize, production increased, and transport improved, again changing the competitive environment. Pennsylvania farms increased in number and decreased in average size; production (though not productivity) rose as cleared acreage rose. A typical Pennsylvania German-area farm in 1850 would be less than a hundred acres, with a high percentage—as much as 90 percent—improved.[7] Farm families in southeastern Pennsylvania continued practicing diversified agriculture, though with shifting emphases. Hay and dairy products assumed greater importance, and farm families also stepped up production of maize, poultry, and pork, all the while continuing to produce wheat, oats, and rye. Although specific emphases had shifted, farming continued to be fundamentally a grain-and-livestock system, and the Pennsylvania barn persisted as the barn type of choice. In fact, the Pennsylvania bank barn ceased to be an unusual sight and became by far the most common barn type in the farm landscape of southeast, south central, and central Pennsylvania.[8]

Treatments of the Pennsylvania barn's function have been limited to noting that it was so well suited to grain-and-livestock mixed husbandry, but when we turn to the broader social context of farming in nineteenth-century Pennsylvania, we find a substantial body of primary evidence that supplies the underpinning for an expanded interpretation of the Pennsylvania barn. It shows that the Pennsylvania barn's famous flexibility extended beyond its purely agricultural function to accommodate a variety of social structures. The Pennsylvania barn could and usually did serve a single family on an owner-occupied farm, but to a surprising extent it also accommodated multiple farms and farm households. It also frequently changed in social function over a family's life cycle. If we regard the Pennsylvania barn within this context, the interior organization found in so many of these grand buildings takes on a new significance.

Tax records, locally gathered agricultural statistics, real estate advertisements, legal records, and extant barns furnish ample evidence that in nineteenth-century Pennsylvania barns were intensively shared. These sources also reveal the spatial dynamics at work. This essay focuses on the period from about 1830 to 1900, and the counties of central, south central, and southeast Pennsylvania, where during that time the Pennsylvania barn was the dominant type, and the rural culture that sustained sharing practices was well developed and widespread. While it is not possible to determine precisely what proportion of the rural population engaged in these practices, census and other figures suggest that in some counties a majority would have had direct experience with them at some point in their lives.

A number of sources show quite clearly that many Pennsylvania farms had a single barn but multiple dwellings. In the 1840s, Israel David Rupp published county histories for several south central and southeastern Pennsylvania counties. In some of these accounts, likely derived from local tax records, he gave figures gathered for an 1838 report on the "Statistics of Agriculture" for these counties. Rupp gave numbers for how many farms there were in Berks and Cumberland counties; and on these farms, how many "Farm Houses," "Tenant Houses on Farms (Not Farm Houses)," and barns. In Cumberland County that year, Rupp reported that there were about 1,400 farms, barns, and farm houses, and another 812 "Tenant Houses on Farms (Not Farm Houses)." Rupp was careful to separate farm houses from tenant houses that were on farms but very explicitly "Not Farm Houses," a clear indication that many farms in the region were occupied and worked by multiple households. Real estate advertisements confirm this pattern. For example, an 1865 ad in the *Franklin Repository* touted a farm with a "two story weatherboarded dwelling house, large bank barn 75 x 45, double corn cribs, wagon shed, other bldgs, and a good Tenant house. Commonly known as the 'mansion farm.'" Another ad featured a "New Bank Barn 72 feet long; Weatherboarded House and Tenant House," also in Franklin County. The *Centre Reporter* observed in its May 7, 1884, issue that "Mr. D. Hess has astonished his barn with a suit of white-wash; . . . he is also erecting a dwelling house for Messrs Alexander and Keller . . . "[9]

These architectural arrangements demonstrate that farms were often worked by more than one household using a single common barn. This organization reflected the complex labor needs on a nineteenth-century Pennsylvania farm. Although agriculture was mechanizing, many processes still demanded hand labor, throughout or in part. Families, though large by today's standards, declined in size over the century, and migration took many away. Pennsylvania farms were highly developed, so in acreage terms alone they had a great deal of land under cultivation. Moreover, diversified production strategies required many different skills.

In addition, the presence of tenant houses frequently represented a longstanding system of farm tenancy that was quite prevalent in this part of Pennsylvania. This was share tenancy. To understand its impact on how the Pennsylvania barn functioned as a collective resource, it is first necessary to explain how share tenancy worked, because it was very different from the Southern, postbellum sharecropping that comes to mind when we think of a "share" of a crop. Tenancy had always been a part of life in rural Pennsylvania. Data were not systematically collected statewide until the 1880 Federal agricultural census, but local court records, tax records, newspapers, landownership maps, and other sources make very clear that it was an important institution long before then. By 1880, tenancy rates statewide averaged about 20 percent, but in the southeastern and central counties, they were higher, ranging from 28 percent in Berks County to 37 percent in Cumberland County. In 1900, fully half the farms in Cumberland County were operated by tenants or managers, and in the other southeastern counties typically over 40 percent were tenanted. So, share tenancy in Pennsylvania's southeast, south central, and central counties was pervasive and may have increased over time during the nineteenth century.[10] When assessing its impact, we should remember that tenancy shifted frequently; over the century and even in a single lifetime, a farm might be owner operated and tenanted in a continuing cycle. Therefore, tenancy probably affected many if not most eastern Pennsylvania farming families over the course of several generations.

The basic terms of Pennsylvania share tenancy involved an agreement, usually verbal, in which a tenant occupied a farm, paying as rent an agreed-upon share of crops to the landowner.

The share came out of all grain crops—not just the most prized wheat crop but other grains such as oats, corn, and rye. Sometimes the share percentage varied with the crop (for example, two-fifths of the wheat and one-third of the others). Tenants normally paid taxes; a local newspaper in Centre County mentioned that "the custom of landlords in this county, is to make their tenants pay *all* the taxes." Tenants also usually "found" (i.e., supplied) part or all of the livestock and sometimes also the implements. The usual term was one year, though some tenants made longer-term agreements. March 1 or April 1 were the favored start dates, in keeping with the seasons. Rural newspapers often noted tenant comings and goings; in April 1883, the *Centre Reporter*'s local news column remarked, "flitting seems to be the order of the day."[11]

Tenants thus faced annual uncertainty and often changed farms, sometimes voluntarily and sometimes unwillingly. On the other hand, unlike Southern sharecroppers, Pennsylvania share tenants usually had considerable latitude over their farming choices, and often brought significant resources to the agreement. Most tenants owned at least some livestock and equipment. Pennsylvania share tenants also enjoyed significant legal protections, developed in a substantial body of case law. Over time, the Pennsylvania courts originated novel legal doctrine—most significantly the notion of the "way-going crop," which held that a tenant had a personal-property right to the crop he had planted. This right was fairly consistently protected in the courts throughout the nineteenth century, and it normally applied to the crop at every stage, even when it was still in the ground. Sometimes the tenant could lay claim even after he had moved from the premises.[12] This legal standing distinguished the Pennsylvania share tenant from the Southern sharecropper, who had no legal claim at all to any part of the crop.

Share tenancy was practiced among all ethnic groups and did not necessarily involve family members, but by the mid-nineteenth century share tenancy in Pennsylvania had come to have a strong link to kinship and was especially common among the Pennsylvania Germans. In Centre County, for example, tax assessment records from 1847 to 1870 show that at least 80 percent of

tenants in the heavily German eastern townships were related to their landlords. This kinship-based system attracted notice from puzzled outsiders, who struggled to comprehend it. In the 1820s a German immigrant schoolteacher named Jonas Gudehus sojourned for a time in eastern Pennsylvania. He noted that the Pennsylvania Germans had a practice of "lending" their land to their sons and then retiring: the American German parent "often lease[s] his children the plantation ('loans out' one says there), moves into the city and leads a carefree life. However, he remains the owner of his possessions as long as he lives and when he dies then his children all get an equal share of the estate." Another observer, Sherman Day, noted in 1843: "A singular practice in the management of the family estate is said to prevail among many of the German farmers in this county [Centre]. The patriarch labors patiently until his eldest son is of age; he then purchases for him a farm adjoining his own, and they labor on together, with a common purse; never keeping any separate accounts until another son is of age and provided for, and taken into the partnership in like manner. If a daughter is married, she is portioned from the common purse; and thus they continue from generation to generation. This fact was communicated by a distinguished jurist of the county."[13] His perception of a "common purse" suggested a benign interpretation, but he did intuit an important aspect of the system.

Kin-based share tenancy arose from Old World historical legacies. Sharecropping in various forms was common all across Europe, as were customs aimed at ensuring maintenance in old age. The practices that so puzzled observers markedly resembled common customs from parts of Europe whence the Pennsylvania Germans had immigrated in the eighteenth century, such as the *Altenteil,* or literally, "old peoples' part." *Altenteil* (also known as *Auszüg,* among other words) encompassed a number of different practices. German rural sociologist H. W. Spiegel observed its workings much later (in interwar Germany) as it applied to peasant landowners who used it as an "anticipated inheritance," i.e., promised land to a child in return for maintenance and/or income. Frequently, the share rent constituted a widow's dower, or provisions in lieu of the dower, after the patriarch passed away. Pennsylvania fathers often lived in the "mansion house," sometimes continuing to farm actively in their own right, other times letting a son (often the youngest) take over. Sometimes they owned several farms and rented them out to several sons or sons-in-law. Many siblings did not even get to rent a farm and worked as farm laborers, sometimes foregoing payment until after the father's death. Children who worked on the farm as share tenants or laborers could hope for a reward when their father died—but in the meantime, they were without independent means. Still, they headed households, had families of their own, and sometimes lived on the farm in separate houses from their parents.[14]

In this context, the barn functioned as a collective resource used by landlords, tenants, and laborers hired by the day or year. The most straightforward of these uses was to have the barn house property belonging respectively to landlord and tenant. Occasionally a tenant might haul his share away immediately for sale, but normally both parties needed storage space. In Potter Township, Centre County, Uriah Slack's 1881 probate file, for example, shows that he had crops stored in at least two different barns: "$^1/_3$ of six acres of wheat in S Slacks Barn; $^1/_3$ of 18 acres of wheat in J Slacks Barn, $^1/_3$ of 4 acres of rye in J Slacks Barn," and "$^1/_3$ of 10 acres of barley in J Slacks Barn." "J" Slack was Uriah's son John A. Slack, and "S" Slack was Uriah's other son Samuel G. Slack. John and Samuel had worked as "laborers" for Uriah as young men, then progressed to being Uriah's tenants just after the Civil War. Sometime in the early 1870s, when he was in his early forties, Samuel Slack, the elder of the two, managed to acquire some land adjacent to his father's property and to marry. John, however, continued to farm on shares for his father, and on his father's death he purchased it from the estate. Uriah's estate laid claim to his thirds, stored in two barns identified with his sons.[15]

In the Slacks' case, two connected farms were pooled to serve an extended family that changed its composition with members' life-cycle position. Documentation shows that they used two barns, and the population census strongly suggests that they essentially shared two dwellings.

In 1870, Uriah, a "Retired Farmer," and his wife Isabella lived with their granddaughter Ellen Pennington. John Slack, his wife and child, and his older brother Samuel lived next door, along with a teenaged domestic servant. Ten years later, by now an elderly widower of 86, Uriah lived as a "Boarder" with Samuel, aged 48 (listed as a "Stock Dealer"), Samuel's wife Mary, their seven-year-old daughter Elizabeth, and Ellen Pennington, now 25, listed as a "Servant." Clayton S. Mast, an eleven-year-old boy, also resided in the household as a laborer. Next door, John A. Slack, 40, lived with his wife, Sarah, and their four children (aged four to twelve) and two teenaged workers, a boy and a girl. Uriah used share tenancy as a means of old-age sustenance, in the *Altenteil* tradition. Architecturally, the *Altenteil* was expressed by two houses that contained households that shifted over time. Today on lands that once belonged to Uriah and Samuel, Uriah's original farmstead hugs the road; across the road, on partially wooded mountain land that Samuel owned, there is a much altered farm site that Samuel may have occupied.[16]

In any event, the Slack family was not anomalous. In Westmoreland County, Jesse Kilgore built a barn on property he rented from his father-in-law, Michael Poorman, who even deferred to Kilgore on where to site the barn. A neighbor later recalled that he had "helped Kilgore to haul about nine loads of hay in the harvest of 1853; put Poorman's part in stack and Kilgore's part in barn." In this case, Kilgore evidently thought that since he had built the barn, his own crops had priority for storage there. His refusal to share interior space may have been a harbinger of future troubles with his landlord, since not long after the two were embroiled in a bitter lawsuit.[17]

Fires often revealed barn sharing in a painfully concrete way. The *Central Press* of Centre Hall, Pennsylvania, reported in 1861 that a barn had burned in Penns Valley, Centre County. The barn had contained hay, corn, a reaper, a wagon, horse gears, and other equipment. The barn's owner, Mrs. Woods, was insured for $700, but "Mr. Marks the tenant lost all as no insurance covered his property." In its account of the 1873 Durst fire, the *Centre Reporter* noted that the farm "was occupied by Adam Krumrine as tenant."

Figure 3. Uriah Slack farm, Potter Township, Centre County, looking northeast. Photograph by the author, 2008.

The fire could not have come at a worse time; a huge crop had just been put up. The "entire crop of this season" went up in flames, along with "all the horsegears, and all of Mr. Krumrine's implements and a separator, belonging to Mr. Durst." Adam Krumrine did see the flames in time to rescue the livestock.[18]

The barn itself belonged to Daniel Durst, who had it insured for $1200. Durst and Krumrine both lost farm machinery, though it seems that Krumrine suffered a total loss in that regard. In all, "about 900 bushels of wheat, 150 bushels of rye, 1200 bushels of oats, [and] 26 tons of hay" were lost. An additional 600 "bushels of shelled corn belonging to Mr. Durst were also burned," and to make matters worse, "Mr. Durst's share of the crop, or rent, [was] not insured." If we assume that terms of the share agreement were like others documented for the region, then Durst probably lost one-third to half of the wheat, rye, and

oats. According to the article, Krumrine had taken out "an insurance of $1600 on his share of the crop." Even a full settlement would not solve the problem of shelter for his animals, though; a poignant sale notice from Krumrine appeared in the same issue of the paper that described the fire: "The undersigned, having been burnt out, offers the following live stock at private sale: Six Head of Work Horses, Three Milk Cows, Eleven Head Young Cattle."[19]

This account demonstrates that barn and yard space housed property that was clearly demarcated in everyone's mind: the landlord's, the tenant's, and the community's. Adam Krumrine's horses would have taken up horse stalls on the ground level, which usually were located at the end of the barn nearest the house, and which often had higher ceilings than the rest of the stable level. Krumrine's cattle would occupy the other stalls, on the ground level. If Durst also

Figure 4. Pencil writings on granary wall, Daniel Durst barn, Potter Township, Centre County. Photo by Timothy Wesley. Used by permission.

stabled animals in the barn, it would have been an easy matter to distinguish them. The animal quarters would lead out to the barnyard where they would all mingle. The two men's farm machinery would sit under the forebay or on the upper-level barn floors. Krumrine and Durst probably stored the wheat, oats, and rye either in sheaves, arranged in mow or loft space, or, if threshed, in a granary. Hay was harvested and stored loose, not baled as it is today, so this crop would have been physically harder to divide, especially if all the hay went into a single mow. Some of the crops could have been stacked outdoors in the barnyard, or shocked in the field.

In the Durst barn, tenancy and barn form are directly linked through physical evidence. Daniel Durst did not wait long to build a new barn after his nephew burned down the old one. The barn still standing today was originally a Pennsylvania barn, 85 feet by 40 feet, and later expanded by an ell. Its interior reveals very concretely that the prior sharing patterns continued after the new barn was built. The 1874 barn had two centrally located threshing floors, and on each gable end was a large mow. A granary containing four large bins, each accessible from an aisle, occupied the southwest portion of the forebay; another, smaller

granary was situated on the forebay side of the easternmost threshing floor. The double floors, double mows, and clearly divided granaries suggest provision for multiple occupancy. The evidence that ties the physical arrangement most directly to share tenancy is literally inscribed on the granary doors. In rough, faded pencil scrawlings, numbers appear in nineteenth-century accounting terms along with fragments of words including "wheat," "third," "taken out," and the names of the tenant and owner for 1874 and 1875, [William] "Goodhard" and Daniel Durst respectively.[20] There could be no more definitive evidence that the divided granary bins could be—and were, in this case—used to correspond to shares of the crop.

Barn floor plans from across the region have consistent patterns showing a flexibility that could be applied either to a single-family farm or to a sharing situation. The floors, mows, and granaries are all clearly demarcated. A single operator could spatially separate his hay, straw, and grains—hay in one mow, straw in another, grains in the granary, machinery on the threshing floor or under the forebay. In sharing situations, the space could be divided so that each party was allocated definite areas—probably specific floor, mow, granary, and stable portions. Indeed, documentary evidence occasionally makes this implicit idea explicit. An 1805 Cumberland County lease, for instance, stipulated that one end of the barn was reserved for the landlord's use.[21]

The Jacob Plank barn in Cumberland County was built in 1852, according to the datestone. This layout has twin mows, floors, and granaries on the upper level, a layout that would readily facilitate sharing. This configuration was common in the region. The tax records are ambiguous about whether Plank had tenants, but they do list him as a "gentleman" in 1860, and we know that by that time he was already sixty years old and had made his fortune in the agricultural-implement business and retired. Thus it is quite likely that Jacob Plank did not farm the property himself but rather let it out, perhaps to one of his several sons. He sold the property in 1860 to a William C. Houser, who by the 1870s was explicitly listed in the tax records as "N[on] R[esident]." The population census for 1860 showed Houser living in the village of Mechanicsburg, yet he was listed as a "farmer" with real estate worth $19,000. Yet another example, in the same township as Plank, is a barn associated with a Martin Brandt. Originally a two-crib log barn, built around 1810, the barn was altered around 1850, resulting in the disappearance of two log walls and a rebuilding in timber framing. Also, the barn was extended to the rear about four feet, and two outshed granaries protruded further still at the back of each mow. This barn not only had twin mows, floors, and granaries, but twin machinery sheds as well. This Martin Brandt (there were several local men of that name) was listed in the 1870 population census as a fifty-six-year-old farmer with no real estate holdings; yet the agricultural census for that year lists him as farming 111 acres worth $20,000.[22]

A barn with an especially dramatic illustration of these features is the Diller barn in Cumberland County. This barn has five central threshing floors; on each gable end, a mow. Its original portion was already big for its time, ninety feet around 1800, but in the middle of the nineteenth century it was enlarged another thirty feet at the west gable end. A new granary was built at the same time.

The Diller barn was on a farm belonging to John Diller, who acquired the land around 1816. The original portion of the barn was probably built around that time. This successful Pennsylvania German patriarch oversaw a large farm. The 1850 census of agriculture shows 325 acres improved along with another 161 unimproved, sustaining a large-scale grain-and-livestock operation that produced 1000 bushels each of wheat and oats, along with 250 of rye and 800 of corn; 8 horses, 10 milk cows, 9 other cattle, 16 sheep, and 38 swine. A thousand pounds of butter were made on the farm that year. Only 7 tons of hay were listed, so we can infer that the farm acreage was given over to crops rather than pasture or meadow.[23] The mows must have been used for straw rather than hay, for bedding for the animals housed beneath.

At first glance, it seems that the Diller barn simply represents an extra-large farm. During John Diller's prime working years, that is probably how it functioned. However, beginning in 1853, the tax records list on his property a "Stone

house and Stone Barn [and] two Log Tennant houses." One of these "Tennant houses" was a miller's dwelling, but the other was likely used for a tenant farmer. This was about the same time the barn was expanded; in 1856, for the first time the tax records mention a "Frame Weather Boarded Bank Barn." John Diller was in his early sixties when these architectural changes were made, and in 1860 he and his wife Elizabeth were living with their thirty-three-year-old son Samuel (who owned no real estate), Samuel's

Figure 5. Granary bins, Daniel Durst barn, Potter Township, Centre County. Photo by the author.

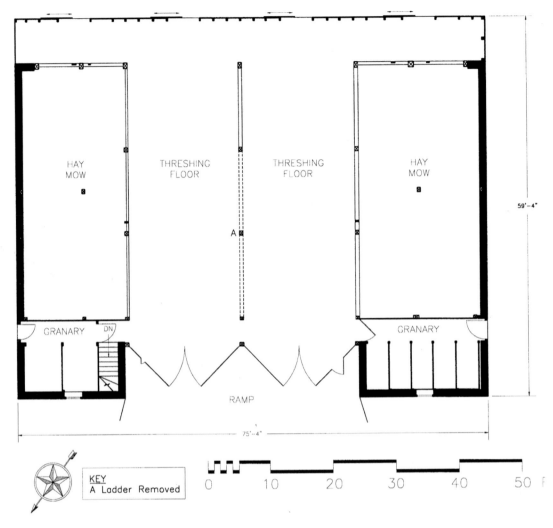

Figure 6. Plank barn, Cumberland County, 1852. Plan of threshing floor level. CAD drawing by Jason B. Smith. Reproduced by permission of Center for Historic Architecture and Design, University of Delaware.

family, two domestics, and a farm laborer. The previous household visited by the census taker, as well as the one he visited immediately after the Dillers', were both young landless farmers and therefore possible occupants of the "Tennant house." Jacob Basore seems the more likely tenant, since he and his young family lived with a farm laborer and a twenty-year-old "Domestic," who could furnish much-needed labor for such a large farm and dairy operation.[24]

The barn was enlarged just as John Diller was about to retire; this timing only makes sense in the context of wider patterns and expectations of share tenancy. The 1870 population and agriculture censuses list John Diller (by now eighty-two years old) as a "retired farmer" with real estate valued at $42,000, living with his son Samuel, who still owned no land. In the 1860s and '70s, Samuel and John Diller Jr. were listed as tenants

in the tax records, along with another farmer who lived next door, Benjamin Mowery. Thus the expanded Diller barn reflects not a single yeoman holding but an operation that was collectively worked by two subordinate sons and their families, along with at least one other household.[25]

Physical and documentary evidence have shown quite clearly that the Pennsylvania barn's interior organization lent itself to joint farming, where a single barn was used to store both landlord's and tenant's shares, and where well-demarcated spaces made accounting clear. In other cases, such as the Slacks', two farms were essentially pooled, with several generations interchangeably utilizing houses and barns. Life-cycle considerations probably made sharing more likely at certain points in a family's evolution; the Diller barn was enlarged, and the Plank barn erected, by retired farmers. Now let us turn to the dynamics of how these arrangements played out in everyday life. Shared barn space could be an expression of cooperation in a common enterprise, but, inherently, the unequal social status and resources of landlord and tenant could also produce conflict and tension, and make the barn a contested place.

Consider what could happen when a tenant was denied barn space he believed was his due. An 1875 legal dispute documents how Cumberland County landlord Johnston Moore allegedly induced his tenant, Jonas Shughart, to agree to farm on shares for him, promising to build a barn to house the tenant's crops. According to court records, Moore "proceeded to build the foundations and stopped, and plaintiff's (Shughart's) [live]stock was without shelter." The agreement was made in April, and by midsummer there was still no action on the barn; so when Moore showed up to oversee quarrying stone for the barn (probably on the farm site),

Shughart "attacked him with a shovel." Subsequently "there was other evidence of threats of injury to defendant when he went to the farm in relation to building the barn." Shughart sued; in a first round, he lost, but on appeal he prevailed, the judge holding that a verbal agreement should be binding, even though Moore claimed he was prevented from building the barn by his tenant's violent actions.[26]

In *Rank v. Rank,* a Lancaster County case tried in 1847, a tenant successfully sued his landlord for damages that resulted from the landlord locking him out of the barn when he wanted to thresh his crop. The court held that because threshing was delayed, the tenant had lost both income (because prices dropped during the delay) and actual grain (because either pests or the landlord had removed some of it in the meantime). In addition, the court ruled that the tenant was entitled not just to the grain but to the valuable straw, declaring that "straw is a constituent part

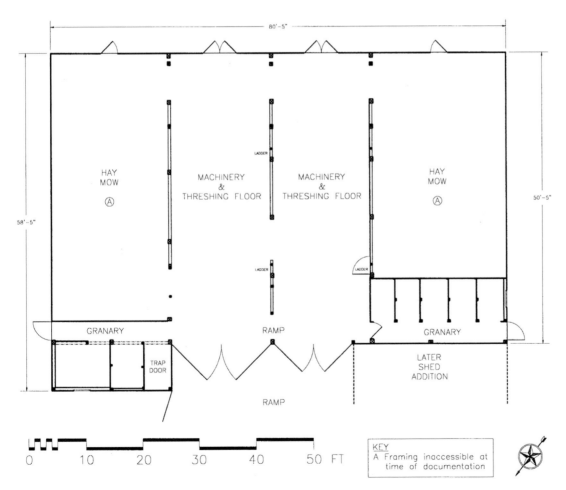

Figure 7. Martin Brandt barn, threshing floor plan. CAD drawing Jason B. Smith. Reproduced by permission of Center for Historic Architecture and Design, University of Delaware.

Figure 8. Diller barn, Cumberland County, bankside. Note the multiple doors admitting both humans and wagons; the gable-end doors from the granary, where grain could be offloaded onto wagons below; and lower-level gable-end door, which led to stables. The projecting forebay can be seen at the extreme left. Photograph by the author.

of the way-going crop."[27] *Rank v. Rank* established that the landlord did not have unlimited control over access to a barn, even if it stood on land he owned.

If we begin to see the Pennsylvania barn in light of incidents like these, we can begin to envision the barn not just as a socially neutral storage facility but as a space with ritual and symbolic significance. The annual reckoning, for example, was a moment of high import, in which the barn became an arena where fundamental economic and social relationships were acted out. Both landlord and tenant had a large stake in making sure the crops were accurately counted and fairly divided. The tenant was usually enjoined to "deliver" the crop to the landlord, and sometimes a specific date was set for the division: the 1848 case of *Briggs v. Thompson* stated, "There was a day fixed for the division of the hay." The ritual was bound by seasonality and custom. Farmer and landlord gathered together after the harvest in the barn, when the crop was presented, surveyed, counted, and divided. Sometimes reckoning took place separately for each crop, each in its own harvest season; at

other times, it seems the parties waited until the entire crop was brought in, in some cases even after it was threshed. Until then, the crop sat in the barn: one court case described "400 bushels of oats in the sheaves in the mow of the barn, unthreshed and not divided or separated."[28]

Whether or not a date was formally specified, crop delivery, counting, and dividing would usually occur "at the barn." Landlords and tenants normally made verbal agreements about the arrangements for delivering the crop, but occasionally these made their way into the written record, especially if there were legal proceedings. For example, in Northumberland County a court summary in the 1862 case of *Garrett v. Dewart* gave the following history leading up to a dispute that involved a tenant farm:

[According to the] articles of agreement the said George Garrett covenanted "to deliver one-half of all the grain, wheat, rye, corn, buckwheat, and oats" raised on the demised premises "to the said Lewis [Dewart] in the mow or corn-crib.... the said Lewis to have one-third of the turnips raised on the place delivered at the barn—the said George to give the

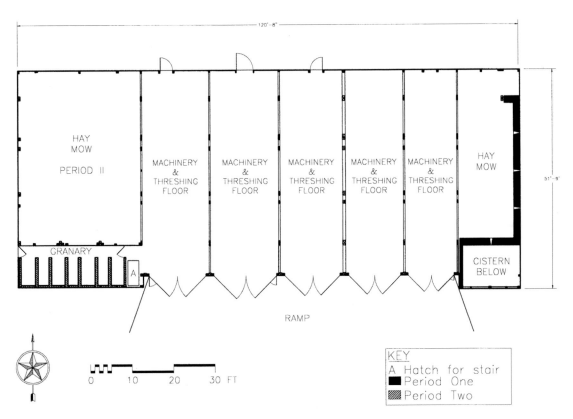

Figure 9. Diller barn, upper level plan. CAD drawing by Rochelle Bohm. Reproduced by permission of Center for Historic Architecture and Design, University of Delaware.

said Lewis all the hay and straw, with the grain in or out, raised on the place, to be delivered either in stack or at the barn."[29]

Dewart did give Garrett the option to deliver some grains at a mill or store house, but in the main the tenant was expected to present the crop either in the barn (where mow and possibly corn crib were located) or directly adjacent to the barn, where hay stacks would be located. Garrett farmed on these terms for Lewis Dewart from 1846 until the landlord died in 1852.

Another case, *Burns v. Cooper*, explicitly described how all parties formally gathered for the division. Tenant Burns, the court averred, had established irrefutably that he had delivered the crop: "the tenant thrashed [the grain], divided it in the barn, in the presence of the lessors and the son of the purchasers of the lessors' title, and took away his own half." The legal commentator asked: "How can the tenant aver that he had not delivered the landlord's share? What more had he to do?"[30] The tenant, previous landlord, and new landlord all gathered at the barn to witness the crop division, the tenant to overtly demonstrate

that he had carried out his part of the bargain, the landlords to observe him doing so. This ritual performance could provide mutual reassurance of a fair division; but we can also imagine it tinged with watchful vigilance, possibly even mistrust and suspicion.

The 1855 case of *Poorman v. Kilgore* highlights the potential for conflict. In this Westmoreland County lawsuit, Michael Poorman was the landlord, and his son Jacob and son-in-law Jesse Kilgore were tenants on shares. This arrangement supposedly had persisted since 1836. Christian Fisher, one of the many neighbors summoned to testify in the trial, told the court: "In the fall, when putting in corn, going in the barn, the old man [Michael Poorman] told me to keep an account of the baskets of corn; he could trust Jesse, but he could not trust Jacob." Here barn space became an arena for regulating tenant behavior. Indeed, especially in situations where kinship-based share tenancy was involved, the barn was a place where unequal power relationships were acted out, where anxieties and resentments could flare. Many tenants were middle-aged adult sons and the annual reckoning was an especially pointed, even humiliating, reminder of their dependency. In 1855, Jacob Poorman was well into middle age—he was forty-three and had a wife and four children—and had farmed on shares under his father for nearly twenty years. Jesse Kilgore was an even older forty-five and had three children living at home. Numerous friends and neighbors testified that Michael Poorman had over the years repeatedly made verbal promises to his son and son-in-law that they would eventually receive title to the property they had rented from him for so long. Indeed, even Jacob's masculinity was implicated in hopes for landownership: his father was said to have declared he would "make a man" of Jacob by giving him land.[31] But Michael reneged. The mistrust between Michael and Jacob must have been mutual. Michael demanded filial deference; Jacob experienced betrayal. He might well remain a tenant into his own old age. In a society where landownership conferred status, this was a bitter prospect to face. In few places was this hierarchical dynamic of power expressed more vividly than on the barn floor at the time when the crop was divided.

Tenants were a category of people for whom barn space could express both dependency and legitimate claims. Widows were another. Barn space could be part of a widow's thirds (her dower)—property legally hers for use during her lifetime. Dower rights prevailed whether or not a husband died with a will. However, for the present study, wills offer the most explicit evidence showing how specific portions of buildings and fields were assigned to a widow, in addition to or in lieu of her dower rights. For example, in 1855 Centre County resident Jacob Crotzer stipulated, "My will is that my sons Samuel and Melcher is to leave my beloved wife Jane the house she lives in as long as she lives she is to have priveilige at the oven and water and in the garden and in the cellar of the other house and stabling for her cattle" [verbatim quotes and punctuation]. P. B. Musser of Spring Mills, Pennsylvania, willed to his wife Catharine "for her use . . . for so long time . . . as she retains my name, all that part of the house in which we now live west of the hall together with half of the cellar, half of the spring house, half of the wash house, half of the stabling in the tithe barn near the house, half of the bake oven

and wood house, the whole of the garden and of the yard in front of the house." Catharine was also entitled to a third of the apples and a third of "all else that may be raised in it [the orchard]" and as much "hay and pasture as is sufficient for the keeping of one cow." John Kerstetter's 1890 will stipulated that his widow will receive "the income and yearly rents of my farm on which we now reside; with so much house room and privilege in the barn, outbuildings and garden as may be necessary for her convenience and comfort all of which I give to her during her life . . . and in lieu of her dower at common law." Some wills contain less specific references to "barn room"; others only implied the widow's claim to barn space by mandating that she be supplied with a cow and horse.[32]

A number of instances show how share tenancy combined with explicit allowances of other kinds of spaces to provide the widow's sustenance; vouchers in probate files often attest that widows collected shares of crops long after their husbands' deaths. In Northampton County in 1852, Joseph Brotzman willed to his wife "the frame house (being the homestead) and garden attached thereto, together with all my household goods and kitchen furniture, with the necessary privileges in the barn, stable and outhouses, and two cows to be fed, stabled and pastured, and as much fire wood and coal as she may reasonably want, to be delivered wherever she may direct on the premises, together with one third part of the wheat, rye, corn, potatoes, and hay that shall be raised and made on the premises hereinafter devised unto my three sons." The widow Brotzman enjoyed explicit claim to house, stable, outhouse, and barn, and implicit claim to space for her third of the crop.[33]

Giving widows space as part of their dower rights was common along the Atlantic seaboard in the eighteenth and early nineteenth centuries. In coastal cities, houses were divided, sometimes with painstaking precision. Bernard Herman has argued that these divisions aimed for an "architectural competency" which varied significantly with a widow's class and with her individual circumstances. Rooms assigned to widows often reflected social associations and expectations, as well as status. Middling widows most often ended up with a few rooms and access to yard or scullery; they often had to then improvise to make these limited spaces serve social, productive, and everyday functions. Sometimes they received access to productive spaces such as shops or bake ovens, which they could use to fashion a livelihood. Holly Mitchell has investigated what happened after the moment when property was divided, to show how widows used their "thirds" to generate income and subsistence, with varying success.[34]

For the landed Pennsylvania patriarch's widow, the ability to draw on barn space afforded productive resources. The widow was guaranteed access to garden, bake oven, and a place to house livestock, which in turn meant that she could continue her dairying activity and raise animals for meat, leather, or fiber. These activities enabled personal subsistence and possibly income. We may assume that widows actively worked in these buildings, feeding, tending, and milking cows. Stabling for horses gave a widow precious geographic mobility and relieved her sons from having to provide her with transportation themselves. To be sure, dower rights (or other resources willed to her) applied only during a widow's lifetime, and frequently husbands bequeathed property only as long as the widow remained unmarried, so a widow's control over these resources was partial and contingent. Nonetheless, for these fortunately endowed women widowhood could mean a life of relative comfort, if seldom of independence.

Widows' solid legal and practical claims to barn space raise the possibility for interpreting another architectural feature of Pennsylvania barns, the datestone. Many barn datestones contain the names of both husband and wife. The Plank barn in Cumberland County, for example, bore a datestone that read: "Built By Jacob Plank and Mary His Wife 1852." Set in a wider context, the message of datestones like these can be interpreted to mean more than pride of ownership. Datestones also expressed not just an individual's success but the standing of an entire family. They validated men's and women's shared farm work in an intricate household economy. And finally, especially in cases where older farmers were building new barns, might a datestone proclaim a wife's (and eventual widow's) rights to

an architectural competency?

The analysis offered here has significant implications for understanding the Pennsylvania barn and its milieu. It is clear that nineteenth-century Pennsylvania farmsteads and farm landscapes should not be viewed as indivisible and unified properties. This finding challenges the tendency to consider the barn only in relation to a single farm or farm household, as an emblem of independent propertied yeoman status. By now it is well recognized that in the nineteenth-century United States, (male) farm owners' purported "independence" rested on labor performed by women, children, tenants, and wage laborers, or (in the South) slaves.

The yeoman ideal also failed to account for extensive neighborhood exchanges. Farming families exchanged resources routinely. Nineteenth-century farm diaries and ledgers are filled with references to these practices. A farmer lacking pastureland, for example, might pasture his horses with a neighbor in exchange for goods or services. Historians Mary Neth, Nancy Grey Osterud, and Douglas Harper have explored how various types of neighborly exchanges knitted rural communities together well into the twentieth century. We can consider Pennsylvania share tenancy one variant of a wider rural culture that emphasized sharing labor, machinery, land resources, and buildings—a necessity in an era when capital and machines had not yet substituted for human networks.[35]

In short, the yeoman myth obscured a reality of deep interdependency. The history of tenancy in Pennsylvania emphasizes that the farm and its neighborhood, extended family, and community are more appropriate levels of landscape analysis than are isolated farms. In turn, a different appreciation of the rural landscape will emerge when we take into account how interconnected were farming households.

A rich tradition of historical scholarship has challenged views of subordinate groups that stress their exploitation and weakness, instead focusing on their agency as they contested prevailing power relationships, with uneven success. A close look at the Pennsylvania barn shows that tenants and widows could and did invoke strong, legally supported claims on barns, fields, and pastures. That these claims were regularly exercised and validated, and architecturally expressed, is clear in abundant historical evidence.

Finally, because so many different people could lay claims to barn space, these spaces had multiple historical meanings. To the proud patriarch, the barn might indeed signify a lifetime of agricultural prosperity, independence, and success; to his sons, it might mingle memories of humiliation with hopes to succeed the father; to his spouse, her "barn room" offered a way toward sustenance during her widowhood. In any case, the Pennsylvania barn was not so much an individual creation as a cultural artifact shaped not only by economics, but by family ties, social structures, and long-standing custom.

NOTES

The author would like to thank Robert Ensminger and Nancy Van Dolsen and two anonymous readers for helpful comments. Unless otherwise specified, all legal citations are from LexisNexis Academic Universe (www.lexisnexis.com/us/lnacademic).

1. *Centre Reporter* (Centre Hall, Pa.), September 18, 1873; "Commonwealth vs. Jacob Durst," Centre County Court Records, bound volume labeled "Centre County Court Records Aug 1871–Nov 1875," Centre County Historical Library, Bellefonte, Pa. The case can be traced in this volume as follows. November Sessions 1873, case no. 446, entry against Jacob Durst for "Indictment, Arson, True Bill, and now Nov. 29, 1873, cause reached and defendant pleads Not Guilty." In entries for January Session 1874, Jacob Durst was found guilty "in manner and form as he stands indicted." The entry for February 3, 1874, notes that Durst was sentenced to "Pay a fine of one dollar and costs of prosecution and undergo an imprisonment by Separate and Solitary Confinement at hard labor, in the Western Penitentiary of Pennsylvania at Pittsburg for a period of one year and Seven Calendar months."

2. Tax Records, Potter Township, Centre County, 1859–1866, Centre County Historical Library; Peter Durst [Jr.] (executors) to Daniel Durst; 257 acres, Centre County Deed book M-2, page 155, dated March 20, 1872, Centre County Recorder of Deeds Office, Bellefonte, Pa.; U.S. Manuscript Population census, 1870, Potter Township, Centre County, entry 440.

3. Much has been written about Pennsylvania barns and outbuildings over the years, including Charles H. Dornbush and John K. Heyl's *Pennsylvania German Barns* (Allentown, Pa.: The Pennsylvania German Folklore Society, 1956), Joseph W. Glass's *The Pennsylvania Culture Region: A View from the Barn* (Ann Arbor, Mich.: UMI Research Press, 1986), Henry Glassie's "Eighteenth-Century Folk Cultural Process in Delaware Valley Folk Building" (*Winterthur Portfolio* 7 [1972]: 29–57), Amos Long Jr.'s *The Pennsylvania German Farm: A Regional and Architectural Folk Cultural Study of an American Agricultural Community* (Breinigsville, Pa.: Pennsylvania German Society, 1972), and Alfred L. Shoemaker's *The Pennsylvania Barn* (Kutztown, Pa.: Pennsylvania Folklife Society, 1959). Henry Glassie established typologies and documented historic Pennsylvania barns. The preeminent recent work is by Robert Ensminger, *The Pennsylvania Barn: Its Origin, Evolution, and Distribution in North America*, 2nd ed. (Baltimore, Md.: The Johns Hopkins University Press, 2003); Ensminger persuasively argues that the forebay bank barn originated in the Swiss Prätigau and traces its various subtypes in North America.

4. James T. Lemon, *The Best Poor Man's Country: A Geographical Study of Early Southeastern Pennsylvania* (Baltimore, Md.: The Johns Hopkins University Press, 1972); James Westfall Thompson, *History of Livestock Raising in the United States, 1607–1860* (Washington, D.C.: U.S. Department of Agriculture, 1942), 84, 138; Percy Wells Bidwell and John Falconer, *A History of Agriculture in the Northern United States, 1620–1840* (1925; repr., Clifton, N.J.: A. M. Kelley, 1975), 7, 137, 177, 227, 110–11; Diane Lindstrom, *Economic Development in the Philadelphia Region, 1810–1850* (New York: Columbia University Press, 1978); John F. Walzer, "Colonial Philadelphia and Its Backcountry," *Winterthur Portfolio* 7 (1973): 161–73; Arthur F. Lord, "The Pre-Revolutionary Agriculture of Lancaster County Pennsylvania," *Proceedings of the Lancaster County Historical Society* 79, no. 1 (1975): 23–42.

5. Daniel Rupp, *History of Berks and Lebanon Counties* (Lancaster, Pa.: G. Hills, 1844), 264.

6. J. Ritchie Garrison, "Farmsteads in the Early Republic," unpublished, undated essay that analyzes data from the 1798 Direct Tax. Cited with permission of the author.

7. The census definition of "improved" varied from one decennial year to another, but generally this meant

cleared land being tilled for crops, put into grass for hay, used as pasture for grazing animals, or put into orchards and vineyards.

8. Lindstrom, *Economic Development in the Philadelphia Region*, 9, 142, 101. County production data are from Rupp, *History of the Counties of Berks and Lebanon*, 263. Statewide figures are derived from published data in 1850 United States Census of Agriculture, tabulated and summarized in Jerome Pasto and K. I. Chen, "Facts on a Century of Agriculture, 1839–1950," *Pennsylvania Agricultural Extension Bulletin*, no. 587 (January 1955). Kuan-I Chen's "Agricultural Production in Pennsylvania, 1840–1950" (PhD diss., Agricultural Economics, Pennsylvania State University, 1954) convincingly demonstrates that for most of the nineteenth century gains in production were the result of additional land under cultivation, not greater productivity per acre. Average farm size in 1850 ranged from 86 acres in Berks County, 92 in Lancaster County, and 130 in Cumberland County; statewide it was 117 acres. These figures are from Pasto and Chen, "Facts on a Century of Agriculture." Joan Jensen, in *Loosening the Bonds: Mid-Atlantic Farm Women, 1750–1850* (New Haven, Conn.: Yale University Press, 1986), discusses butter production. See also Elinor Oakes, "A Ticklish Business: Dairying in New England and Pennsylvania, 1750–1812," *Pennsylvania History* 47 (1980): 195–212. For an overview of markets important to the southeastern Pennsylvania farm economy, see Jo N. Hays, "Overlapping Hinterlands: York, Philadelphia, and Baltimore, 1800–1850," *Pennsylvania Magazine of History and Biography* 116 (1992): 295–321.

9. I. D. Rupp, *History and Topography of Dauphin, Cumberland, Franklin, Bedford, Adams, and Perry Counties* ... (Lancaster City, Pa.: G. Hills, 1846), 367; *Franklin Repository*, October 25, 1865, and July 13, 1864, accessed online through Pennsylvania Civil War Newspapers Web site, http://digitalnewspapers .libraries.psu.edu/Default/Skins/civilwar/Client .asp?skin=civilwar&AppName=2. *Centre Reporter*, May 7, 1884. See also the *Centre Reporter*, July 24, 1868. Nancy Van Dolsen, in *Cumberland County: An Architectural Survey* (Carlisle, Pa.: Cumberland County Historical Society, 1990), especially 284–92, notes the prevalence of tenant houses and "mansion houses" in Cumberland County.

10. Lee Soltow and Kenneth W. Keller, "Tenancy and Asset Holding in Late Eighteenth-century Washington

County, Pennsylvania," *Western Pennsylvania Historical Magazine* 65 (January 1982): 1–17; Lucy Simler, "Tenancy in Colonial Pennsylvania: The Case of Chester County," *William and Mary Quarterly* 3d ser., 43, no. 4 (October, 1986): 542–69. Tenancy data are from the United States Census of Agriculture. Published summaries are now available online at http://www .agcensus.usda.gov/Publications/Historical_Publica tions/index.asp. The *Centre Reporter*'s June 30, 1910, cover story noted that just 56.3 percent of farms in the county were owner operated.

11. Terms of tenancy described in *Democratic Watchman* (Bellefonte, Pa.), August 8, 1862; Jacob Spangler, Probate File no. 4358, 1873, Centre County Historical Library; *Centre Reporter*, March 16 and March 30, 1905. Notices of tenant comings and goings in *Centre Reporter*, January 5, 1905, April 5, 1883; April 12, 1883; January 19, 1888; and December 22, 1910.

12. Pennsylvania law contrasted sharply with that of other areas, notably the postbellum South, where the landlord's claim on the crop eventually came to dominate. See Harold Woodman, *New South, New Law: The Legal Foundations of Credit and Labor Relations in the Postbellum Agricultural South* (Baton Rouge: Louisiana State University Press, 1995), 67–70. In Iowa, as well, the landlord had a legal right to place a lien on his renter's crop. See Donald Winters, *Farmers without Farms: Agricultural Tenancy in Nineteenth-Century Iowa* (Westport, Conn.: Greenwood Press), 1978. The doctrine of "way-going crop" was explicated in many cases including *Shaw v. Bowman*, [no number in original], Supreme Court of Pennsylvania, 91 Pa. 414; 1879 Pa. Lexis 362, October 23, 187; 9 *Forsythe v. Price*, [no number in original], Supreme Court of Pennsylvania, Middle District, Harrisburg, 8 Watts 282; 1839 Pa. Lexis 54, May, 1839.

13. The relationships among landlords and tenants were determined in the following manner: the tax records show landowners and their tenants. There is also a section for tenants that indicates the owner of the property where the tenant lives. For the eastern townships, I noted all the landlords who paid taxes on at least fifty acres, and I noted the tenants on these properties who shared a surname; then I added the tenants with different surnames who were verified as sons-in-law through the probate records or local histories and genealogies. The figure is likely an underestimate, because it hasn't been possible to identify all of

the sons-in-law. I do not have definitive proof that all these arrangements were on shares, but I have uncovered very few instances of cash rental arrangements. Moreover, the 1880 manuscript agriculture census, which distinguished between share rental and cash rental, showed the overwhelming form of tenancy was farming on shares. Tenancy status is corroborated by the population manuscript census (where tenants appear as farmers with a zero real estate holding). For methods of identifying farm tenants elsewhere, see John T. Houdek and Charles Heller Jr., "Searching for Nineteenth-Century Farm Tenants: An Evaluation of Methods," *Historical Methods* 19, no. 2 (1986): 55–61. Nineteenth-century accounts from Jonas Gudehus, "Journey to America," trans. Larry M. Neff, in Albert Buffington, ed., *Ebbes fer Alle—Ebber Ebbes fer Dich,* Pennsylvania German Society Publication 14, 1980, 304. Sherman Day's observations were published in his *Historical Collections of Pennsylvania* (Philadelphia: n.p., 1843), 200. I have not been able to identify the "jurist" to whom he referred.

14. On Old World forms of sharecropping and their relationship to inheritance see Hermann Rebel, "Peasant Stem Families in Early Modern Austria: Life Plans, Status Tactics, and the Grid of Inheritance," *Social Science History* 2, no. 3 (Spring 1978), 255–91; H. W. Spiegel, "The *Altenteil*: German Farmers' Old Age Security," *Rural Sociology* 4, no. 2 (June 1939): 203–18; Carl Wehrwein, "Bonds of Maintenance as Aids in Acquiring Farm Ownership," *The Journal of Land & Public Utility Economics,* 8, no. 4 (November 1932), 396–403; Jon Gjerde and Anne McCants, "Individual Life Chances, 1850–1910: A Norwegian-American Example," *Journal of Interdisciplinary History,* 30, no. 3 (Winter 1999), 377–405. Linda Pickle, *Contented among Strangers: Rural German-Speaking Women and Their Families in the Nineteenth-Century Midwest* (Champaign: University of Illinois Press, 1996), 61, associates the term *Altenteil* with the widow's crop share. The Centre County probate files contain numerous descriptions of house and outbuilding space allowed widows. See for example James Sankey, Probate File no. 4347, 1868, Centre County Historical Library. The term "mansion house" or "Mansion farm" appears frequently in probate papers. See for example Francis Alexander, Probate File no. 103, 1872, Centre County Historical Library.

15. Uriah Slack Probate File, no. 4545, 1881, Centre County Historical Library; U. S. Manuscript Popula-

tion census, 1850, Potter Township, Centre County, page 74; U.S. Manuscript Agriculture census, 1850, Potter Township, Centre County, no page number, line 18; U. S. Manuscript Population census, 1860, Potter Township, Centre County, page 85; U.S. Manuscript Agriculture census, 1860, Potter Township, Centre County, page 9, line 23; U.S. Manuscript Population census, Potter Township, Centre County, 1870, page 40; U.S. Manuscript Agriculture census, Potter Township, Centre County, 1870, page 7, line 26; U.S. Manuscript Population census, Potter Township, Centre County, 1880, Enumeration District 235, sheet 21, line 1; U.S. Manuscript Agriculture census, Potter Township, Centre County, 1880, Enumeration District 235, page 13, line 1; Tax Records, Potter Township, Centre County, 1848, 1850, 1854, 1856, 1858, 1860, 1863, 1865, 1867, 1870, 1872, 1873, 1875, 1878, 1880, 1881. Centre County Recorder of Deeds, Deed Book Q, 250–51; Deed Book 69, 192–93; Deed Book B2, 660; Deed Book S2, 421–22; Uriah Slack Probate File.

16. U.S. Manuscript Population census, 1860, Potter Township, Centre County, page 85; U.S. Manuscript Agriculture census, 1860, Potter Township, Centre County, page 9, line 23; U.S. Manuscript Population census, Potter Township, Centre County, 1870, page 40; U.S. Manuscript Agriculture census, Potter Township, Centre County, 1870, page 7, line 26; U.S. Manuscript Population census, Potter Township, Centre County, 1880, Enumeration District 235, sheet 21, line 1; U.S. Manuscript Agriculture census, Potter Township, Centre County, 1880, Enumeration District 235, page 13, line 1. The Slack farm is shown in the Potter Township page of the *Atlas of Centre County: From Actual Surveys, by and under the direction of Beach Nichols* (Philadelphia: A. Pomeroy, 1874).

17. *Poorman v. Kilgore,* [no number in original], Supreme Court of Pennsylvania, 26 Pa. 365; 1855 Pa. Lexis 240, 1855.

18. *Central Press* (Centre Hall, Pa.) July 19, 1861; *Centre Reporter* (Centre Hall, Pa.), September 18, 1873.

19. Ibid.

20. The tax records for 1874 and 1875 show that William "Goodhart" was Daniel Durst's tenant. Centre County tax records, 1874, 1875, Potter Township, Centre County Historical Library. The evidence in this paragraph was gathered in fieldwork in 2005–2006.

21. Nancy Van Dolsen, *Cumberland County, Pennsylvania: An Architectural Survey* (Ephrata, Pa.: The Science Press, 1990) 285.

22. Ibid., 190–92; Entries for William C. Houser, Tax Records, Cumberland County, Monroe Township, 1862-3-4; 1865-6-7, 1871-2-3 (Cumberland County Historical Society, Carlisle, Pa.); U.S. Manuscript Population Census for 1860, Cumberland County, Mechanicsburg Borough, page 9. Information on Brandt from "Architecture and Landscape of the Pennsylvania Germans," guidebook for the 2004 Vernacular Architecture Forum annual conference, unpublished, Tours section, 18–19; U.S. Manuscript Population Census, 1870, Monroe Township, Cumberland County, page 182, lines 13–18; US Manuscript Agriculture Census, 1870, Monroe Township, Cumberland County, page 7, line 9. Robert Ensminger has suggested that the Martin Brandt barn may have been originally constructed as a hybrid log-and-frame barn, rather than renovated to a hybrid form. However, the layout still features twin spaces regardless of construction sequence.

23. U.S. Manuscript Agriculture Census, 1850, Westpennsboro Township, Cumberland County, page 57, line 15; Tax Records, Westpennsboro Township, Cumberland County, 1820 through 1872, Cumberland County Historical Society.

24. Tax Records, Westpennsboro Township, Cumberland County, 1820 through 1872 (Cumberland County Historical Society, Carlisle, Pa.); U.S. Manuscript Population Census, 1860, Westpennsboro Township, Cumberland County, page 29.

25. Tax Records, Westpennsboro Township, Cumberland County, 1820 through 1872; U.S. Manuscript Population Census, 1870, Westpennsboro Township, Cumberland County, page 551; U.S. Manuscript Agriculture Census, 1860 and 1870, Westpennsboro Township, Cumberland County. Another example in the Westpennsboro Township is the George McKeehan farm, Historic Site Survey Files, Cumberland County Historical Society, Carlisle, Pa. At one point three brothers lived on the patriarch's farm, which had several houses, at least two barns, and tenant houses. The sons are listed on the tax records as tenants. Van Dolsen, *Cumberland County,* also notes numerous instances of retired farmers living with children.

26. *Shughart v. Moore,* Supreme Court of Pennsylvania, 78 PA. 469; 1875 Pa. Lexis 165, May 24, 1875.

27. *Rank v. Rank,* [no number in original], Supreme Court of Pennsylvania, 5 Pa. 211; 1847 Pa. Lexis 27, May 21, 1847.

28. *Briggs v. Thompson,* [no number in original] Supreme Court of Pennsylvania, 9 Pa. 338; 1848 Pa. Lexis 251, October 9, 1848; *King v. Bosserman,* no. 5, March T., 1900 Superior Court of Pennsylvania 13 Pa. Super. 480; 1900 Pa. Super. Lexis 183, March 12, 1900, Argued April 23, 1900.

29. *Garrett v. Dewart.,* [no number in original], Supreme Court of Pennsylvania, 43 Pa. 342; 1862 Pa. Lexis 178, November 17, 1862.

30. *Burns et al. v. Cooper,* [no number in original] Supreme Court of Pennsylvania 31 Pa. 426; 1858 Pa. Lexis 182.

31. *Poorman v. Kilgore,* [no number in original] Supreme Court of Pennsylvania 26 Pa. 365; 1855 Pa. Lexis 240; U. S. Manuscript Population Census, 1850, Unity Township, Westmoreland County, page 353; U. S. Manuscript Agriculture Census, 1850, Unity Township, Westmoreland County, page 167.

32. Dower is explained in Richard Chused, "Married Women's Property Law: 1800–1850," *Georgetown Law Journal,* June 1983: 1359–425; Marylynn Salmon, *Women and the Law of Property in Early America* (Chapel Hill: University of North Carolina Press, 1986); Lisa Wilson, *Life after Death: Widows in Pennsylvania, 1750–1850* (Philadelphia: Temple University Press, 1992); Elizabeth Bowles Warbasse, "The Changing Legal Rights of Married Women 1800–1861," (PhD diss., Radcliffe College, 1960, repr. 1987), chapter 1, discusses dower as it pertained to real estate.

Joseph Crotzer, Probate File no. 810, 1856, Centre County Historical Library; will dated November 17, 1855. Tax records show the sons as tenants of the father. For other examples in Centre County, see John Bierly, Probate file no. 489; George Gramly, Probate file no. 1519; Israel Weaver, Probate file no. 8102. P. B. Musser, Probate file Probate file nos. 3112, 1873, Centre County Historical Library. See also *Santee v. Santee,* [no number in original], Supreme Court of Pennsylvania, 64 Pa. 473; 1870 Pa. Lexis 394, March 2, 1870; and John Kerstetter, Probate file no. 5831, 1890, Centre County Historical Library.

For references to barn room, see *South Mahoning TP. v. J. F. Marshall et al.,* no. 81, Supreme Court of Pennsylvania, 138 Pa. 570; 21 A. 79; 1891 Pa. Lexis 1135, October 20, 1890. John Stover, Probate file no. 4274, 1836, Centre County Historical Library, offers cow and horse but makes no explicit mention of space.

33. For widows' vouchers extending over years, see Henry Vonada, Estate file no. 5320, 1886, Centre County Historical Library. Brotzman's case is in Estate of Joseph Brotzman, Deceased, no. 58, Supreme Court

of Pennsylvania, 133 Pa. 478; 19 A. 564; 1890 Pa. Lexis 923 March 11, 1890, argued March 24, 1890.

34. Bernard L. Herman, *Town House: Architecture and Material Life in the Early American City, 1780–1830* (Chapel Hill: University of North Carolina Press, 2005), 155–92; Holly Bentley Mitchell, "The Power of Thirds: Widows and Property in Portsmouth, New Hampshire, 1680–1830," (PhD diss., Brandeis University, 2007); Nora Pat Small, e-mail communication of December 27, 2007.

35. Mary Neth, Preserving the Family Farm: Women, Community, and the Foundations of Agribusiness in the Midwest, *1900–1940* (Baltimore: The Johns Hopkins University Press, 1995); Douglas Harper, *Changing Works: Visions of a Lost Agriculture* (Chicago: University of Chicago Press, 2001); Nancy Grey Osterud, *Bonds of Community: the Lives of Farm Women in Nineteenth-Century New York* (Ithaca, N.Y.: Cornell University Press, 1991).

WHITNEY A. MARTINKO

"So Majestic a Monument of Antiquity"

Landscape, Knowledge, and Authority in the Early National West

In the spring of 1791, the Ohio Company of Associates was consumed with questions about the ornamentation of town squares. In the young town of Marietta, the first legal settlement in the Northwest Territory, the Associates formulated a detailed outline of how each public space should be planted and maintained. In one instance, they legislated that the square named Quadranaou be planted with a specific pattern of sugar maple, white maple, and mulberry trees and directed that "the Elevated square with the Ascents leading to the same be immediately put into Grass, and hereafter no other ways occupied—[and] the whole to be left in good Post and Rail fence." Likewise, they delegated the care of a raised road called the Sacra Via to their most respected leader; he was expected to "attend particularly to its preservation in its present form and seed it to Grass."[1]

While the Associates directed the care of these spaces, they had not constructed the central features of these squares (Figure 1). The geometric earth forms at their centers were part of a mysterious complex of earthworks at the junction of the Ohio and Muskingum rivers, which Company leaders had scouted in the 1780s. The Company chose this site for its new town, and rather than ignoring or destroying the features, the men venerated and publicized them. Two centuries later, archaeologists would identify these features and objects excavated from within them as the products of the native Adena and Hopewell peoples, who lived in the Ohio River Valley between 1000 BC and 500 AD (Figure 2).[2] But in the early republic, the features provided enigmatic evidence of former inhabitants of the American continent. After all, the Native Americans who lived in the Ohio country professed no specific knowledge of the structures. By labeling

Figure 1. A rare three-dimensional depiction of the Marietta earthworks before settlement, likely sketched by Rufus Putnam. Printed in Harris, *Journal of a Tour*, n.p., Special Collections, University of Virginia Library.

the earthworks and the objects uncovered from them "American antiquities," western migrants convinced citizens throughout the United States that these landmarks would inform the history of their new nation.

As the traffic of settlers and travelers increased in the Ohio Valley after 1800, the importance of antiquities to national culture shifted. After Ohio became a state in 1803, its residents sought recognition as authorities on the landscape by contrasting their own observations with those of outsiders, calling them generic, exaggerated, or both. In publishing their own findings and theories, residents began to link the collection and discussion of antiquities primarily to Ohio and only secondarily to the nation as a whole. In the 1810s, this search for local authority prompted some Ohioans to establish institutions, correspondence networks, and publications throughout the state to produce information about the West, in the West.

This study of the ways that Ohioans created knowledge about western lands, and in turn, about themselves, engages two bodies of historical literature: works about western landscape and identity and studies about the development of American intellectual networks and cultural institutions. Historians have long recognized that "from the beginning Americans had sought

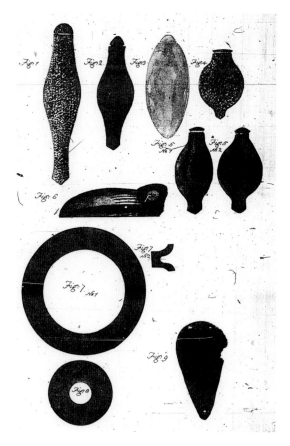

their identity in their relationship to the land they had settled."[3] In order to appraise how westerners built state and regional identities, some historians have discussed the importance of the Land Ordinance of 1785 in imposing a grid on the landscape. Others have argued that the economic relationships that developed along the Ohio River and subsequent transportation networks unified Ohioans.[4] Yet in explaining identity vis-à-vis landscape, these studies invoke a process by which settlers internalized a landscape feature as a symbol or common experience without detailing how this process transpired and created a shared identity.[5] In another body of literature, historians have detailed the formation of transatlantic intellectual networks during colonial expansion and the effect that American independence had on this system. Yet none has examined how similar processes occurred during western expansion in the United States. Scholars who have studied American institutions in the early nation have focused on the museums,

societies, and universities themselves, tending to neglect the networks that sustained them. As a result, their works rarely recognize the participation of westerners in eastern institutions or the influence of communication networks and broader cultural discussions in the shaping of similar establishments in the West.[6]

This study of antiquities in the Ohio country between 1785 and 1820 joins these two historiographies and pays careful attention to the chronology and geography of the conversation surrounding the subject.[7] In so doing, it reveals some of the ways westerners created knowledge about their surrounding landscape in order to define their place in the new nation. This process of creating knowledge entailed three steps: collection of empirical information, interpretation, and communication of the conclusions. Residents of the Northwest sought authority by manipulating this process. Nationally minded Ohio Company settlers retained their connections with New England institutions, and by sending information east, they viewed themselves as extending a network of elite intellectuals. As inaccurate and unflattering accounts of the Ohio landscape and its residents proliferated in travel literature, ordinary Ohioans began to refute these accounts by publishing descriptions of antiquities. In the process, they encouraged a new hierarchy of criteria for authority: residence would carry more weight than social distinction in evaluating descriptions of the West. Leading Ohio antiquaries steered this discussion by collecting information from state residents, compiling it within the state, and communicating it as a western product. By articulating their regional pursuits within the framework of the state, they made Ohio the center and standard for the study of American antiquities and the proposed leader of western development.

To be sure, hope for individual gain motivated these westerners to engage in the antiquities discussion. Some sought economic profit by selling texts about antiquities or by publicizing the subject to entice land investors. Others tried to garner personal prestige as intellectual or cultural leaders. Yet westerners' engagement with antiquities reveals a broader goal that united these specific ones: they all sought to reconcile history and progress to assuage anxieties about cultural development in the West. Their contemporaries constantly debated whether settlers aided the nation by civilizing the frontier or whether they signaled its cultural regression. In response, westerners appropriated antiquities as the tokens of a venerable culture. Specifics of the surrounding dialogue, such as theories about the origins of ancient civilization or the meanings of ceremonial artifacts, did not matter in this light. The mere acts of collecting and describing antiquities conveyed the civility of Ohioans and allowed them to publicize their cultural perspicacity and their land improvements that yielded ancient artifacts. To be sure, the development of towns, roads, canals, and farms destroyed the ancient landscape in its purest form. But by engaging the subject of antiquities, Ohioans pursued their individual attempts at profit and recognition by reconciling a vision of history and of progress that identified the state as the cultural leader of the early American West.

The Ohio Company and the Origins of the American Antiquities Discussion

When Ohio Company settlers arrived at the junction of the Ohio and Muskingum rivers in April of 1788, they set to work plotting their city around a cluster of earthworks. Rufus Putnam surveyed "the Ancient works or Town" and wrote that "the situation of the City-plat is the most delightful of any I ever saw, and those traces of ancient walls, mounds, etc., are truly surprising."[8] A month later, John May "spent the day in viewing and reconnoitering the spot where the City is to be built" and found "the situation delightfully agreeable, well calculated for an elegant City—the old ruins are a masterly piece of work of great extent." May judged the landscape the most elegant feature of the place, writing of the "many traces of art in different places" in contrast to the "surveying buildings etc. in a very backward state."[9] Town planners gave the earthworks Latin names, built public squares around two of the mounds, and determined to "perpetuate the figure and appearance of so majestic a Monument of Antiquity" for ages to come.[10] Early travelers viewed the earthworks as

evidence of "the ingenuity of man in very remote and former ages" and frequently remarked that the earthworks fell "within the ground-plot of the city of Marietta," where the Company preserved them as public property (Figure 3).[11] As prominent men keenly interested in the formation of national culture, Ohio Company members appropriated the remarkable characteristics of the western landscape as elements of national importance.

In planning this first settlement of the Northwest Territory, Ohio Company leaders strove to set an example for future western settlement and expansion. Founded as a joint stock company in March of 1786 by a group of New England veteran Revolutionary officers, the Company enlisted investors to fund the purchase of a large tract of land northwest of the Ohio River. When Company Secretary Winthrop Sargent first visited the area in July 1786, he noted that "the good lands about the Ruins of the Antient Town or City [are] very advantageous," and Ohio Company founders chose this site for their future town.[12] In 1787, Company representatives bought one and a half million acres from Congress; the first contingent of settlers arrived on the banks of the Muskingum and Ohio rivers one year later (Figure 4).[13] Although the developers anticipated financial profits and personal prestige, the founders of the Ohio Company structured their organization and settlement with loftier goals of provided a model example of republican living in the United States, one that fostered a meritocratic yet stable society.[14] Within this framework, Company leaders' attention to natural history reflected their overarching belief that settlers should collect information about western lands as a service to the nation.

In the late eighteenth century, many Americans regarded the frontier as a wild land that would resist the advancement of civilization and diminish the manners, social organization, and intellect of settlers.[15] Western residents themselves entertained these concerns. In 1787, Major Ebenezer Denny, stationed at Fort Harmar on the Muskingum River, lamented that the "highly cultivated mind" of Ohio immigrant Polly Symmes was "about to be buried in the wilderness."[16] In

1790, shareholder Thomas Wallcut cited disorganized Company meetings as "symptoms of decay" in Marietta and confessed his fears that the town would "be a short lived society."[17] Other settlers recognized those fears and combated them with letters boasting of their settlement's social refinement. In 1788, Rowena Tupper wrote to a New England friend regarding her new life "in a savage land, which might greatly raise your curiosity." She addressed her former companion's "various conjectures concerning our situation" and assured her that "we are much happier than you concive [sic] of. The country has been so often spoken of, that it is *needless* for me to say more than that, it answears [sic] every expectation."[18] Firsthand accounts of the Ohio country permeated New England communities, yet Tupper felt compelled to assure her friend that "the society far exceeds whatever [her] ideas had formed" and that she did not fear regressing to an uncivilized life. Few doubted the potential for economic development of Ohio's fertile lands, especially given reports contrasting their temperate climate and rich soils to "the northern frozen deserts" of Vermont and Maine.[19] Still, even settlers sometimes worried about the prospects for cultivating society on such lands and struggled to convince their peers of western civility.

By the early 1780s, a handful of published descriptions about complex earthworks had generated little more than fleeting curiosity among a few intellectuals.[20] Two years before settlement began, Ohio Company leaders started to publicize widely the earthworks as evidence of a lost civilization. They believed that remnants of the ancient landscape evinced the civilized history of their nascent town and proved that the frontier could sustain social and economic development.[21] They also celebrated that the Ohio Valley earthworks "demonstrat[ed] the physical antiquity of America" and allowed them to insert their new nation into discussions of ancient civilizations.[22] By 1787, they had made "antiquities" the standard term used to describe the Ohio earthworks and related objects, associating them with ancient ruins in Europe. In fact, the Ohio Valley might someday form the seat of American civilization and prosperity.

In particular, Company leaders framed Ohio antiquities as a parallel to the ruins of the Roman republic. In striving to establish an American republic, they looked to classical texts, places, persons, and images as models to emulate in their new nation.[23] Many Americans viewed the earthworks as sites of communal government and ceremony, an interpretation that suggested the republican political and social heritage of the new nation. Marietta leaders enhanced this republican vision when they named earthworks after places in ancient Rome.[24] The former Revolutionary officers who led the Company even imagined that the earthworks, or "fortifications," symbolically linked their military service to an ancient warrior civilization not unlike the Roman army.[25] Though most Americans received only practical educations, these references to ancient Roman culture were highly legible to ordinary citizens because elements of the classical past permeated popular culture.[26]

American interest in western earthworks increased as Ohio Company associates publi-

Figure 3. This map shows the Marietta town grid plotted over the earthworks and was likely sketched by Rufus Putnam. Printed in Harris, *Journal of a Tour*, n.p., Special Collections, University of Virginia Library.

cized their existence and related them to contemporary American culture. Elites across the nation quickly generated a wide-scale debate about the earthworks' origins. By the late 1780s, individuals with no connections to the Ohio country cited evidence from the western landscape to create a history that bolstered the respectability of the new nation. These men proposed a number of potential builders of the earthworks, ranging from Spanish explorers to ancestors of socially advanced South American Indians to the forefathers of the Indians who still lived in the Ohio country.[27] The origins debate continued for decades; no regional or institutional consensus emerged, and arguments often culminated in racial theories unrelated to analysis of antiquities themselves.[28] By the time that the first permanent settlers arrived on the Company tract, "the world ha[d] heard much" of the fortifications.[29] Those settlers likely would have echoed James Backus, who after viewing the Marietta earthworks in May 1788, was "not convinced of their origin."[30]

In an age when contemporary revolutions fired interest in theorizing the structure and history of civilization, books that described cycles of humanity in which great civilizations rose and fell greatly influenced the discussion of American earthworks. American readers—even those on the frontier—stocked their libraries with books about classical history and looked to them for theories that readily explained the western earthworks and their absent engineers.[31] Individuals who discussed western antiquities most frequently invoked the Scottish philosophers' materially based stages of civilization. When George Turner requested a copy of Winthrop Sargent's "Remarks on the Ancient Works at Muskingum" in 1787, he hoped to learn about the New World's "early Inhabitants—their probable Descent—and the causes of their Decay," a process that Turner believed occurred independently of Old World civilizations. He reflected on reports of American antiquities:

In the couple of innumerable ages, might not America have seen—and perhaps in Succession—the Rise, Progress, and Decline of Empire? Might

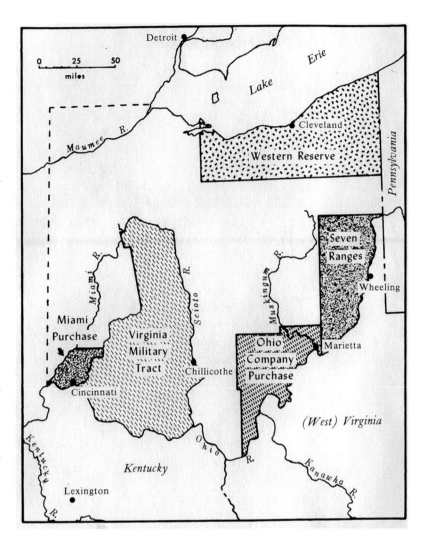

she not have fostered the Arts and Sciences, while the now enlightened Parts of the Earth were covered with Barbarians? And may not the last period of her perfect Civilization be too remote in Antiquity for the most durable of her Monuments to have withstood the leveling Hand of Time?[32]

Turner's questions showed the influence of Edward Gibbon's work, which inspired innumerable conversations about the trajectory of European civilization in the 1770s and 1780s. These discussions gave Turner cause to wonder whether "those ancient Remains on the Muskingum, with others which have come to our Knowledge, are among the last efforts of expiring Civilization."[33] Other correspondents contemplated the Ohio

Figure 4. The Ohio Country, showing land tract purchases and the future borders of the state, admitted in 1803. Robert L. Brewer, "The Ohio Country," in Andrew Cayton, The Frontier Republic (Kent, Ohio: Kent State University Press, 1986), frontispiece, reprinted with permission from The Kent State University Press.

earthworks within this framework of societal development. In 1791, Jonathan Heart deduced that builders of such elaborate earthworks must have lived "not altogether in an uncivilized state; they must have been under the subordination of law, (and) a strict and well-regulated police."[34] A writer calling himself "Lucius" reasoned that "since a middle stage of society is most favorable, to population, and barbarism baleful, would any chuse to deny that population, especially among western Indians, might be vastly more numerous in past ages than in the modern?"[35] In 1790, a Kentucky resident described ancient ruins in the Illinois territory as evidence for the future decline of Europe because "at certain periods there seem to be revolutions in nature, which entirely obliterate the memory of the past."[36] Each author tried to place the builders of the Ohio Valley ruins in the historical social order of world civilizations.

Since conclusions about the earthworks' history held broad implications for the young nation's future, the antiquities discussion raised epistemological concerns about the study of the ancient landscape. Many Americans looked to scientific methods to uncover secrets of the ancient past from the landscape. After requesting information from the Muskingum in 1788, James Winthrop reminded Winthrop Sargent, "There is no danger of being too minute. The danger is of not being critical. You will do great service by furnishing the Academy with particular drawings of these things wherever found. It may be of great service in the history of mankind." Ancient buildings or markings "cannot be copied too accurately, as by a comparison of these things with the familiar productions of other countries, and something with history, we may trace useful resemblances . . . and the degree of civilization may be tolerably ascertained."[37] Yet other men worried that knowledge about the earthworks' creators might be lost forever. In 1796, Benjamin Smith Barton instructed readers that the age of antiquities necessitated the use of "imagination and conjecture," which caused him to "leav[e] the sure road of historical inquiry, for the narrow, and too often uncertain, path of the antiquary."[38] This predicament of studying ancient forms worried

many intellectuals and caused George Turner to exclaim, "how contemptible is the Knowledge of Man—how limited our historical Information—and, we may add, how disgraced with Superstition and Error!"[39] With their potential to inform, earthworks raised equally pressing questions about the methods used to study the history of North America.

Americans used the study of antiquities as one subject of scientific inquiry that would boost the power and interests of the newly independent United States. They strove to show that the design of their new republic promoted intellectual pursuits, and natural historians took an especially keen interest in this process.[40] In the words of historian John C. Greene, "Patriotism, economic interest, and scientific curiosity all dictated that the works of nature in the New World be described, catalogued, and placed at the service of the new nation."[41] Many men agreed with Jeremy Belknap that "the Trans-Allegheny Country is an object of very great Importance" in these pursuits and offered the perfect subject for this inquiry.[42] Antiquities presented Americans with the opportunity to study natural history themselves rather than collect specimens as middlemen in the British colonial framework, as they had done before Independence. After the Revolution, Americans continued to share information with Europeans, who maintained a great interest in North American natural history. But the former colonists now staked a claim for national identity by collecting objects at a growing number of American colleges and by publishing studies domestically.[43] Contributing empirical data and artifacts to this effort enabled Ohio Company settlers to position themselves as the premier sources of information about the nation's ancient and natural history. While the Ohio Company preserved many earthworks *in situ,* they believed that ancient artifacts belonged in eastern institutions.[44] Leaders like Manasseh Cutler and Winthrop Sargent strengthened their intellectual networks in anticipation of moving west, meeting with correspondents and visiting museums as they traveled to transact business.[45] When Cutler journeyed to New York and Philadelphia to arrange the Company's land purchase, he met with Ezra Stiles, Benjamin

Rush, and Benjamin Franklin; visited academic leaders, libraries, and museums at four colleges; and toured Charles Willson Peale's museum and the curiosity cabinet at Independence Hall. Though familiar with popular institutions, Ohio Company associates sent ancient artifacts specifically to academic institutions where they would "furnish matter for the contemplation of the republic of letters, and for useful deductions in natural science."[46]

Amid these intellectual pursuits, the western landscape earned the Ohio country a reputation as an extraordinary place. The publication of a mock epic poem, *The Anarchiad,* was one of the first publications to generate this popular image. The Connecticut Wits—Joel Barlow, Lemuel Hopkins, David Humphreys, and John Trumbull—had learned about the Muskingum earthworks from letters written by Ohio Company leaders and soldiers stationed at Fort Harmar. Concerned with the political and cultural development of the United States, the authors wrote *The Anarchiad* both to warn against the dangers of antifederalism and to establish a model for American poetry.[47] Set in the ancient landscape of the Ohio Valley, the poem appeared in ten newspaper installments between October 1786 and May 1787 and immediately gained a wide readership. Continually published under the headline "American Antiquities," the epic began as a letter from "Antiquary"—the collective pseudonym for the authors—to the Ohio Company members Return J. Meigs and William Dana. Antiquary identified himself as a member of "a society of cricks and antiquarians, who have made it their business and delight, for some years past, to investigate the ancient as well as natural history of America," and he claimed that he had uncovered manuscripts, printed texts, and artifacts in the earthworks. He attempted "to quench the thirst for novelty from the burning spring on the Ohio" by publishing the poem, which he characterized as "still more valuable to the republick of letters" than any previous findings. Speaking to the popular interest in western antiquities, Antiquary wrote, "I need scarcely premise the ruins of fortifications, yet visible, and other vestiges of art in the western country,

had sufficiently demonstrated that this delightful region had once been occupied by a civilized people." By using "a chemick preparation" to restore an ancient text, Antiquary demonstrated that scientific analysis would inform Americans of their ancient predecessors.[48] Despite the poem's fantastical narrative, the authors grasped the mythic potential of the western landscape and rooted in it their broad concerns about the development of American culture.

Ohio Company affiliates augmented this image of the incredible Ohio landscape as they flooded New England with descriptions of western curiosities. The unique landscape of the Ohio country prompted writers to create a new set of topographical terms to describe it.[49] Still, Ohio settlers often lamented that no picture or description could communicate accurately the remarkable characteristics of the earthworks, as when Rufus Putnam assured Manasseh Cutler that "Mr. Sargent's painting gives but a faint idea of what is to be seen on the spot."[50] Sometimes these descriptions crossed into the terrain of fantasy. In 1789, Winthrop Sargent reported the discovery of a bug that buried itself and then sprouted as a plant. Among members of the American Academy of Arts and Sciences, this account "raised, not a laugh (for that would have been unbecoming a philosophical body); but a smile; and some whispers were circulated: 'This is a fine Ohioism.'"[51] Within a year of the settlement of Marietta, some New Englanders associated stories of fantastic flora and fauna specifically with the Ohio country. Still, scientific reports of Ohio Company associates outweighed mythical accounts, and the Northwest Territory continued to supply Americans with information for serious discussion of antiquities.

After Ohio Company members settled in Marietta, their enduring ties to New England society motivated and facilitated the study of antiquities in this national context. These men promoted strong cultural nationalism, or the "effort to cultivate American accomplishments in intellectual endeavors, to the exclusion of European influences."[52] Most belonged to intellectual communities fostered by universities and philosophical societies in Boston, Cambridge, New Haven, and Philadelphia, and acted as western liaisons to these institutions. Men like Manasseh Cutler and Winthrop Sargent immersed themselves in the pursuit of scientific knowledge.[53] In 1788, several easterners proposed a sustained exchange of information with Winthrop Sargent. Like Jeremy Belknap, they asked for "Information from Time to Time respecting the discoveries and improvements which may be made in that region of fertility and curiosity" and offered information from the East in return.[54] James Winthrop traded blueprints of a barometer to Sargent for "observations, which you may think [of] communicating. Those upon the climate and native productions of the country, upon antiquities, arts, tools, will be useful."[55] Many men maintained connections with state as well as national institutions, as Jared Mansfield did when he corresponded regularly with the Connecticut Academy of Arts and Sciences as well as the American Academy.[56]

Their fascination with antiquities distinguished Ohio Company associates from their western counterparts. Settlers and travelers paid little attention to earthworks in western Virginia and Kentucky in the last two decades of the eighteenth century.[57] As more prominent landowners moved to the Northwest in the years before Ohio statehood in 1803, Ohio Company members stood out among their elite territorial peers. Regardless of their attention to the land as surveyors, boosters, and agriculturalists, Ohio leaders in the Miami Purchase and the Virginia Military District displayed a less than keen interest in antiquities.[58] Thomas Worthington's infrequent mention of earthworks represented the low interest in antiquities held by many leading landowners. During his stay with the Putnam family in Marietta in 1796, Worthington made no note of earthworks in his description of the "lovely" land and town.[59] In 1804, Hugh Williamson sent a long list of questions to Worthington regarding "indian antiquities" after a Kentuckian had mentioned Worthington as a "gentleman who has paid considerable attention to that subject."[60] After waiting many months for a reply, Williamson wrote again and still received no response. One of Worthington's rare comments on earthworks encapsulates his disinterest: he once wrote to his wife that "an Indian mound will afford a lovely situation for a summer house, and commands views of the whole town."[61] Despite a number of earthworks near Worthington's mansion and in nearby Chillicothe, he never joined the national debate about who built the mounds or what they signified.

Elites who were interested in antiquities set high standards for discussion of the subject because antiquities informed America's history and contemporary culture. Leaders characterized their study as an activity for elites with time for leisure. A writer describing the French settlement at Gallipolis expressed this sentiment in 1791, when he praised settlers for first "improving the surface [rather] than searching into the bowels" of the land to learn about "the Botany, Mineralogy, and Antiquities of our country."[62] Participants in the antiquities discussion also frequently judged information by the social respectability of sources. For instance, when Thomas Jefferson doubted the veracity of accounts of bricks and iron tools discovered in the Ohio Valley, he wanted to know whether General Parsons had seen the evidence for himself.[63] When Jonathan Heart relayed numerous observations of the Marietta antiquities to Dr. Benjamin Smith Barton, he described the character of his contacts and admitted that some information might not be "that satisfactory information which the nature of your work probably requires."[64]

Nevertheless, intellectual standards of the elite did not inhibit popular discussion of antiquities. As gentlemen travelers and prominent residents sent information east to intellectual institutions, ordinary settlers who quickly populated the Northwest also read about antiquities, unearthed artifacts, and described the earthworks in letters. James Winthrop had foreseen this swift development of the Ohio country and had warned Winthrop Sargent that "care should be taken to prevent people from building on, or plowing up such sacred ground."[65] As western lands attracted growing numbers of people to its territory, with promises of prosperity, adventure, and curiosities, keeping the ancient earthworks intact proved increasingly difficult.

Western Antiquities in the Early National Culture of Geography and Travel

For some Americans, accounts of western antiquities proved too remarkable to believe without a firsthand look. Geographer Gilbert Imlay predicted correctly when he wrote that the Northwest would "draw men of science to trace and investigate [its] various phenomena" from which "the world will receive much pleasure and instruction."[66] But the unique characteristics of western lands also attracted adventure seekers and travelers. Public discussion of antiquities intensified curiosity about the West, inspiring many trips down the Ohio River and creating an audience for travel narratives. As one Marietta visitor explained, "I had been willing to persuade myself that [the earthworks] were only the sports of nature, and that imagination might have formed mole hills into pyramids and walls fifty or sixty feet high. I do assure you my opinion was wholly changed upon my late survey, and I am now convinced from a view of the Muskingum works . . . that nations must once have existed in these interior parts of America."[67] Even when seeing was believing, many travelers still thought that they were "dealing a little in the wonderful."[68] One man credited the earthworks with improving his health, writing that his mind "was constantly occupied and amused with the new and interesting scenery and the wonderful antiquities in this neighborhood."[69] Accounts by ordinary travelers proliferated alongside those written by notable public figures and provided intriguing descriptions of antiquities to Americans without connections to western travelers, educated elites, or philosophical societies.

A set of common experiences characterized these journeys down the Ohio River in the 1790s.[70] Few adventurers failed to note their initial impressions of earthworks. Most visitors to Marietta, whether they planned to stay for one day or a lifetime, visited the local earthworks upon arrival. When James Backus first disembarked, he immediately "went out to view the Town and commons" and was "pleased with the large Mound of old ruins as they are called."[71] After traveling from Connecticut, Benjamin Dana and his cousin Israel Putnam arrived at Marietta on April 30, 1794, and "the next day [they] walked about town & went out & saw the Grand Mound & the Square" before boarding another boat bound for the town of Belpre.[72] Francis Baily's travel diary suggests that many Ohio Valley earthworks had become tourist attractions by the mid-1790s. When he climbed to the top of the Grave Creek mound, on the Virginia side of the River, he found a tree with a "number of names carved by those whom curiosity had drawn to visit this place."[73] In Marietta, he noted that there was a "covered way" leading from the river directly to the earthworks.[74] By 1800, the Ohio landscape showed stark evidence of travelers' activities encouraged by the tourist culture developing in the Ohio Valley.[75]

Settlers exacerbated these changes to the landscape, and many destroyed earthworks. At the beginning of the nineteenth century, people moved to Ohio to develop the land for personal and national profit. While many Ohio Company men articulated a desire to preserve all of the "vestiges of antiquity," some recognized the impossibility—and undesirability—of this task. One early settler judged that the Company would maintain a few earthworks for public use, but that "the rest of the works can remain, when the city is built, on paper only."[76] In Cincinnati, travelers frequently remarked that roads bisected mounds and exposed ancient objects to passersby.[77] In 1800, fewer than 50,000 people lived in the Ohio territory, but by 1810, the population exceeded 230,000 (Figure 5). This nascent citizenry, anchored in the southern half of the state, eagerly sought to develop Ohio into an economic hub of the nation.[78] While many residents expressed curiosity about the earthworks, most concerned themselves with land development.

Nevertheless, discussion of antiquities increased as settlers and travelers poured into the Ohio Valley. Books and newspaper articles attested to sustained national interest in the subject. Travel writers and booksellers increasingly appealed to readers by distinguishing between books that generally described western lands and those that addressed antiquities.[79] Newspapers across the country also published short travel accounts about American antiquities. These articles commonly appeared in multiple periodicals, printed everywhere from Charleston, South Carolina, to western New York, to Portland, Maine. Editors republished one report more than fifty times within the span of fifteen years. In March of 1792, the *Philadelphia National Gazette* published five paragraphs "from the manuscript of a late traveller" under the headline, "Remarkable Antiquities in Interior America." Twelve newspapers borrowed the text over the following three months. Four years later, the *New-York Time Piece* published the article again, removing the phrase "from the manuscript of a late traveller." This spawned another set of reprintings, with some columns retaining mention of the author's recent travels. The article's largest print cycle came after the *Richmond Enquirer* in Virginia revived it on July 21, 1807. Over the next eight months nearly two dozen newspapers published the piece yet again. The reprinting cycles of this one article show that public interest, not simply new information, guided newspaper content about antiquities.

This discussion grew alongside a widespread fascination with geography. In the early republic, geography books and maps abounded, mak-

ing knowledge of the land central to conceptions of the nation itself.[80] Popular geography books like Gilbert Imlay's *Topographical Description of the Western Territory of North America* (1792) and Jedidiah Morse's *The American Geography* (1789) limned vivid images of western terrain in the minds of readers, who provided a ready market for multiple editions of the texts.[81] The prevalence of detailed descriptions of antiquities prompted readers to picture earthworks and curiosities in their visions of the Ohio River Valley, making the subject an unavoidable topic for travel writers. In Morse's *Geography*, the Northwest Territory earned a special section entitled "Antiquities and Curiosities."[82] When Thaddeus Mason Harris returned to Boston after a trip to Ohio in 1803, he "was advised, on my return, to communicate the Geographical articles to the public" and published his journal so that it would contribute information "to the common stock of the topographical knowledge of our country."[83] By describing antiquities, geographers enhanced the symbolic, nationalistic significance of the ancient earthworks and artifacts.

Like Americans in the East, westerners expressed a great interest in geography and

Figure 5. Ohio County Population in 1810. Map created by the University of Virginia Library, Historical Census Browser, based on data from the Interuniversity Consortium for Political and Social Research (ICPSR).

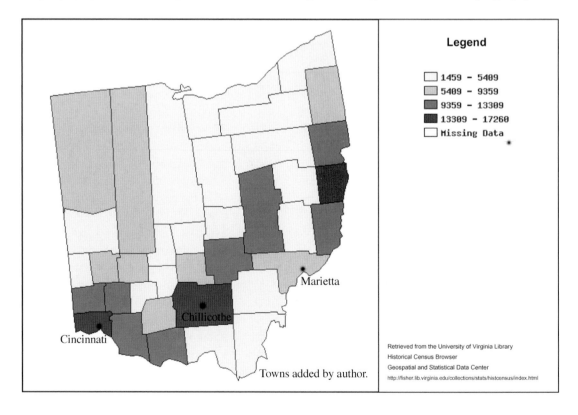

eagerly consumed geography books, natural histories of the land, and maps. Because geography books portended to teach literacy and to entertain, they appealed to a particularly wide segment of the population.[84] Benjamin Franklin Stone remembered poring over Morse's *Geography* during his childhood in the Ohio territory; Thomas Wallcut noted that Marietta residents read Thomas Hutchins's geographical writings and Thomas Salmon's *New Geographical and Historical Grammar*; and elite Ohioans insisted that their children study geography.[85] Settlers and travelers inevitably entered Ohio with their preconceptions shaped by geography books and travel narratives. Some used the texts as field guides and noted when their observations did not match.[86] Maps of the West proliferated, and diagrams of the Marietta earthworks became popular on both sides of the Atlantic (Figure 6).[87] For many Americans, the measured, schematic images provided their first glimpse of the western landscape. In *Weatherwise's Federal Almanack* (1788), Boston printer John Norman published one of the first popular images of earthworks, a crude map of "the Ruins of a City" with a description of nearby land along the Muskingum River. Anticipating readers' desire for more information, he advertised "a pamphlet containing a Geographical Description of the Western Country" and a "large Map of said Country" for sale at his print shop.[88] Several printers made engravings from Rufus Putnam's surveys, and Winthrop Sargent published the first detailed sketches of ancient artifacts in a pamphlet in 1796. Ten years later, Jared Mansfield wrote of one Ohio map: "There is no doubt that [the cartographer] will obtain something very handsome by it as a vast number of people in this state would purchase such a map, & perhaps many of the Eastern States."[89] As a result of this geographic print culture, travelers frequently viewed local features in the context of a national perspective, such as when Jesup Couch judged a mound at Grave Creek to be "the largest mound in the Union" during a trip in 1804.[90]

As well as situating Ohio in the nation's geography, the framework of the state structured historical consciousness of the Ohio country. Settlers had begun to conceive of a history for

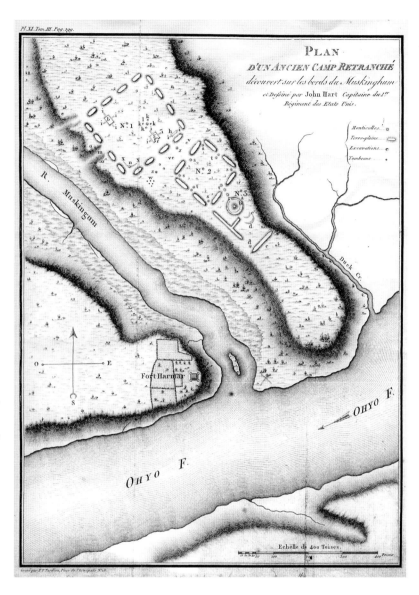

the Ohio territory since its settlement under the Northwest Ordinance. In 1795, John Cleves Symmes already "[thought] it a duty I owe to my country and to myself" to write a history of Ohio settlement in the Miami Purchase.[91] When Ohio entered the Union in 1803, the political entity of the state had developed an important meaning in America's geographic culture, and early historians appropriated it as a framework for a coherent history of the region. Thaddeus Mason Harris arrived in Marietta on April 23, 1803, a mere two months after Ohio entered the Union, but he nevertheless appended a detailed historical report of Ohio to his travel narrative in

Figure 6. "Plan D'un Ancien Camp Retranché découvert sur les bords du Muskingum et Defsiné par John Hart Capitaine du 1er Régiment des Etats Unis" (Paris, 1801), courtesy of the Ross County Historical Society, Chillicothe, Ohio.

1805.[92] Despite his limited travel and his overt loyalties to the Federalist leaders at Marietta, Harris extrapolated from his experiences to create a geography and a history for the state. He tied his narrative so closely to state boundaries that he felt compelled to justify his descriptions of antiquities that "[fell] without the limits of the State of Ohio."[93] After statehood, travelers continued to follow the same route down the Ohio River, but they cast their comments about local phenomena as reflections of the entire state.

Between 1800 and 1820, travel writers appropriated the subject of antiquities as a way to comment on the manners and cultural development of western residents. By 1810, wealthy travelers and Europeans seeking to judge American development formed the bulk of travelers down the Ohio River.[94] They often criticized westerners by celebrating the merits of antiquities and disparaging the settlers' disregard for them. One of the most notorious critics and best-selling authors, Thomas Ashe, defined the preservation of an ancient object as "a monument of former times, and of the taste of the present inhabitants."[95] Describing a mound in Chillicothe, Ashe judged that its associations and aesthetic beauty "ought to have endeared it to the heart and made it an object fit for the most sacred contemplation of the mind." When he found that Chillicothe residents had damaged it and several other earthworks, his respect "for the inhabitants fled before this testimony of the depravity of their taste and vulgarity of their minds."[96] According to Ashe's definition, the study of "Indian antiquity" demanded "perseverance [and] erudition" from individuals with "curiosity, leisure, and intelligence."[97] By explicitly linking antiquities with high culture, travel writers used the intellectual framework established by Ohio Company men to criticize western residents who did not preserve earthworks.

Conflicting accounts of western antiquities, and the cultural commentary attached to them, prompted concerns over who had the authority to characterize western lands and residents. Authors of travel narratives often claimed to be disabusing readers of false accounts, but many of these self-proclaimed corrective narratives also misrepresented their subjects. In turn,

some readers rebuked unreliable authors. In a particularly scathing review, a writer identifying himself as "Iota" contended that Thomas Ashe's *Travels in America* (1808) comprised a "miserable compilation" of information copied from a traveler's guide called *The Navigator*.[98] He suggested that the title "Crudities hastily gobbled up in a tour" would have best suited the book, whose accounts "were interlarded with the most gross aspersions of the character of the settlers, the most odious misrepresentations of the effects of the climate, and the most extravagant exaggeration on the subject of the antiquities in the Western Territory."[99] Based on "personal Knowledge and correct information," Iota listed specific errors made by Ashe and scolded fellow readers for their poor judgment of travel narratives. He considered it "mortifying" that a Massachusetts native had written an excellent description of Ohio "in which is a very accurate account of indian antiquities, [but] not enough copies could be disposed of to pay for the paper on which it was printed; while the base imposition of a pretended visitor of the same country, should meet with the most rapid and extensive sale. But such is American patronage!" Iota ended his diatribe with a warning of the dangers of letting outsiders offer definitive accounts: *Suis neglectis, alienos fovalis.* By neglecting to buy books written by their countrymen, Americans encouraged foreigners to write about the United States and profit from their mischaracterizations.

Other Americans who shared Iota's concerns sought to publish verified accounts of western earthworks. Hugh Williamson, writing from New York, was one. He wrote, "What nation of the other continent gave birth to our Indians or what degree of art they may have possessed in their highest state of cultivation are questions hitherto immerged in the dark shades of oblivion. Any light that can be cast upon this subject must be acceptable to people in Europe as well as to every inquisitive citizen of the United States."[100] Williamson condemned two published works, "one of them from Europe, by gentlemen who are hardly willing to admit the existence of Indian fortifications." He "had embraced the opinions from the information of intelligent friends, very different from those writers" and sought to verify his opinions through trusted gentlemen with first-hand accounts of the earthworks.[101] At a time when accounts of antiquities had been first exaggerated and then refuted, Williamson viewed the problem in international terms and sought to set the record straight.

Yet between 1805 and 1820, Ohio residents increasingly considered anyone living outside the bounds of their state an outsider when it came to describing Ohio lands. In response, they repudiated inaccurate descriptions of their state's landscape for themselves in an effort to prove their intelligence and refinement in the face of eastern condescension. Although the nation had successfully admitted new states into the Union on equal footing, Americans remained unsure of the cultural and social parity of the residents of these frontier states. Well after Ohio achieved statehood in 1803, "the old woman" New England still sometimes "accuse[d] Miss Ohio of being awkward and indolent."[102] Even residents of the state sometimes expressed similar concerns about the refinement of Ohioans. When Jesup Couch suggested that "the manners of the people [were] much vitiated" in Marietta, he worried that their behavior would reflect poorly on the state as a whole.[103] A few writers appraised this lack of social cultivation sympathetically. In 1810, Christian Schultz Jr. commended the unassuming quality of Ohioans, writing that "inhabitants of the Ohio country in general have very little of that unmeaning politeness, which we so much praise and admire in the Atlantic States. They are as yet the mere children of nature, and neither their virtues nor their vices are calculated to please refined tastes."[104] Yet even the most favorable accounts of the state of western culture recognized that a decided air of inelegance lingered over Ohio. As one means of changing this, the state's residents inserted themselves into the antiquities discussion that frequently criticized them.

Ohio Residents Speak for the West

As many westerners realized that descriptions of the Ohio landscape bore on their own reputations, Ohioans engaged antiquities as one way to counter negative portrayals of their landscape and themselves. By 1805, many residents resented the fact that travelers had "frequently given to the world such crude and indigested statements, after having visited a few ancient works, or, heard the idle tales of persons incompetent to describe them, that intelligent persons residing on the very spot, would never suspect what works were intended to be described."[105] Rather than sending information and artifacts east like the earliest Ohio Company settlers had done, residents of the young state changed the dynamic of the study of antiquities to respond directly to these concerns prompted by travelers' accounts. They transformed the discussion of Ohio's ancient landscape in three ways. First, a number of ordinary Ohioans began to study and to communicate their knowledge of local antiquities to newspapers and writers. Second, as growing settlement and development of Ohio lands made preservation of ancient landscape features problematic, Ohioans began to represent these features in print and in local institutions. And third, Ohioans framed the study of antiquities in terms of the state, even as they sought to promote the cultural development of the entire western region. As a result of these efforts, westerners came to dominate the national discussion about American antiquities, and by 1820, they had made residence an important criterion in speaking with authority about the West.

Between 1805 and 1810, ordinary Ohioans began to publish their discoveries of antiquities and to gain more respect in the discourse about the subject. Unlike the erudite Ohio Company leaders, these spokesmen did not often identify with elite eastern society or institutions. One Ohioan wrote to the *Ohio Fredonian,* "I had waited a long time for some one more adequate to the task than I can pretend to be, to give a description of these curiosities, which appear to be worthy of the attention of the greatest antiquarian. But since I find this not likely to be done, I have commenced it myself, which may probably pave the way for others much more capable of performing the task."[106] The writer acknowledged his modest position but signed the letter "Hermes," alluding to his status as a messenger. Whether such modesty was feigned or sincere, writers like Hermes asserted themselves as the most qualified commentators on Ohio antiquities by virtue of their western residence.

Almanacs published in Ohio between 1805 and 1810 also reflected Ohioans' growing desire to speak for themselves. William M'Farland, the author of *Browne's Western Almanac, or, The Cincinnati Almanac* (1805), noted his "happ[iness] in being the instrument of furnishing the public with the first Almanac ever calculated and published by a citizen of the State of Ohio."[107] In the next year's edition, Robert Stubbs replaced the universal aphorisms, home remedies, and statistics printed by other American almanacs with detailed information about Ohio. His call for descriptions of the land from state residents had generated so many responses that he planned to publish them in a separate pamphlet. Like those concerned with antiquities, Stubbs believed that Ohio residents "[had] it in their power to furnish the public with more specific intelligence."[108] Over the next several years he filled the almanac with descriptions of towns, natural features, and antiquities culled from letters, newspapers, and Thaddeus Harris's *Tour of Ohio* (1805). In the 1809 edition, Stubbs reprinted the letter from Hermes that described earthworks near Chillicothe and encouraged more Ohio residents to contribute to the discussion. That same year, Stubbs toured Ohio and published firsthand accounts of its geography. While most almanacs calibrated only calendrical details to specific locales, *Browne's Western Almanac* appealed to readers with detailed descriptions of the Ohio landscape.[109]

After 1810, writers from all locales increasingly cited Ohio residents as the primary sources of correct information about the western landscape. Eastern newspapers reprinted more local reports from Ohio newspapers in order to satisfy their readers' interest in antiquities. Nonresident book authors attested to the accuracy and originality of their landscape descriptions by seeking endorsements from respected periodicals and individuals, which publicized the authors' firsthand knowledge and connections to Ohio residents.[110] In recommending Samuel R. Brown's book *The Western Gazetteer, or Emigrant's Directory* (1817) to the "enterprising Farmers and

Mechanics of the Atlantic states," one advertisement explained, "where personal knowledge was wanting, [Brown] has availed himself of the correspondence of many of the most intelligent gentlemen resident in the West."[111] Cincinnati resident Dr. Daniel Drake employed the same strategy. In an 1816 advertisement for his book *Natural and Statistical View or Picture of Cincinnati and the Miami Country* (1815), Drake solicited a commendation from Josiah Meigs, Commissioner of the United States General Land Office and son of Marietta founding father Return J. Meigs. Meigs possessed great knowledge and authority on western lands, and he thought it his "duty to say" that Drake's book "contains more *correct, scientific*, and truly valuable information, relative to its object, than any or all other works that have been published."[112] In another advertisement, Drake quoted the *Port Folio* to explain that "the principal value of this work arises from the number and importance of the facts it contains derived from the personal observations of the author."[113] Since travel narratives about Ohio abounded, authors gathered endorsements of their intimate knowledge of western lands in order to distinguish their books.

As alluded to by the references to "gentlemen" in book endorsements, Ohio elites continued to participate in the study of antiquities. A number of locally and regionally prominent citizens encouraged and organized popular discussion of the ancient landscape. Caleb Atwater and Daniel Drake became the most notable of these Ohio antiquaries. Born in Massachusetts in 1778, Atwater moved from New York to Circleville, Ohio, in 1815 and immediately characterized himself as a westerner. After three years, Atwater touted his residence in Ohio as he widely publicized "his intention of publishing Notes of that State."[114] Drake had lived in the West since the age of two, when his family migrated from New Jersey to Kentucky. He moved to Cincinnati, Ohio, in 1800, and practiced medicine there until 1817, when he accepted a professorship at Transylvania University in Lexington, Kentucky. After a year, he returned to Cincinnati to start a medical school, stoking a cultural rivalry between the two towns.[115] Drake frequently moved back and forth across the Ohio River until his death in 1852.[116]

The structure of communication networks developed by these Ohio antiquaries resembled earlier ones between New Englanders and westerners, with the important exception that they valued local reports most highly rather than social status of the correspondent. In 1820, Caleb Atwater served as postmaster of Circleville, Ohio, struggled to earn a living despite an education at Williams College, and identified himself as a "professional man, constantly engaged in various branches of business"—hardly the profile of a wealthy man of leisure.[117] Yet Atwater located people around the state who shared his antiquarian interests and solicited information and sketches from them. His correspondents included Samuel Williams, a chief land office clerk at Chillicothe; early Marietta settlers Judge Paul Fearing, Dr. Samuel Hildreth, and Return J. Meigs Jr.; the Perry County Surveyor; a U.S. Indian agent stationed at Piqua; and a judge and a minister from Chillicothe (Figure 7).[118] Atwater called these men gentlemen, recommended some of them for membership in the American Antiquarian Society, and acknowledged many more in his publication *Description of the Antiquities Discovered in the State of Ohio and Other Western States*.[119] The large contingent of Ohioans accepted into the American Antiquarian Society established the state as a formidable source of scholarly inquiry.[120]

Despite the erudition of Atwater's correspondents, interaction between ordinary Ohioans and these deputies democratized the process of information collection. This process established a distinct sphere of western knowledge that implicitly and explicitly challenged cultural domination by elites and easterners.[121] As residence became the prime qualifier for information about antiquities, antiquaries addressed their calls for information to a broader segment of the population. Rather than targeting gentlemen, be they residents or travelers, antiquaries contacted people who lived near earthworks. Some calls still specifically addressed the educated segment of the western population, such as Atwater's hope that "the literati of the west will rally around [the] banner" of Kentucky antiquary John D. Clifford.[122] But most calls for information urged anyone with information about earthworks to collect and communicate it, either privately to antiquar-

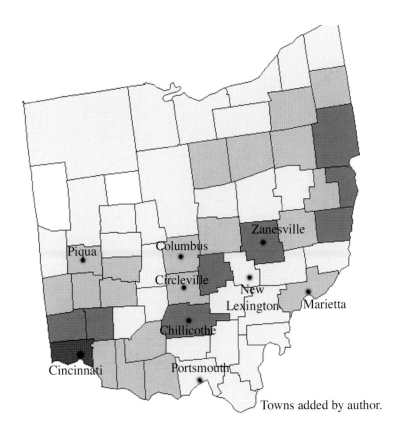

Towns added by author.

ies or through publications. When the Western Museum Society established their institution in Cincinnati in 1818, members advertised that they would "with pleasure receive and preserve such *Natural and Artificial Curiosities* as are worthy of being introduced into a well regulated cabinet." Anyone could approach them with artifacts for consideration: "These [objects] may be handed to one of the Managers, or carried to the south wing of the College edifice, where compensation will be made if required."[123] Information collection had become more egalitarian since the earliest years of Ohio Valley settlement when New England antiquaries limited participation to social elites. While antiquaries often referred to their close correspondents as gentlemen, any literate or curious Ohioan could contribute to knowledge of antiquities by virtue of living near them.[124] Newspaper accounts and antiquaries' correspondence show that Ohioans responded to these calls. Well-diggers discovered an ancient skeleton; statehouse builders unearthed antiquities in Columbus; and more than one farmer reported finds to Atwater.[125] By 1820, gentlemen travelers no longer dominated the field;

Figure 7. Locations of Caleb Atwater's Chief Correspondents. Map adapted from the University of Virginia Library, Historical Census Browser.

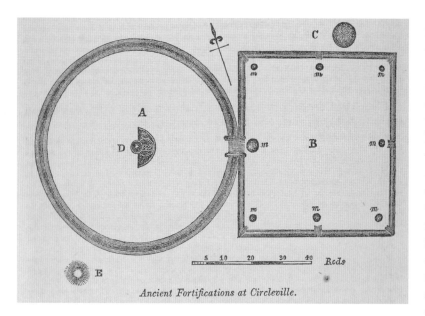

Ancient Fortifications at Circleville.

Figure 8. Diagram showing the earthworks at Circleville. Henry Howe, *Historical Collections of Ohio* (Cincinnati, 1847), 410, Special Collections, University of Virginia Library.

residents of western states spoke for themselves.

As settlement progressed, some Ohioans made great efforts to preserve earthworks, usually as sites of recreation in cities and outside growing towns. Marietta residents maintained the earthworks that the Ohio Company founders had venerated. In Pickaway County, Ohio, in 1810, Daniel Dresbach emulated the Marietta founders by directing the incorporation of earthworks into the town of Circleville (Figures 8 and 9).[126] In 1804, Jesup Couch recorded a glimpse of typical activities at these sites; in Marietta, he and a friend shot pistols "for amusement" and then "walked up to the fortifications, [were] introduced to Gen. Putnam who walked with us about the fortifications & then invited us to tea."[127] A year later, he noted when he and friends rode horses "out to the fortification" beyond Chillicothe before returning to town to enjoy a night of drinking and socializing.[128] Chillicothe residents frequented these "ancient fortifications near the Banks of the Scioto" because many undoubtedly agreed with Mahlon Burwell that their "situation [was] quite romantic."[129]

Still, most town planners retained ancient earthworks sparingly. In many southern Ohio cities, builders preserved just one or two mounds and leveled the majority of complexes in constructing roads and buildings. Cincinnati exemplified this practice of selective incorporation. In 1815, Daniel Drake reported, "Evening walks are more habitual, in which the river bank and the adjacent

hills—the *Columbian garden*—and the *mound,* at the *west end,* [we]re the principal resorts."[130] Cincinnatians retained antiquities *in situ* when they could transform them into useful space. However, as long as a few examples remained intact, town residents valued urban expansion more highly. One German traveler's journal reveals that others agreed with this approach: "Having seen on the map of the city of Cincinnati, the indication of some Indian mounds, I went in search of them, but was unsuccessful, for the very good reason that the hills had been demolished and in their place houses built."[131] When land development threatened the maintenance of ancient sites, settlers often valued new roads, buildings, and farms more highly than the preservation of earthworks.

Before the settlement of Marietta, James Winthrop had cautioned Winthrop Sargent to prevent the plowing and destruction of earthworks, but in the following years, a sense of inevitable destruction accompanied discussions of antiquities. For instance, when builders of the new statehouse in Columbus uncovered a number of skeletons and artifacts in 1814, they professed great interest in the objects but concluded that "the mound must be all taken away, and the earth in which the bones lay [be] found to answer the purpose intended."[132] Many westerners recognized that "the rapidly increasing population and cultivation of our country" had led to the destruction of features of the ancient landscape.[133] In *The Western Gazetteer,* Samuel Brown impugned General Anthony Wayne for cutting down a mound in order to house a sentinel, a sign that "venerable antiquity has not been respected."[134] After learning that a Chillicothe resident had leveled a mound "to make room for a fine brick house," Brown lamented that "this want of respect for *aboriginal antiquities,* is too often evinced by the people of the west."[135] As the pace of development increased, so too did the urgency with which advocates documented mounds, collected artifacts, and encouraged preservation.

This process precipitated a paradox. The progress that antiquaries lamented created cities and towns whose cultural institutions would support the study of antiquities. By 1820, over 580,000 people lived in Ohio, mostly in the southern half of the state (Figure 10). Cincinnati became a center of western development, rivaled only by Lexington, Kentucky.[136] As Ohioans improved land and settled the state, they uncovered evidence that informed discussions about antiquities. Writers increasingly attributed these discoveries to farmers and construction laborers, linking land development to increasing knowledge about the ancient past. Settlement encouraged the establishment of western newspapers, printing presses, museums, schools, and societies, which helped Ohioans to claim earthworks as a distinctly western cultural capital.

As the state economy boomed, leading antiquaries embraced the potential for cultural development. In recognizing the threats to the ancient landscape, men like Atwater and Drake published studies of antiquities and developed institutions that would hold artifacts from the landscape. By representing the landscape on the page and transferring specimens from the land to collections, these men opened up Ohio lands for development while preserving the information that they provided about the state's ancient history. During its early years, the Western Museum represented the grandest and most explicit attempt by leaders to establish local institutions that preserved and publicized information about western lands.[137] In 1818, Daniel Drake and four Cincinnati civic leaders founded the Museum near Cincinnati College to "make an extensive and permanent collection of the natural productions and antiquities of the Western Country."[138] Although Drake believed that American antiquities did not "awaken inspiration, nor infuse melancholy" like "the classical ruins of Asia and Europe," he judged them worthy of admiration and contemplation.[139] Traveling to see antiquities and curiosities in their natural settings remained the best way to study the subject, but Drake hoped that the Museum would preserve objects that might otherwise be destroyed by the changing of the landscape and make these specimens accessible to a wide audience. The Society planned to collect artifacts from across the United States and even the world, but the founders primarily sought to build its collections with objects from the West.[140] Although the directors restricted membership to those who could pay a fifty-dollar fee, they planned public lectures and advertised that before the galleries opened "decent strangers will be cheerfully admitted if they apply to any member of the Society, or to . . . the managers."[141] Other antiquaries made similar efforts on a smaller scale, such as when Caleb Atwater encouraged curious residents to come view artifacts that he displayed at the Circleville post office.[142]

Figure 9. "Bird's Eye View of Circleville, Ohio, in 1836." This town plat was drawn from memory in 1870 by G. F. Wittich. *History of Franklin and Pickaway Counties, Ohio* (Cleveland: Warner Brothers, 1880), 174, The Chillicothe and Ross County Public Library, Chillicothe, Ohio.

Figure 10. Ohio County population in 1820. Map created by the University of Virginia Library, Historical Census Browser, based on data from the Interuniversity Consortium for Political and Social Research (ICPSR).

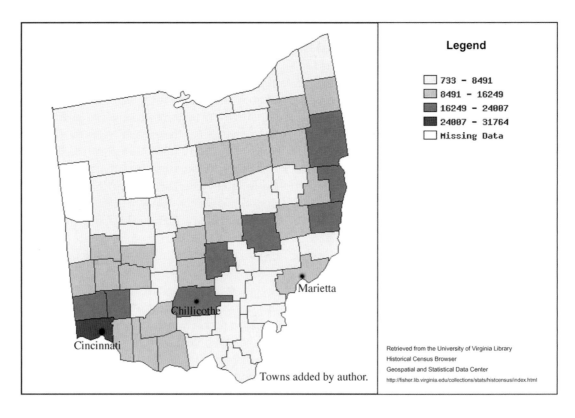

Legend

☐ 733 – 8491
▨ 8491 – 16249
▨ 16249 – 24007
■ 24007 – 31764
☐ Missing Data

Marietta

Chillicothe

Cincinnati

Towns added by author.

Retrieved from the University of Virginia Library
Historical Census Browser
Geospatial and Statistical Data Center
http://fisher.lib.virginia.edu/collections/stats/histcensus/index.html

These efforts to establish cultural institutions and publications in Ohio occurred during a decade of anxious attempts to define national culture and to prove the successful development of the West. During the War of 1812, cultural nationalism surged and Americans viewed the study of history and natural history as a service to the nation.[143] The American Antiquarian Society, founded in 1812 in Worcester, Massachusetts, embodied this spirit by collecting and preserving the nation's ancient artifacts and historical documents.[144] Many westerners joined the Society, which attempted to foster a truly national membership, and supported its national scope and aims. In an address to the Cincinnati School of Literature and the Arts in 1814, Drake outlined how Americans needed to develop their own intellectual base by borrowing some knowledge from Europe but creating new knowledge in their own country. In his words, "Old states are abundant in the means of imparting elementary knowledge; new ones, in occasion for applying it practically."[145] Though by "states" he meant nations, his discussion of the intellectual relationship between old and new geopolitical enti-

ties also applied to the expanding United States. In his address, Drake readily admitted the comparatively low cultural development of the West: "Learning, philosophy, and taste, are yet in early infancy, and the standard of excellence in literature and science is proportionably low."[146] Yet he encouraged the development of western institutions, arguing that intellectual pursuits could flourish on the frontier.

With these goals of national improvement in mind, Ohioans defined their studies of western antiquities in the context of the state. Unlike earlier settlers who regarded themselves as Americans or New Englanders in the West, these men identified their interests and perspectives in terms of their adoptive state. While statehood did not automatically unite residents, it did provide a framework for common experiences and concerns.[147] A number of New England natives living in Cincinnati in 1818 inscribed this relationship in a Thanksgiving Day toast. They honored their "friends in the East" and the "New-England System of Education," but they reserved their highest dedication for the "State of Ohio." The revelers professed, "It has become the land of our home, the theatre of our lives, and the scene of our hopes. Let us use every exertion to promote its present and future interests."[148] Though they held much in common with near neighbors in Kentucky and Indiana, they defined their lives and interests through the state. As one writer phrased it in 1815, "whatever relates to the improvement of our agriculture, manufactures, and commerce; to the perfection of our political and social institutions, and to the economicks, statisticks and history of our infant state, is of the greatest consequence."[149]

By simultaneously defining themselves as westerners, Ohioans promoted their state as the embodiment of the entire region. This characterization of their land and themselves encouraged others to judge the success and potential of western settlement by looking to Ohio as the representative example of ideal American expansion. Ohio antiquaries enhanced the image of Ohio as the heart of the successful West by distinguishing themselves from their western peers south of the Ohio River in Kentucky. At first glance, antiquaries in these two states shared goals and methods. Like Atwater and Drake, Kentuckians John Clifford and C. S. Rafinesque appealed to citizens for information, participated in national organizations, and established themselves as their state's leading antiquaries.[150] They also made great efforts to support cultural and intellectual development in their state, such as the *Western Review*, a literary magazine founded specifically to publish writings by western authors on western presses.[151] Yet Clifford and Rafinesque, like Atwater and Drake, defined their authority by state and county lines. Though a native and frequent resident of Kentucky, Drake wrote extensively about the Ohio landscape while publishing nothing about Kentucky. When Atwater and Rafinesque fiercely criticized one another's work, Rafinesque called specifically to "some intelligent citizens of Ohio" to fill in the gaps rather than pursuing the project himself.[152] Moreover far fewer Kentuckians discussed antiquities in their state. In 1820, only three state residents belonged to the American Antiquarian Society, while Ohio boasted nine members.[153] Ohio antiquaries pointed to the discrepancy of antiquarian interest between the

states to highlight their own cultural and intellectual achievements.

Publications and institutions that centered on the western landscape proved to be one of the most successful ways for Ohioans to show the development of the West and its contribution to the nation. As the decade progressed, some Americans recognized Ohioans' efforts to foster a virtuous civility through cultural institutions. The editor of the *Daily National Intelligencer* viewed Daniel Drake's 1814 literary address as "flattering proof of the progress of the arts in a quarter which a very few years past was an untravelled forest."[154] In 1815, John Quincy Adams celebrated the development of the western states, concluding that the "moral and political character" of Yankee emigrants to the West, "far from degenerating, improves by emigration." He denounced the "prejudices harboured against them by the New-England Junto federalists" and called for recognition of their progress.[155] More than one writer pointed to Ohio to prove that "the whole Western Country is continually assuming a more flourishing condition, and with its settlements extending all the advantages which can belong to its prosperity."[156]

In this framework of state qua region, Ohioans engaged the antiquities conversation to define themselves as westerners writing about the West. As such, they refused to defer either to eastern scholars remote from their subject or to travelers who, "riding at full speed, had neither the industry, the opportunity, nor the ability to investigate a subject so intricate."[157] When Atwater set out to publish a book about Ohio, he announced his "great interest in this first attempt to publish a work of the kind in the west."[158] Ohioans characterized national circulation of objects and information as secondary to the collection of information within the West. Settlers of the Northwest Territory had emphasized their similarities to peers in New England, but this generation of antiquaries distinguished themselves from easterners. Atwater revealed disdain when he wrote, "A gentleman in one of our Atlantic cities, who has never crossed the Alleghenies, has written to me that *he* is fully convinced that [the earthworks] were raised for religious purposes."[159] He and Drake defined their communities in the West and sought influence among their local peers, believing that "those who attain to superiority in the community of which they are members, are relatively great."[160] As shown by their establishment of distinctly western institutions, Ohioans worked to make the West the master of its own image.[161]

Ohioans claimed authority for themselves in the antiquities discussion by organizing terminals of information collection, interpretation, and distribution within their state. Without a doubt, men like Atwater and Drake still exchanged information and objects with easterners. They participated in eastern institutions by developing affiliations with societies, writing letters, and doing business with eastern counterparts.[162] Atwater belonged to the American Antiquarian Society, and he and his western contemporaries published in national magazines, participated in an international discourse of racial origins, and relied on eastern publishers to print books and engrave images. In 1819, he acknowledged that he was "obliged to [his] friends in the East" for success in publishing his first book.[163]

However, these Ohio men defined the knowledge that they communicated as a product of the West. To begin, antiquaries' networks of local informants throughout the state emphasized the importance of intimate knowledge of the land that only residents could obtain. When Atwater expanded his studies beyond Ohio's borders, he categorized earthworks by state and did not simply label them western antiquities. He recruited informants within each state and encouraged others to do the same if they wrote about antiquities outside their home states.[164] *Archaeologia Americana,* which included Atwater's *Description of the Antiquities,* identified members of the Society primarily by their state residence.[165] By narrowing the geographic range of their studies to match the geopolitical bounds of the state, antiquaries increased the depth of their expertise and their ability to leverage this knowledge in broader debates over western development.

Furthermore, Ohio antiquaries applied conclusions of their studies primarily to the state and the region while withholding broad suppositions about the continent's history.[166] Men like Atwater and Drake believed that the evidence they gathered could speak to universal issues, such as "the great truths of our religion" or the trajectory of civilizations.[167] Yet they interpreted this body of information locally.[168] As a result, national societies looked to western members as crucial sources of knowledge, not simply raw data, about the ancient landscape. President James Monroe wrote directly to Atwater to learn about Ohio antiquities.[169] National societies served to collect knowledge from across the country, and westerners sent information to the American Antiquarian Society "to be kept for the inspection of the Philosophers and Historians of posterity."[170] Representative knowledge depended on an aggregate of information collected from all areas of the West, and a national perspective gave way to an interest in one's own locale.

Ohioans' efforts to make themselves authorities on the ancient western landscape succeeded because Americans sustained a popular interest in the ancient landscape. Descriptions of antiquities continued to pervade newspapers, travel narratives, and geography books through the first quarter of the nineteenth century. In 1819, Caleb Atwater estimated that he could immediately sell the entire stock of his book about Ohio antiquities at the impressive price of five dollars apiece "either on this or on the other side of the mountains."[171] Interest in antiquities reached such a pitch that one man stole the manuscript "Western Antiquities" from the widow of the Reverend John P. Campbell, expecting to reap a large profit by publishing it as his own work.[172] By the end of the decade, Atwater sensed a "renewed vigour" surrounding the subject and reported that "new discoveries are daily made."[173]

As popular interest and discoveries of antiquities grew with expansion, Ohio became the paradigm for study. Travelers and early settlers described earthworks in Michigan, Illinois, Missouri, the Louisiana Territory, and western New York throughout the 1810s, and by the end of the decade, the headline "Antiquities of the West" could denote earthworks in many areas.[174] To describe these new discoveries, writers consistently employed the standards established in Ohio. The Western Museum in Cincinnati

Mound at Marietta.

Figure 11. This engraving shows the common artistic sytle of depicting earthworks by the 1840s. Note the individuals at center and the steps leading to the top of the mound. Henry Howe, *Historical Collections of Ohio* (Cincinnati, 1847), 516, Special Collections, University of Virginia Library.

became a locus of inquiry into curiosities of western lands. In 1819, one Cincinnatian wrote, "It must be obvious to everyone acquainted with the Western Country, that Cincinnati is a very eligible situation for a seat of learning."[175] When Indiana residents discovered what they believed to be a silver mine, several individuals brought samples of the material to the Museum for investigation by curator Robert Best. Through scientific analysis, Best concluded that the ore contained no traces of silver and that "a fraud has been practised by some person for the purpose of speculation."[176] Anyone who desired more information about the matter could visit the Museum to see samples and the results of Best's chemical analysis. Along with Cincinnati's other institutions, the Museum prompted many to remark that the city "ha[d] grown in wealth and population beyond all parallel in history" and that "the Muses have taken up their abode there."[177] By 1820, the Western Museum had gathered resident experts to analyze information from settlers farther west and to communicate their findings from the growing city of Cincinnati. Westerners no longer had to regard the East as the only locus of knowledge about the continent; Ohioans

had developed publications and institutions that served the same purpose.

Westerners recognized the importance of connections to national institutions and made no claims to the parity of their organizations with eastern societies, or even of American cultural independence from Europe. However, some Ohioans seized on the topic of antiquities in order to promote the cultural development and respectability of their state. Ordinary Ohioans' interest in the subject, along with the sustained efforts made by more prominent men like Atwater and Drake, increased Ohio's prominence in this national framework by promoting the state as an exemplar of cultural development and a regional center of knowledge. By the 1820s, western settlers who pushed toward the Mississippi could look to Ohio as a model for western social development.

The westward progression of American settlement did not inevitably necessitate development of western cultural institutions and intellectual pursuits. Though many of the western organizations and publications begun in the 1820s failed or strayed from their founders' goals, they evinced how one generation of Ohio residents responded to concerns over cultural authority. A look at the American antiquities discussion shows that Americans consistently debated the state of western development from the moment that the Ohio Company began to plan a settlement in the Northwest. The first settlers inspired lasting curiosity about antiquities, a subject that a variety of people engaged to comment on social development in the West. As competition among voices grew in the early nineteenth century, Ohio residents sought to distinguish themselves as authorities on the subject and to establish their state as a model of western development.

After Caleb Atwater published his *Description of the Antiquities Discovered in the State of Ohio and Other Western States* in 1820, westerners continued to discuss, document, collect, and theorize about antiquities even as development destroyed them. Interest in the subject spawned popular works like William Henry Harrison's *Discourse on the Aborigines of the Valley of the Ohio* (1838) and Ephraim Squier and Edwin Davis's monumental tome *Ancient Monuments of the Mississippi Valley* (1848).[178] The 1840s ushered in antiquarian and local history movements that sought to define the expanding nation, and the proliferation of histories about the state of Ohio, such as Caleb Atwater's *History of the State of Ohio, Natural and Civil* (1838), Henry Howe's *Historical Collections of Ohio* (1847), and Samuel Hildreth's *Pioneer History: Being an Account of the First Examinations of the Ohio Valley and the Early Settlement of the Northwest Territory* (1848), included detailed descriptions of the state's ancient earthworks.[179] Landscape painters created images of ancient American inhabitants and terrain, which hung on museum walls, scrolled across the stage on moving panoramas, illustrated volumes of Ohio histories, and backed traveling lecturers (Figure 11).[180] At mid-century, the ancient American landscape held a very visible place in popular culture and literature.

Ohioans continued to engage with the local landscape as they sought to define their place in the state, the West, and the nation. Since the first legal expansion into the Northwest Territory, Americans had examined and explained the physical evidence of ancient civilization as a means of addressing these broad concerns. Ohio Company settlers and many of their contemporaries reached westward in order to promote their designs for the young United States, using discussion of antiquities to elevate conceptions of the western territory and to create a usable history for the new nation. As public interest demanded more information about antiquities and western lands, travelers viewed the Ohio River Valley as a prime destination and published accounts of their journeys. When residents of the new state of Ohio felt unfairly characterized, they consciously sought to link authenticity of information with western residence. A select group of antiquaries encouraged and coordinated these efforts and labeled their studies of Ohio as intellectual products of the West. By encouraging the development of cultural institutions and centering the antiquities discussion on Ohio, residents promoted their state as the prototype for social development during western expansion.

More broadly, Ohioans negotiated an identity for their state that promoted its economic development and its social sophistication. These efforts earned the state distinction. By the 1820s, many Americans agreed, "Ohio, by her early attention to her most vital interests, bids fair to equal any of her elder sisters in the confederacy."[181] In a nation that judged the success of civilization by its economic progress and its cultural refinement, Ohioans shaped the discussion of antiquities in order to emphasize simultaneously their development of the land and their appreciation of its history. By doing so, they distinguished their state's leadership in the West and its value to the nation.

NOTES

The author would like to thank Professors Peter Onuf and Charles McCurdy, Andrew Sandoval-Strausz, Philip Herrington, Laura Kolar, and an anonymous reviewer for *Buildings & Landscapes* for their comments on various iterations of this essay. Patricia Fife Medert of the Ross County Historical Society and Kimberly Feinknopf-Dorrian of the Ohio Historical Society also deserve especial thanks for help with sources.

1. *The Records of the Original Proceedings of the Ohio Company*, 2 vols. (Marietta: Marietta Historical Commission, 1917), 2:80–81.

2. For archaeological overviews of these cultures, see A. Martin Byers, *The Ohio Hopewell Episode: Paradigm Lost and Paradigm Regained* (Akron, Ohio: University of Akron Press, 2004), and Darlene Applegate and Robert C. Mainfort Jr., *Woodland Period Systematics in the Middle Ohio Valley* (Tuscaloosa: University of Alabama Press, 2005).

3. John F. Sears, *Sacred Places: American Tourist Attractions in the Nineteenth Century* (New York: Oxford University Press, 1989), 4. Sears argues that Americans turned to the landscape to define themselves and their national culture in the 1820s and 1830s.

4. Peter Onuf most prominently addressed the legacy of the Northwest Ordinance in *Statehood and Union: A History of the Northwest Ordinance* (Bloomington: University of Indiana Press, 1987). Landscape historian John Stilgoe translated this political framework into an emphasis on the system of grids overlaid on the Northwest Territory, arguing that the design made Americans "conscious of their nationality, of their new identity as citizens of a political entity larger than the old parochial colonies." Stilgoe, *Common Landscape of America, 1580 to 1845* (New Haven, Conn.: Yale University Press, 1982), 107. Kim Gruenwald, a historian of the region's economy, has argued that the Ohio River defined the region for residents and became the key to claiming lands farther west. Gruenwald, *River of Enterprise: The Commercial Origins of Regional Identity in the Ohio Valley* (Bloomington: University of Indiana Press, 2002), 24, 157.

A number of studies have proven the value of studying land through a cultural framework. Most recently, Frazer McGlinchey delineated a landscape mythology created by the leaders of the Ohio Company and argued that the conflict between this myth and frontier realities illustrates the tenuousness of their grasp on western lands. Frazer McGlinchey, "'A Superior Civilization': Appropriation, Negotiation, and Interaction in the Northwest Territory, 1787–1795," in *The Boundaries between Us: Natives and Newcomers along the Frontiers of the Old Northwest Territory, 1750–1850*, ed. Daniel Barr, 118–42 (Kent, Ohio: Kent State University Press, 2006). Also, a number of literature scholars recently have studied the connection between culture and land, reiterating "the truism that national identities are directly connected to, and dependent on, the possession of real lands, both in terms of how lands are conceptually grasped and in their actual physical possession." Jeffrey Hotz, *Divergent Visions, Contested*

Spaces: The Early United States through the Lens of Travel (New York: Routledge, 2006), 3.

5. For example, in Gruenwald's account, Ohio settlers developed common experiences through travel and trade on the Ohio River and viewed it as a symbol of future westward expansion.

6. Some scholarship about the Lewis and Clark expedition has addressed how this endeavor contributed to a distinctly American scientific study. Many recent studies have placed this national endeavor in the global networks of exploration and scientific study, such as Alan Taylor's essay, "Jefferson's Pacific: The Science of Distant Empire, 1768–1811," in *Across the Continent: Jefferson, Lewis and Clark, and the Making of America*, ed. Douglas Seefeldt, Jeffrey L. Hantman, and Peter S. Onuf, 16–44 (Charlottesville: University of Virginia Press, 2005). However, studies of scientific expeditions examine Euro-Americans who traveled west with a set agenda and then returned to the East. This study of antiquities interrogates the expansion of intellectual networks among Americans who settled on the western frontier.

For more on intellectual networks and institutions in America, see Susan Parrish, *American Curiosity: Cultures of Natural History in the Colonial British Atlantic World* (Chapel Hill: University of North Carolina Press, 2006); M. H. Dunlop, "Curiosities Too Numerous to Mention: Early Regionalism and Cincinnati's Western Museum," *American Quarterly* 36, no. 4 (Autumn 1984): 524–48; Joel J. Orosz, *Curators and Culture: The Museum Movement in America* (Tuscaloosa: University of Alabama Press, 1990); and H. G. Jones, ed., *Historical Consciousness in the Early Republic: The Origins of State Historical Societies, Museums, and Collections, 1791–1861* (Chapel Hill: University of North Carolina Press, 1995). Of these works, Dunlop's essay addresses the subject of antiquities most directly. Yet his cursory attention to the antiquities discussion led him to conclude too simply that most westerners "were most especially indifferent, even hostile, to the prehistoric remains that dotted the landscape" (527).

7. The discussion of American antiquities has inspired a limited historiography. The first such study, *Archaeology of the United States, or Sketches, Historical and Bibliographical, of the Progress of Information and Opinion Respecting Vestiges of Antiquity in the United States*, written by Samuel F. Haven in 1856 (reprint: New York: AMS Press for Peabody Museum of Archaeology and Ethnology, 1973), remains the most

comprehensive. Many modern historical studies treat Americans' attention to antiquities as a monolithic discussion, interspersing accounts from the 1780s with ones from the 1840s. Roger Kennedy's *Hidden Cities* comprises the most extensive study of the subject, but the book's composition and focus on racial debates fail to capture the larger context of the discussion. Angela Miller's art historical study of mid-nineteenth-century depictions of the ancient American landscape probes Americans' cultural conceptions of earlier civilizations. Her insightful study establishes the connection between antiquities and national identity, yet her tight chronological focus on the 1850s does not address the extended discussion of the topic. Similarly, Charles Boewe's compilation of John D. Clifford's essays about antiquities, published in 1819 and 1820, does not account for prior attention to the subject. Roger Kennedy, *Hidden Cities: The Discovery and Loss of Ancient North American Civilization* (New York: Free Press, 1994); Angela Miller, "'The Soil of an Unknown America': Lost World Empires and the Debate over Cultural Origins," *American Art* 8, no. 3/4 (Summer/ Autumn 1994): 8–27; Charles Boewe, ed., *John D. Clifford's Indian Antiquities* (Knoxville: University of Tennessee Press, 2000).

8. Rufus Putnam Diary, April 11, 1788, typescript, VFM193, Archives of the Ohio Historical Society, Columbus; Rufus Putnam to Manasseh Cutler, May 16, 1788, in Manasseh Cutler, *Life Journals and Correspondence of Rev. Manasseh Cutler, LL.D.*, ed. William Parker Cutler and Julia Perkins Cutler (Cincinnati, 1888), 380.

9. John May Journal, May 27, 1788, *The Western Journals of John May, Ohio Company Agent and Business Adventurer* (Cincinnati: Historical and Philosophical Society of Ohio, 1961), 48.

10. Archer Butler Hulbert, ed., *The Records of the Original Proceedings of the Ohio Company*, 2:79–80, 209; Thomas Wallcut Diary, February 26, 1790 (microfilm: roll 3), Thomas Wallcut Papers, Massachusetts Historical Society, Boston.

11. Gilbert Imlay, *A Topographical Description of the Western Territory of North America* (London, 1797), 21; Letter to Mr. Thomas, May 16, 1788, in Imlay, *Topographical Description*, 597; Thaddeus Mason Harris, *A Journal of a Tour into the Territory Northwest of the Alleghany Mountains, Made in the Spring of the Year 1803* (Boston, 1805), 123.

12. Winthrop Sargent Diary, July 27, 1786 (microfilm: reel 1), Winthrop Sargent Papers, Massachusetts Historical Society, Boston.

13. Andrew R. L. Cayton, *The Frontier Republic: Ideology and Politics in the Ohio Country, 1780–1825* (Kent, Ohio: Kent State University Press, 1986), 14, 17.

14. For more on this subject, see Timothy J. Shannon, "The Ohio Company and the Meaning of Opportunity in the American West, 1786–1795," *New England Quarterly* 64, no. 3 (September 1991): 394–402.

15. Martin D. Snyder, "The Hero in the Garden: Classical Contributions to the Early Images of America," in *Classical Traditions in Early America*, ed. John W. Eadie (Ann Arbor: University of Michigan Press, 1976), 143, 166–67; John A. Jakle, *Images of the Ohio Valley: A Historical Geography of Travel, 1740 to 1860* (New York: Oxford University Press, 1977), 48.

16. Ebenezer Denny, *Military Journal of Major Ebenezer Denny* (Philadelphia: Historical Society of Pennsylvania, 1859), 326.

17. Thomas Wallcut Diary, February 16, 1790.

18. Rowena Tupper to Mrs. Stone, November 18, 1788, box 2, folder 1, Marietta Collection, Ohio Historical Society, Columbus.

19. Manasseh Cutler to Winthrop Sargent, March 24, 1786, *Life Journals and Correspondence of Rev. Manasseh Cutler, LL.D.*, 188; Letter to Mr. Roberts, May 16, 1788, in Imlay, *Topographical Description*, 596; Alan Taylor, *Liberty Men and Great Proprietors: The Revolutionary Settlement on the Maine Frontier, 1760–1820* (Chapel Hill: University of North Carolina Press, 1990).

20. The Ohio Company founders became the first people to study the complex earthworks in depth and to relate them to contemporary American culture. Travelers, missionaries, and soldiers had noted them beginning in the early eighteenth century, and *The Royal American Magazine* had published a description and diagram of "an old Fort and Intrenchment in the Shawanese country" sketched by a traveler in 1772. By 1780, these scattered reports had prompted some speculation about the origins of ancient Americans, and James Bowdoin, president of the American Academy of Arts and Sciences, had encouraged further investigation. Thomas Jefferson's skepticism represented a more typical response. In his 1781 work *Notes on the State of Virginia*, he did not mention reports of large, geometric earthworks in the western part of the state and described small barrows in central Virginia as representative western earthworks. After excavat-

ing a mound on his property, he wrote, "I know of no such thing as an Indian monument: for I would not honor with that name arrow points, stone hatchets, stone pipes, and half-shapen images. Of labor on the large scale, I think there is no remain as respectable as would be a common ditch . . . unless it be the Barrows, of which many are to be found all over this country." He concluded, "That they were repositories of the dead, has been obvious to all." Jefferson later acknowledged the complexity and scope of Ohio Valley earthworks after westerners published more extensive accounts of these landscape features. "A Plan of an old Fort and Intrenchment in the Shawanese country," *The Royal American Magazine* (Boston), January 1775, 29, available at American Periodical Series Online; Thomas Jefferson, *Notes on the State of Virginia,* ed. William Peden (1781; Chapel Hill: University of North Carolina Press, 1955), 97; John C. Greene, *American Science in the Age of Jefferson* (Ames: Iowa State University Press, 1984), 343. For accounts of early reports of western earthworks, see Anthony F. C. Wallace, *Jefferson and the Indians: The Tragic Fate of the First Americans* (Cambridge, Mass.: Harvard University Press, 1999), 131–39, and Jakle, *Images of the Ohio Valley,* 68–69.

21. David Waldstreicher, *In the Midst of Perpetual Fetes: The Making of American Nationalism, 1776–1820* (Chapel Hill: University of North Carolina Press, 1997), 60. Settlers promoted these ideas in newspapers, private correspondence, and booster pamphlets.

22. Benjamin Smith Barton and Winthrop Sargent, "Papers Relative to Certain American Antiquities" (Philadelphia, 1796), 11, available at Early American Imprints, series 1: Evans.

23. Meyer Reinhold, "Survey of the Scholarship on Classical Traditions in Early America," in *Classical Traditions,* ed. Eadie, 19, 21, 35–36.

24. The Company named the earthworks Capitolium, Quadranaou, Conus, and Sacra Via. Hulbert, ed., *The Records of the Original Proceedings of the Ohio Company,* 2:79–80, 209. See John E. Stambaugh, *The Ancient Roman City* (Baltimore: The Johns Hopkins University Press, 1988), for more on ancient Rome.

25. When a Mr. St. John suggested the name Castropolis for the new town, he explained, "The elevated spot which most probably will be chosen for the site of the new City, being now covered with remains of Fortifications, erected by a Warlike and Civilized nation, it should receive a Name, which might transmit to poster-

ity, some records of this extraordinary Circumstance; in commemoration therefore of this singular fact, as well as of its being undertaken by Military Men." St. John to Winthrop Sargent, September 25, 1787 (microfilm: reel 2), Sargent Papers, Massachusetts Historical Society, Boston; Jeremy Belknap to Ebenezer Hazard, September 29, 1787, Belknap Papers, *Collections of the Massachusetts Historical Society,* vol. 3, no. 5 (Boston, 1891), 493.

26. Americans across the nation invoked classical history with pseudonyms, art, rhetorical structure, and town names; one reference to the ancients evoked this entire field of classical thought. James McLachlan, "Classical Names, American Identities," in *Classical Traditions,* ed. Eadie, 84. For a full discussion of the Aeneas and Adamic myths and egalitarianism in early American education, see John C. Shields, *American Aeneus: Classical Origins of the American Self* (Knoxville: University of Tennessee Press, 2001), esp. 259, 268–277.

27. Figures like Noah Webster speculated that Fernando de Soto had built the works during the sixteenth century. Naturalist Dr. Benjamin Smith Barton, likely "Lucius," believed that advanced southern Indian tribes had pushed as far north as the Muskingum to fight their barbarous neighbors, who had come over a narrow pass from northeast Asia. General Samuel Parsons associated the earthworks with contemporary natives, thinking it improper "to open the mounds of earth supposed to contain the bones of the dead whilst the Indians were in treaty with us." Jeremy Belknap to Winthrop Sargent, September 17, 1788 (microfilm: reel 2), Sargent Papers, Massachusetts Historical Society, Boston; "Antiquity," *Worcester Massachusetts Spy,* May 29, June 5, June 19, 1788, 1; "Lucius," "A Few Observations," *Hartford Connecticut Courant,* December 8, 1788, 1. Parsons feared that opening the mounds might anger native leaders and prevent the settlement of a treaty. Charles S. Hall, *Life and Letters of General Samuel Holden Parsons* (New York: Archives of J. Pugliese, 1968), 493.

28. For more information about origins of antiquities, see Kennedy, *Hidden Empires.*

29. Letter to Mr. Roberts, May 16, 1788, in Imlay, *Topographical Description,* 597.

30. James Backus Journal, May 27, 1788, box 14, Woodbridge-Backus Papers, Ohio Historical Society, Columbus.

31. Americans were particularly fond of Alexander Adam's *Roman Antiquities,* Edward Gibbon's *History of the Decline and Fall of the Roman Empire,* Basil Kennett's *The Antiquities of Rome,* and C. F. Volney's *The Ruins, or, A Survey of the Revolutions of Empires.* These conclusions are drawn from the author's survey of newspapers available at America's Historical Newspapers. Joyce Chaplin writes, "It was Gibbon, above all, whom Americans read as avidly as they might have a novelist, in an age when history was a form of literature that entertained as well as instructed." Chaplin, *An Anxious Pursuit: Agricultural Innovation and Modernity in the Lower South, 1730–1815* (Chapel Hill: University of North Carolina Press, 1993), 30–37, 45–51.

These patterns held true in the West as well as the East. In 1803, a bookseller in Lexington, Kentucky, noted that "Classics has a great sale here" and that he quickly sold his entire supply of classical texts. Quoted in Richard W. Clement, *Books on the Frontier: Print Culture in the American West, 1763–1875* (Washington, D.C.: Library of Congress, 2003), 47. One Ohio settler noted reading "Volney's Ruins, two Vol. a valuable work by a Frenchman" in Chillicothe, Ohio. Jesup N. Couch Journal, April 8, 1805, "From Reading in Connecticut to Chillicothe, Ohio," Archives of Ohio Historical Society (photocopy 1945.191, Ross County Historical Society, Chillicothe, Ohio). John Cleves Symmes grounded his grandsons' early reading in Kennett's book. John Cleves Symmes to John Cleves Short and Charles Wilkins Short, May 9, 1804, *The Intimate Letters of John Cleves Symmes and His Family* (Cincinnati: Historical and Philosophical Society of Ohio, 1956), 12.

After the turn of the nineteenth century, Americans expanded their interest in classical history to include the ancient histories of Egypt, India, and all of Europe. In stores and advertisements across the nation, booksellers consistently placed volumes about America's western territories alongside books about ancient civilizations. The most popular of these included Thomas Maurice's *Indian Antiquities or Dissertations of Hindostan,* Sir William Jones's *Antiquities of Asia,* William Russell's *History of Ancient Europe,* and John Robinson's *Antiquities of Greece.* This observation is based on the author's survey of book advertisements available at America's Historical Newspapers. A typical example: Imlay's *Topographical Description* was advertised next to *Roman Conversations on the History and Antiquities of Rome (New Haven Connecticut Journal,* December 26, 1793, 3). Also, the full title of Jones's book was *Disserta-*

tions and Miscellaneous Pieces Relating to the History and Antiquities, the Arts, Sciences, and Literature, of Asia but was commonly abbreviated to *Antiquities of Asia.*

32. G. Turner to Winthrop Sargent, June 15, 1787 (microfilm 96, series 11, roll 1, box 1, folder 2), Winthrop Sargent Papers, *Papers of Thirteen Early Ohio Political Leaders* (Columbus: Ohio Historical Society, 1976).

33. Ibid.

34. Jonathan Heart to Benjamin Smith Barton, January 5, 1791, in Imlay, *Topographical Description,* 300.

35. "Lucius," "A Few Observations upon the Western and Southern Indians," *Hartford Connecticut Courant,* December 8, 1788, 1.

36. "Extract of a letter from Louisville, Kentucky, dated March 19," *New-York Daily Gazette,* May 10, 1790, 2. Similarly, a newspaper article in 1801 referred to "the revolutions of time" that had erased ancient American civilization. "Antiquity," *Jenks' Portland Gazette* (Maine), May 4, 1801, 2.

37. James Winthrop to Winthrop Sargent, February 26, 1788 (microfilm: reel 2), Sargent Papers, Massachusetts Historical Society, Boston.

38. Benjamin Smith Barton to Joseph Priestley, May 16, 1796, in Barton and Sargent, "Papers Relative," 5.

39. Turner to Sargent, June 15, 1787, Sargent Papers, *Papers of Thirteen Early Ohio Political Leaders.*

40. Greene, *American Science,* 6–7, 31.

41. Ibid., 188.

42. Belknap to Sargent, April 26, 1788, Sargent Papers, Massachusetts Historical Society, Boston.

43. For instance, letters from a German professor of botany and a Swiss zoologist awaited Manasseh Cutler when he returned to Massachusetts from the Ohio Valley. They requested information about western botany and antiquities. In 1788, Rufus Putnam sent an annotated map of the Muskingum earthworks to Paris, where it was reprinted. Manasseh Cutler to Winthrop Sargent, November 19, 1788 (microfilm: reel 2), Sargent Papers, Massachusetts Historical Society, Boston.; Rufus Putnam, "Plan of the Ruins of an Ancient Town or Fortified Camp near the Confluence of the Muskingum and Ohio Rivers" (Paris, 1788), no. 33, Karpinski Collection, Ohio Historical Society, Columbus. Parrish, *American Curiosity,* 106, 118–19, 130, 134; Greene, *American Science,* 5–12; James McLachlan, "Classical Names, American Identities," in *Classical Traditions in Early America,* ed. Eadie, 85. These efforts occasionally resulted in scientific innovations in the

West, such as when Manasseh Cutler first counted tree rings to determine the age of a site. Cutler Journal, September 6, 1788, *Life Journals and Correspondence*, 418.

44. "New-Haven, June 5," *Hartford Connecticut Courant*, June 9, 1788, 2; Heart to Barton, January 5, 1791, in Imlay, *Topographical Description*, 303.

45. Cutler Journal, July 3–14, 1787, *Life Journals and Correspondence*, 219–83. Many Ohio settlers visited Peale's Museum when they stopped in Philadelphia on their way west. Elizabeth Mansfield penned an account of her visit in 1803, and Cutler wrote a remarkably detailed description of his visit in 1787. Elizabeth Mansfield to Harriot Lysson, December 1803, box 1, folder 2, Mansfield Papers; Cutler Journal, July 13, 1787, *Life Journals and Correspondence*, 259–61; David R. Brigham, *Public Culture in the Early Republic: Peale's Museum and Its Audience* (Washington, D.C.: Smithsonian Institution Press, 1995).

46. "New-Haven, June 5," *Hartford Connecticut Courant*, June 9, 1788, 2.

47. J. K. Van Dover, "The Design of Anarchy: *The Anarchiad, 1786–1787*," *Early American Literature* 24, no. 3 (1989): 237–46; Emory Elliott, *Revolutionary Writers: Literature and Authority in the New Republic, 1725–1810* (New York: Oxford University Press, 1986), 93, 99; John P. McWilliams Jr. *The American Epic: Transforming a Genre, 1770–1860* (New York: Cambridge University Press, 1989). For full text of the poem, see David Humphreys et al., *The Anarchiad: A New England Poem (1786–1787)*, ed. Luther G. Riggs (Gainesville, Fla.: Scholars' Facsimiles and Reprints, 1967).

48. "American Antiquities," *New-Haven Gazette, and the Connecticut Magazine*, October 26, 1786, 287.

49. W. Bruce Finnie, "Ohio Valley Localisms: Topographical Terms, 1750–1800, *American Speech* 38, no. 3 (October 1963): 178–87.

50. Rufus Putnam to Manasseh Cutler, May 16, 1788, in Cutler, *Life Journals and Correspondence*, 380.

51. Jeremy Belknap to Ebenezer Hazard, January 24, 1789, Belknap Papers, 104.

52. Orosz, *Curators and Culture*, 4.

53. Greene, *American Science*, 21, 63, 89. Sargent often presented papers about antiquities to the American Philosophical Society and sent specimens to their collections. Barton to Priestley, May 16, 1796, in Barton and Sargent, "Papers Relative," 5. This letter was republished in *Transactions of the American Philosophi-cal Society* 4 (1799): 177–78.

54. Jeremy Belknap to Winthrop Sargent, April 26, 1788, (microfilm: reel 2), Sargent Papers, Massachusetts Historical Society, Boston.

55. James Winthrop to Winthrop Sargent, February 26, 1788 (microfilm: reel 2), Sargent Papers, Massachusetts Historical Society, Boston.

56. For examples, see Jared Mansfield to Stephen Twining, November 15, 1802, and Jared Mansfield to William Lyon, September 27, 1803, box 1, folder 2, Jared Mansfield Papers, Ohio Historical Society, Columbus.

57. Travel accounts and popular geographic publications about these areas sometimes mentioned antiquities as curiosities. John Filson briefly described "curious sepulchres, full of human skeletons" (33) in the section entitled "Curiosities," and he referred to "the remains of two ancient fortifications" near Lexington, where "pieces of earthen vessels have also been plowed up." He compared these ancient remains to the material culture of contemporary Indians and concluded that Europeans, probably Welshmen, built them. John Filson, *The Discovery, Settlement, and Present State of Kentucke* (Wilmington, 1784), 33, 97–98. Thomas Hutchins did not mention antiquities in *A Topographical Description of Virginia, Pennsylvania, Maryland, and North Carolina, Comprehending the Rivers Ohio . . .* (Boston, 1787). Travelers did mention Grave Creek Mound, in western Virginia, frequently, but most of these writers were travelers to Ohio, not residents of western Virginia or Kentucky settlers.

58. The author surveyed the papers of Thomas Worthington, John Cleves Symmes, of New Jersey, Edward Tiffin, of England (via Charles Town, western Virginia), Jared Mansfield, of Connecticut, and Nathaniel Massie, of Virginia. Worthington Papers (microfilm 96, series 15), *Papers of Thirteen Early Ohio Political Leaders*; John Cleves Symmes, *The Correspondence of John Cleves Symmes, Founder of the Miami Purchase, Chiefly from the Collection of Peter G. Thomson*, ed. Beverley W. Bond Jr. (New York: Macmillan Company, 1926); Symmes, *Intimate Letters*; Edward Tiffin Papers (microfilm 96, series 12), *Papers of Thirteen Early Ohio Political Leaders*; Mansfield Papers; Nathaniel Massie Papers (microfilm 181; Ohio Historical Society); Linda Elise Kalette, *The Papers of Thirteen Early Ohio Political Leaders: An Inventory to the 1976–77 Microfilm Editions* (Columbus: Ohio Historical Society, 1977).

59. Thomas Worthington Diary, June 27, 1796 (1948.109), Territorial Papers Manuscript Collection,

Ross County Historical Society, Chillicothe, Ohio.

60. Hugh Williamson to Thomas Worthington, April 23, 1804 (microfilm 96, series 15, roll 3, box 2, folder 7), Thomas Worthington Papers, *Papers of Thirteen Early Ohio Political Leaders.*

61. Sarah Worthington King Peter, *Private Memoir of Thomas Worthington, Esq.* (Cincinnati, 1882), quoted in Kennedy, *Hidden Cities,* 76. Although Kennedy says that antiquities interested Worthington, he musters very little evidence to support this claim. The author's survey of Worthington's papers at Ohio Historical Society and Ross County Historical Society revealed no mention of antiquities by Worthington.

62. This writer looked forward to the day when settlers could study these subjects, after their town began to prosper. "Scioto," *Philadelphia General Advertiser,* October 31, 1791, 3.

63. "New-Haven, August 23," *New-Haven Gazette,* August 23, 1787, 213.

64. For instance, Heart described a Mr. Wells as "a gentleman of very nice observation and philosophical inquiry." Heart to Barton, January 5, 1791, in Imlay, *Topographical Description,* 297; "Lucius," "A Few Observations," *Hartford Connecticut Courant,* December 8, 1788, 1.

65. Winthrop to Sargent, Febrary 26, 1788 (microfilm: reel 2), Sargent Papers, Massachusetts Historical Society, Boston.

66. Imlay, *Topographical Description,* 282.

67. "Extract of a Letter from Pittsburgh November 18," *Philadelphia National Gazette,* December 5, 1791, 43.

68. "Antiquity," *Jenks' Portland Gazette* (Maine), May 4, 1801, 2.

69. Harris, *Journal of a Tour,* 57.

70. Between 1770 and 1819, more than 40 percent of all western travelers journeyed down the Ohio River. See maps of travelers' routes and destinations in Jakle, *Images of the Ohio Valley,* 167–70.

71. Backus Journal, May 27, 1788, box 14, Woodbridge-Backus Papers.

72. Benjamin Dana Journal, April 30, 1794, typescript, box 4, folder 1, Marietta Collection.

73. Francis Baily Diary, December 10, 1796, *Journal of a Tour in Unsettled Parts of North America in 1796 and 1797,* ed. Jack D. L. Holmes (Carbondale: Southern Illinois University, 1969), 64. In one case, a traveler and his company decided to stay here overnight to view "the surprizing forts and the 'big Mound,' in this vicinity." Harris, *Journal of a Tour,* 61.

74. Baily Diary, February 21, 1797, *Journal of a Tour,* ed. Holmes, 83.

75. John Sears has argued that tourism did not begin in earnest in America until the 1820s because the country and the population did not meet the requirements of traveling to tour: money, leisure time, transportation, safety, and a mythology of place. Evidence from the Ohio landscape, particularly surrounding antiquities, suggests that scholars should reconsider the nature of pre-1820 leisure activities and travel. Even if a variety of factors motivated travelers to journey down the Ohio, most of them sought out earthworks as a pleasure destination on their trips because of the mythology that surrounded them. Sears, *Sacred Places,* 3.

76. Letter to Mr. Roberts, May 16, 1788, in Imlay, *Topographical Description,* 598.

77. Winthrop Sargent to Benjamin Smith Barton, September 8, 1794, in Barton and Sargent, "Papers Relative," 1.

78. Gruenwald, *River of Enterprise,* 82–83; U.S. Department of Interior, Census Office, *Compendium of the Third Census: 1810,* available at the University of Virginia, Historical Census Browser, based on data from the Interuniversity Consortium for Political and Social Research (ICPSR).

79. For example, authors named their books to emphasize travel and antiquities. Advertisements commonly mentioned that Denon's *Travel in Egypt* was "descriptive of Antiquities" and that Priscilla Wakefield's *Family Tour through the British Empire* "includes antiquities." *New York Morning Chronicle,* June 3, 1806, 1; *Alexandria Daily Advertiser* (Va.), April 1, 1805, 4; "Massachusetts. Boston, May 30," *Worcester Massachusetts Spy,* June 5, 1805, 3.

80. Martin Brückner, *The Geographic Revolution in Early America: Maps, Literacy, and National Identity* (Chapel Hill: University of North Carolina Press, 2006).

81. Jeffrey Hotz terms this process "mental mapping." Hotz, *Divergent Vision, Contested Spaces,* 6.

82. Jedidiah Morse, *The American Geography* (1789; London, 1794), 460.

83. Harris, *Journal of a Tour,* vi.

84. Brückner, *Geographic Revolution,* 146.

85. Benjamin Franklin Stone, "Autobiography of B. F. Stone," typescript, box 3, folder 1, Marietta Collection; Wallcut Diary. In frequent letters, John Cleves Symmes encouraged his grandsons to study the subject. John Cleves Symmes to John Cleves Short, October 21, 1804, *Intimate Letters*, 16–17.

86. When Francis Baily arrived in Marietta in 1797, he compared his observations of the Ohio River with the information that Gilbert Imlay and Thomas Hutchins had published. Baily Diary, February 21, 1796, *Journal of a Tour*, 83.

87. Rufus Putnam, "Plan of the Ruins," no. 33, Karpinski Collection; "Plan D'un Ancien Camp Retranché découvert sur les bords du Muskingum et Dessiné par John Hart Capitaine du 1er Régiment des Etats Unis" (Paris, 1801), 1949.105, Ross County Historical Society.

88. *Weatherwise's Federal Almanack for the Year of our Lord, 1788* (Boston, 1787), available at Early American Imprints, series 1: Evans.

89. Jared Mansfield to William Lyon, July 5, 1807, box 1, folder 2, Mansfield Papers.

90. Couch Journal, October 9, 1804.

91. John Cleves Symmes to Jonathan Dayton, June 17, 1795, *Correspondence of John Cleves Symmes*, 169.

92. In this historical compendium, Harris printed a variety of documents, treaties, and maps related to the lands that would become the state of Ohio.

93. Harris, *Journal of a Tour*, 161–62.

94. In the words of historian John Jakle, these travelers were "close to America's cultural mainstream," and many sought to gain profit or reputation by publishing their accounts. Jakle, *Images of the Ohio Valley*, 14, 47.

95. Thomas Ashe, *Travels in America, Performed in 1806* (1808; New York, 1811), 181.

96. Ibid., 181.

97. Ibid., 126.

98. First published in 1801, Zadok Cramer's *Navigator* advised travelers going down the Monongahela, Allegheny, Ohio, and Mississippi rivers and became popular enough to demand many subsequent editions.

99. "From the Anthology," *Washington Monitor* (D.C.), May 13, 1809, 106.

100. Williamson to Worthington, April 23, 1804 (microfilm 96, series 15, roll 3, box 2, folder 7), Worthington Papers.

101. Hugh Williamson to Thomas Worthington, January 7, 1805 (microfilm 96, series 15, roll 3, box 3, folder 1), Worthington Papers.

102. Quoted in Waldstreicher, *In the Midst of Perpetual Fetes*, 264.

103. Couch Journal, October 12, 1804.

104. Christian Schultz Jr., *Travels on an Inland Voyage through the States of New-York, Pennsylvania, Virginia, Ohio, Kentucky, and Tennessee . . . Performed in 1807 and 1808* (New York, 1810), 20.

105. Caleb Atwater, "Description of the Antiquities Discovered in the State of Ohio and Other Western States," in *Archaeologia Americana, Transactions and Collections of the American Antiquarian Society* (Cambridge, Mass., 1820), 109.

106. Reprinted in *Richmond Enquirer* (Va.), August 16, 1808, 4.

107. William M'Farland, *Browne's Western Calendar, or, The Cincinnati Almanac for the Year of Our Lord, Eighteen Hundred & Six* (Cincinnati, 1805), available at Early American Imprints, series 2: Shaw–Shoemaker.

108. Robert Stubbs, *Browne's Western Calendar, or, The Cincinnati Almanac for the Year of Our Lord, Eighteen Hundred & Seven* (Cincinnati: n.p., 1806), Early American Imprints, series 2: Shaw–Shoemaker.

109. Other Ohio almanacs published during this time included information about state and county political office holders, circuit court sessions, and distances between towns. While almanacs about other states sometimes included similar information, Ohio almanacs published this information more extensively and consistently. Some state almanacs advertised that readers could apply calendrical calculations to surroundings states, and others named multiple states in their titles, such as *Charless' Kentucky, Tennessee, and Ohio Almanack* (Lexington, 1804). Yet *Browne's Western Almanac* distinguished itself by labeling itself a product of Ohio and publishing extensive geographic information about the state while advertising its applicability to the western region. Conclusions about Ohio almanacs are based on the author's survey of almanacs published in Ohio and Kentucky between 1801 and 1810, and in 1813, 1817, and 1820, available at Early American Imprints, series 2: Shaw–Shoemaker.

110. Iota had accused Thomas Ashe of lifting text from *The Navigator*, and readers criticized John Melish for copying prose from Morse's *Geography*. Melish

claimed that his observations enabled him to "[give] *a new picture* of the country." "Philadelphia, April 29, 1813. to the Editor of the New-York Medical and Philosophical Register," *Albany Argus* (N.Y.), June 11, 1813, 2.

111. "Literary Notice," *Saratoga Courier* (N.Y.), June 18, 1817, 2. Another review of his book included "commendations" printed by the *Analectic Magazine* and *Port Folio*. "Cincinnati," *Boston Daily Advertiser,* April 2, 1816, 4.

112. "Circular to the Registers of the Land Offices of the United States. General Land-Office, April 20, 1817," *New Haven Columbian Register,* May 10, 1817, 1; "Western Geography," *Washington Daily National Intelligencer* (D.C.), March 5, 1816, 4. Emphasis original to text.

113. "Cincinnati," *Boston Daily Advertiser,* April 2, 1816, 4.

114. *Boston New-England Palladium,* June 2, 1818, 1; *Bellows Falls Vermont Intelligencer,* June 8, 1818, 2.

115. Drake addressed this rivalry and defended his actions regarding the two medical schools in two pamphlets, the twenty-three-page "An Appeal to the Justice of the Intelligent and Respectable People of Lexington" (Cincinnati, 1818), and the thirty-five-page, "A Second Appeal to the Justice of the Intelligent and Respectable People of Lexington" (Cincinnati, 1818), available at Early American Imprints, series 2: Shaw–Shoemaker.

116. Joyce Appleby, ed., *Recollections of the Early Republic* (Boston: Northeastern University Press, 1997), 40–41.

117. *Archaeologia Americana,* 3.

118. Ibid., 14–16; Atwater, "Description of the Antiquities," in *Archaeologia Americana,* 172.

119. The American Antiquarian Society first published this as a compilation of Atwater's letters and associated correspondence; Atwater later published it independently. Caleb Atwater to Samuel Williams, March 25, July 10, September 4, November 23, 1819, folder 8, Williams Papers.

120. In 1820, Drake and Atwater served as Ohio's two counsellors. Four other Ohioans served as receiving officers, and three more Ohioans served as corresponding members. The Ohio officers spread across the state, hailing from Marietta, Cincinnati, Chillicothe, Circleville, Zanesville, and Columbus. Kentucky had three officers, all from Lexington. Incidentally, Winthrop Sargent, the former Ohio Company leader, served as the sole member from Mississippi. *Archaeo-*

logia Americana, 14–16.

121. Andrew Cayton and Peter Onuf, *The Midwest and the Nation: Rethinking the History of an American Region* (Bloomington: University of Indiana Press, 1990), 54.

122. Atwater, "Letter to the Editor," in *Clifford's Indian Antiquities,* ed. Boewe, 65.

123. "Western Museum Society," *Chillicothe Weekly Recorder,* July 9, 1819, 382. Emphasis original to text.

124. The notes of Rev. John P. Campbell provide notable examples of this trend, because he recorded information from a number of Indians "of truth and respectability." "Aborigines of the West," *Boston Recorder,* July 24, 1816, 120.

125. "Antiquities of Western America," *Poulson's Philadelphia American Daily Advertiser,* November 4, 1814, 2, reprinted from the *Western Intelligencer;* "OHIO. (Chillicothe) Nov. 27," *Richmond Enquirer,* December 16, 1809, 1.

126. John W. Reps, "Urban Redevelopment in the Nineteenth Century: The Squaring of Circleville," *Journal of the Society of Architectural Historians* 14, no. 4 (December 1955), 23–26; John W. Reps, *Town Planning in Frontier America* (Princeton, N.J.: Princeton University Press, 1969), 299–302.

127. Couch Journal, October 16, 1804.

128. Couch Journal, March 30, 1805.

129. Mahlon Burwell Journal, October 9, 24; December 7, 1814 (MG 24, G 46), Mahlon Burwell and Family Fonds Collection, National Archives of Canada, Ottawa. Burwell was a loosely guarded captive held at Chillicothe during the War of 1812. Thanks to Patricia Fife Medert for this source.

130. Drake, *Natural and Statistical View,* 168. Residents of Chillicothe, Ohio, often made local mounds the destinations of leisure activities. Emphasis original to text.

131. Karl Barnhard, Duke of Saxe-Weimar Eisenach, *Travels through North American during the Years 1825 and 1826* (Philadelphia, 1828), 137. While Marietta retained their earthworks, Circleville undertook an extensive project to level the earthworks and reconfigure their town on a rectangular grid.

132. "Antiquities of Western America," *Poulson's Philadelphia American Daily Advertiser,* November 4, 1814, 2. Reprinted from the *Western Intelligencer.*

133. John D. Clifford, "Letter I," *Western Review,* September 1819, in *Clifford's Indian Antiquities,* ed. Boewe, 1.

134. Samuel R. Brown, *The Western Gazetteer; or Emigrant's Directory* (Auburn, N.Y., 1817), 282–83.

135. Ibid., 307. Emphasis original to text.

136. When Ohio became a state, Lexington was the most populous western city. Cincinnati's population eclipsed it within a decade. For an excellent history of printing in Cincinnati and Lexington, see Clement, *Books on the Frontier*, 27–50.

137. Under later proprietorship of a showman, beginning in 1829, the Western Museum lost its intellectual focus and became a place of popular entertainment, complete with a mermaid, life-size wax figures, and a model of Hell. These developments did not reflect the original intent of museum founders a decade earlier. Dunlop, "Curiosities Too Numerous to Mention," 524–48.

138. Orosz, *Curators and Culture*, 105–7; *The Cincinnati Directory* (Cincinnati, 1819), 39, available at Early American Imprints, series 2: Shaw–Shoemaker. The fervor for global antiquities continued in America and integrated itself into museum culture. Museum proprietors advertised antiquities as attractions, and an Italian artist in New York even created a "marvellous gallery" filled with Roman antiquities and model rooms for visitors' enjoyment. *New York Mercantile Advertiser,* July 6, 1812, 3.

139. Daniel Drake, "Anniversary Discourse of the State and Prospects of the Western Museum Society," 20.

140. Ibid., 27.

141. *Cincinnati Directory* (1819), 40.

142. *Woodstock Observer* (Vt.), September 11, 1821, 3, reprinted from *Chillicothe Weekly Recorder*.

143. For more on cultural nationalism, see Orosz, *Curators and Culture*, 4, 7, 127–28.

144. Louis Leonard Tucker, "Massachusetts," *Historical Consciousness in the Early Republic*, ed. Jones, 17.

145. "Literature, Arts, Sciences &c. Anniversary Address," *Chillicothe Weekly Recorder,* February 16, 1815, 260. In 1820, Drake acknowledged the establishment of many societies and institutions as progress, yet he believed that they needed to grow before they could be labeled successful. Daniel Drake, "An Anniversary Discourse, on the State and Prospects of the Western Museum Society" (Cincinnati, 1820), 28–31.

146. Daniel Drake, "Anniversary Address, Delivered to the School of Literature and the Arts, at Cincinnati, November 23, 1814" (Cincinnati, 1814), 4–5, available at Early American Imprints, series 2: Shaw–Shoemaker.

147. Politics often divided Ohioans, and settlers acknowledged a sense of different regional origins. For example, upon arriving in Marietta from New Haven, Connecticut, in 1803, Elizabeth Mansfield was relieved to be "once more in a place of safety and among New England people." Elizabeth Mansfield to Harriot Lysson, December 1803, box 1, folder 2, Mansfield Papers. For more information about the statehood debate, see Cayton, *The Frontier Republic*.

148. "From the Cincinnati, (Ohio,) Gazette. The New-England Thanksgiving," *New-York Daily Advertiser,* January 5, 1818, 2.

149. " Literature, Arts, Sciences, &c. Anniversary Address," *Chillicothe Weekly Recorder,* February 16, 1815, 260.

150. Clifford had worked for his family's Philadelphia mercantile business until financial problems drove him to Lexington, Kentucky, in 1808. Here, he worked as a merchant and became a trustee of Transylvania University, founded the Kentucky Athenaeum and Museum Cabinet, and wrote about Kentucky's antiquities. Rafinesque, a European merchant with a deep interest in natural history, had traveled the world by the time he arrived in Lexington in 1818. The following year, he accepted a professorship in botany and natural history at Transylvania University and bounded his research by Kentucky's borders, seeking to produce information specific to the state. Boewe, introduction to *Clifford's Indian Antiquities,* ed. Boewe, xiv–xvii; Rafinesque, "Alleghawee Antiquities," in *Clifford's Indian Antiquities,* ed. Boewe, 88.

151. Boewe, introduction to *Clifford's Indian Antiquities.*

152. Although economic historian Kim Gruenwald has claimed that solidarity among Ohio Valley residents peaked in the 1820s, the antiquities discussion shows that fissures had already developed in discussions of the land and its history. Gruenwald, *River of Enterprise,* 117.

153. Kentucky had only one counsellor (Alexander K. Marshall), one receiving officer (John D. Clifford), and one corresponding member (Rev. Horace Holley, president of Transylvania University), all of Lexington. *Archaeologia Americana,* 14–16.

154. "Western Literature," *Washington Daily National Intelligencer* (D.C.), April 6, 1815, 2.

155. John Quincy Adams, "Emigration Westward," *Baltimore Patriot,* March 15, 1815, 2.

156. *Salem Essex Register*, March 25, 1812, 2.

157. Atwater, "Description of the Antiquities," in *Archaeologia Americana*, 109.

158. Caleb Atwater, "Letter to the Editor," *Western Review*, October 1819, in *Clifford's Indian Antiquities*, ed. Boewe, 65; "American Antiquities. Communication," *Worcester Massachusetts Spy*, September 1, 1819, 2.

159. Ibid., 145.

160. Drake, "Anniversary Address, Delivered to the School of Literature," 5.

161. When forced to transfer their collections, antiquaries made significant efforts to keep them in the West. In 1824, C. S. Rafinesque refused to donate Clifford's artifacts to the American Antiquarian Society, granting them to a Cincinnati museum instead. Boewe, introduction to *Clifford's Indian Antiquities*, ed. Boewe, xxvi. Later in the nineteenth century, many of these western antiquities did eventually move east to institutions like the New-York Historical Society, the Peabody Museum of Archaeology and Ethnology at Harvard University, and British museums like the Blackmore. This later transfer of antiquities eastward deserves its own consideration in another study.

162. Greene, *American Science*, 127.

163. Caleb Atwater to Thomas Worthington, May 24, 1819, Early Statehood Papers Collection, Ross County Historical Society. Westerners without ready access to eastern resources suffered the consequences, as when Kentuckian John D. Clifford could not publish sketches of artifacts because Lexington, Kentucky, lacked advanced woodcut technologies. Boewe, introduction to *Clifford's Indian Antiquities*, ed. Boewe, xxiii.

164. Atwater, "Letter to the Editor," in *Clifford's Indian Antiquities*, ed. Boewe, 65.

165. *Archaeologia Americana*, 5.

166. Ohio antiquaries came to no consensus on the specific origins of the earthworks. Daniel Drake believed that antiquities evinced a transmission of arts from long ago, suggesting "a derivation of the existing tribes from the people whose monuments overspread our country." Daniel Drake, *Washington Metropolitan* (D.C.), July 27, 1820, 2. This view was espoused by other leaders like former Congressman Hugh Williamson, who believed that war had decimated native civilizations and reduced them to a savage state, and by Barton, who believed that some native tribes had descended from these ancient Americans while others had not. Hugh Williamson, *Observations on the Climate in Different Parts of America, Compared with the Climate in Corresponding Parts of the Other Continent . . .* (New York, 1811); Barton and Sargent, "Papers Relative," 12.

Caleb Atwater, despite his belief in monogenesis of the human race, believed that the decline of a civilization could not erase artistic knowledge. He argued that the builders of the earthworks migrated south into Mexico and South America, where Europeans found their descendants in the fifteenth century. Atwater, "Antiquities of the West," *New Haven Columbian Register*, March 28, 1818, 4; Atwater, "For the Weekly Recorder. Antiquities," *Chillicothe Weekly Recorder*, August 18, 1819, 6.

167. Ibid.

168. Rafinesque, "Letter to Caleb Atwater," in *Clifford's Indian Antiquities*, ed. Boewe, 81.

169. "Aboriginal Antiquities in the West—Address to His Excellency James Monroe, President of the U. States," *New Haven Columbian Register*, March 21, 1818, 4.

170. "Columbus, (O.) April 1," *Bellows Falls Vermont Intelligencer*, April 26, 1819, 3.

171. Caleb Atwater to Samuel Williams, June 21, 1819, folder 8, Samuel Williams Papers, Ross County Historical Society.

172. *Chillicothe Weekly Recorder*, August 9, 1815, 39. Henry H. Frost's theft of the manuscript led Ohioans to question his religious credentials and to denounce his moral character and authority to preach.

173. *Archaeologia Americana*, 5.

174. "For the Alexandria Gazette. Antiquities of the West," *Alexandria Gazette* (Va.), May 12, 1818, 2.

175. *Cincinnati Directory* (1819), 39.

176. "From the Cincinnati Gazette," *New York American*, September 18, 1820, 2. Settlers of the Far West also looked to Ohio when they could not "procure books, from which to make references, or draw comparisons." Ibid. "For the Alexandria Gazette. Antiquities of the West," *Alexandria Gazette* (Va.), May 12, 1818, 2.

177. *Washington Metropolitan* (D.C.), July 27, 1820, 2.

178. Boewe, introduction to *Clifford's Indian Antiquities*, ed. Boewe, xx; Terry A. Barnhart, "Toward a Science of Man," in David L. Browman and Stephen Williams, *New Perspectives on the Origins of Americanist Archaeology*, 87–116 (Tuscaloosa: University of Alabama Press, 2002).

179. For more on antiquarianism in the 1840s, see David Hall, "Reassessing the History of New England," in *New England: A Bibliography of Its History,* xix–xxxi (Hanover, N.H.: University Press of New England, 1989).

180. Miller, "'The Soil of an Unknown America,'" 8–27. Charles Sullivan painted two particularly interesting views of Ohio mounds in the 1830s, one of the Miamisburg mound and one of the complex of earthworks at Marietta. Both are in the collections of the Ohio Historical Society (call numbers H 53136 and H 26256, respectively). The histories written by Hildreth and Howe include engravings similar to the Sullivan paintings and the images discussed by Miller.

181. "From the Cherry Valley Gazette. New Villages," *Hartford Connecticut Courant*, August 20, 1822, 2.

JAY D. EDWARDS

Shotgun

The Most Contested House in America

Known by a variety of names in Louisiana, the shotgun house was first formally named by Fred B. Kniffen in his 1936 article on Louisiana house types.[1] Since the pioneering work of John Michael Vlach in the 1970s, the shotgun house in New Orleans has functioned as a bellwether of political commitment to entire subcultures, including their associated social and racial predispositions. Theories of the origins of the shotgun lie deeply enmeshed in larger cultural debates on race and authority in the city. Some see the shotgun as a response to constrained urban lots while others see the building type inextricably linked to the city's substantial nineteenth-century African

American population. These biases lay relatively submerged and unstated, but with the receding flood waters of Hurricane Katrina, when roughly 40 percent of the city's housing stock was severely damaged or destroyed, the competition between groups and classes for scarce resources and limited funding has brought these contests to the fore (Figure 1).[2] In New Orleans, it seems everyone has a well-defined idea about what should be preserved and what should be bull-dozed. Irreconcilable theories of the origins and value of the shotgun house go to the very heart of the question of what is to be saved. Entire sections of the city are at stake (Figure 2).

Figure 1. Shotguns destroyed by Katrina in the Ninth Ward, September 2005. FEMA photograph, courtesy CADGIS Laboratory, Louisiana State University.

In New Orleans, the fate of thousands of vernacular houses rests on decisions made by planning commissions and recovery agencies and on their conceptions of the relative value of specific historic architectural types and neighborhoods. As the nation has discovered, Katrina recovery funding has been difficult to acquire. Many thousands of homeowners who lost their homes have gone without meaningful support. Large sections of the city remain almost entirely abandoned thirty-four months after the storm (Figure 3). A sizable proportion of the abandoned and endangered houses are shotgun related, but it is other building types and older neighborhoods considered to be more viable or more culturally significant that are being given priority.

A series of professional, city-sponsored redevelopment plans have favored placing resources into the more highly elevated (and less damaged) sections of the city while transforming heavily flooded residential areas such as the Seventh and the Ninth Wards into depopulated green zones. New Urbanist planning is often touted as the best hope for salvation of the city. The Bring Back New Orleans Commission offered a decisively New Urbanist plan for the city, which included the essential elimination of the majority of the existing housing stock of the "shotgun crescent" of New Orleans.[3] The more recent "Unified New Orleans Plan" suggests that those neighborhoods where a "cluster of residents" rebuild for themselves should be supported by public funds. Thinly repopulated areas (including much of the nineteenth-century shotgun crescent) would be abandoned (Figure 4). So draconian have been these plans, and so biased in the direction of removal rather than recovery, that an alternate plan, "The People's Plan," was sponsored by the national NGO (nongovernmental organization) Acorn, three American universities, and the National Science Foundation. It addresses the problems of recovery in Planning Districts 7 and 8 (the Seventh through the Ninth Wards), and particularly the Ninth Ward.[4]

Those sections of Orleans Parish most severely affected by flood waters immediately after Katrina were also the areas where the highest percentage of African American residents lived.[5] They are also the areas with the lowest

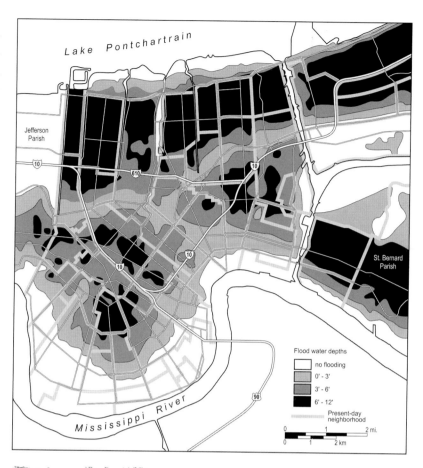

percentages of recovery and of returned families, as measured by voter turnout in the 2006 mayoral election and by mail delivery figures. By one estimate, "as many as 130,000 black residents still live outside the city." It is not surprising that there is widespread belief among the city's African American residents that they have been disproportionately impacted. "Political forces are continuing in the direction of New Orleans not being rebuilt." As one Associated Press dispatch presciently warned, "Hurricane Katrina [may] prove to be the biggest, most brutal urban-

Flood water depths
no flooding
0'– 3'
3'– 6'
6'– 12'
Present-day neighborhood

Figure 2. Map of flood depths in Orleans Parish after Katrina, based on Lidar data supplied by the CADGIS Laboratory, drafted by Mary Lee Eggart for the Fred B. Kniffen Cultural Resources Lab, Louisiana State University.

Figure 3. Wrecked shotgun in the Lower Ninth Ward, December 2005. Photograph by author.

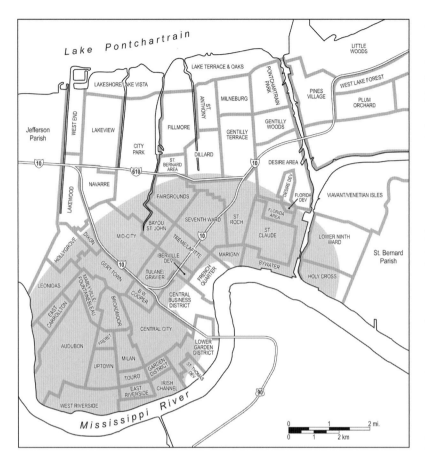

Figure 4. The shotgun crescent and New Orleans neighborhoods. Drafted by Mary Lee Eggart. Data based on 1933 aerial photography of Orleans Parish, courtesy John Anderson, director, Cartographic Information Center, Louisiana State University.

renewal project Black America has ever seen." In September 2007, about sixty-nine percent of the city's Pre-K population had returned, leaving a deficit of some 61,000 families. Many of the new post-Katrina returnees, however, are new to the city, meaning that an even larger proportion of previous residents—mostly African-Americans—have failed to return. "There is a struggle here in New Orleans about who gets to be part of this city after the storm."[6] Hanging above these controversies is the question of preservation priorities. Just how important is the architectural and historic value of the shotgun house? Part of the reason for its uncompetitive position in the scale of vital cultural resources may lie in the historical perceptions that surround the shotgun in the popular imagination.

Getting Architectural History Right

The value of the shotgun house depends largely on one's view of its role in the history and culture of New Orleans. The prevailing architectural

narrative is that the shotgun is best explained as an adaptation to narrow urban lots of the early nineteenth century. As first articulated by architectural historian Sam Wilson Jr., the shotgun house finds its genesis as a local invention of the 1830s. Wilson's landscape-determinist theory has become the accepted account for shotgun origins in New Orleans, but the position requires scrutiny.

Wilson and numerous architectural historians who follow him claim that the shotgun was created as an adaptation to the peculiar nature of lot layout in the French Quarter and the expanding Creole faubourgs (new satellite neighborhoods) that surrounded it. As laid out by Second Colonial Engineer, Adrien de Pauger, in 1722, the standard colonial urban lot was sixty French feet wide (63 feet 11 inches English measure) by 120 (127 feet 10.5 inches E.M.). Two "key lots" in each square were 150 French feet deep (roughly 159 feet E.M.) by the standard sixty-foot width (Figure 5a). French inheritance laws required that each child receive an equal division of the inheritance, so by the early nineteenth century, many of these lots had been subdivided into increasingly narrow linear strips, thirty feet (32 feet E.M.), or even twenty or fifteen feet wide, but still often 120 or 150 feet deep (Figures 5b and 5c).

Adapted to the narrow lots of New Orleans, "Creole cottages" dominated the streetscapes of working class neighborhoods from the 1790s, their roof ridges running parallel to the street (Figure 6). In the last decade of the eighteenth century, buildings with roof ridges running perpendicular to the street were generally limited to rear service structures. With the economic development and rapid expansion of the city between 1810 and 1840, many working class people prospered, and new generations of taller Creole cottages were developed (Figure 7). Their spatial limitations were still problematic, so residents continued to experiment with other ways of expanding their living spaces within the confines of the narrow lots.[7]

The Civil War contributed to the breakup of the large extended family. In its wake, the growth of the Savings and Loan Industry stimulated a high demand for relatively inexpensive

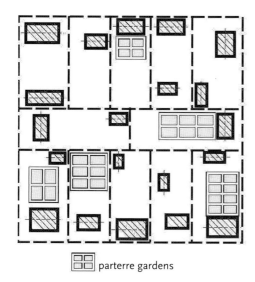

parterre gardens

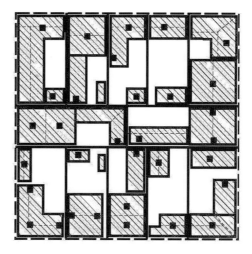

N. Rampart St.

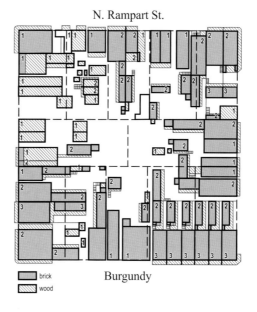

brick
wood

Burgundy

Figure 5a. French Colonial block. Plan of a typical square in the Vieux Carré illustrating placement of houses and gardens during the French Colonial period. Each square was approximately 320 English feet on a side, and each lot was 10 *toise*, or about 64 English feet wide. Drafted by Mary Lee Eggart for the Fred B. Kniffen Cultural Resources Lab, Louisiana State University.

Figure 5b. Spanish Colonial block. Plan of a typical square in the Vieux Carré illustrating the configuration of lots and buildings following the second great New Orleans fire of 1794. Single-story Creole cottages and multistory *porte-cochère* townhouses are now set at the front of the properties, with service buildings and patios in the rear. Tall brick party walls separate many of the lots. Plan by Mary Lee Eggart.

Figure 5c. Distribution of buildings in Vieux Carré Square 103 in 1986. The old 64-foot-wide lots are now subdivided into as many as three properties each. Dashed lines illustrate the location of original Colonial property lines. Plan by Mary Lee Eggart.

single-family houses. Artisan and working class families could now afford to purchase linear wooden houses seventy to ninety feet long (four to six rooms). "The [Creole Cottage] type proliferated throughout the city for a half century until it began to evolve into the shotgun about 1845."[8] Because their roofs sloped toward the front and back, it was difficult and expensive to expand Creole houses linearly towards the rear. A three-room, sixty-foot-deep Creole house was about all a one-and-a-half-story-tall gabled roof would cover (Figure 7). At this point, according to Wilson, developers and builders of spec (speculative) housing in New Orleans simply reoriented the roof ridge of the traditional working class Creole house, aligning it with the long dimension of the narrow urban lot and creating the shotgun house. This provided a form that could be more conveniently expanded to any desired length within the confines of the restrictive geometric units of these French urban lots. Those who believe that the shotgun is largely a late-nineteenth-century addition to the cultural landscape generally tend to undervalue its significance when considered against other typical New Orleans houses, for example Greek Revival mansions, Creole cottages and *porte-cochere* townhouses.

In 1975, John Michael Vlach offered an alternative view. His dissertation described the findings of a year of comparative study on the shotgun-type houses of Louisiana, Haiti, and the Yoruba culture of southwest Nigeria.[9] Vlach argued that the shotgun house of Louisiana found its origins in a small rural Haitian folk cottage called the "*ti kay*" or small house. It probably originated as a rural African maroon house type in the mountains of central Hispañola in early colonial times. Vlach described it as a syncretism of an indigenous Arawak house combined with West African dimensional and proportional preferences and (eventually) French building technologies and European materials. One byproduct of the diasporas of the Haitian revolution (1791–1803) was that this house was reconstituted by Haitian

Figure 6. An 1820s-style Creole cottage with *abat vent* and architrave, St. Peter Street, Vieux Carré, by Charles de Armas, June 4, 1862. Courtesy New Orleans Notarial Archives (006.114); detail.

Figure 7. A 1830s style 1 1/2 story, two-bay Creole cottage, 830 N. Rampart Street, by Childe Hassam (1927). The buildings are extant. Lithograph courtesy Prints and Photographs Division, Library of Congress.

Figure 8. A (circa 1830) shotgun maisonette, with *abat vent*, 616-618 Marigny Street, Faubourg Marigny, by Charles de Armas, May 4, 1860. Courtesy New Orleans Notarial Archives (065.003), detail. The lot is over 54 feet wide, the house about 21.5 feet wide. The mirror-image lot behind contains a 33-foot-wide classic four-room Creole cottage with room to spare. Both lots have carriageways providing access to the sheds and stables at the rear.

builders in New Orleans between circa 1810 and 1840 (Figure 8).

Vlach pointed out that shotgun-like house forms were abundant in Haiti. Sources unavailable to him at the time of his study demonstrate

their prevalence in the towns of the French colony of Saint-Domingue since early in the eighteenth century. A watercolor painting of the town of Les Cayes on the southwestern peninsula circa 1729, by a French sailor, clearly shows no fewer than twelve shotgun-like houses and what appears to be a church and a public building in the shotgun form (Figure 9). Shotguns are also depicted on plantations from this period.[10] Based on its current geographical distribution, the shotgun was dominant in the central and southern sections of the French colony and abundant in the center of the colonial city of Gonaïves, in northwestern Haiti.

In several waves, substantially more than twelve thousand refugees from the Haitian Revolution arrived in Louisiana between 1791 and 1809. They included roughly equal proportions of colonial French, African slaves, and *affranchis* (free people of color, called *gens de couleur libres* in New Orleans). This latter, largely mulatto, population had become a *petit bourgeoisie* class in Saint-Domingue. Men worked as planters, as small businessmen, and as artisans—carpenters, house builders, cabinetmakers, carriage makers, masons, barbers, upholsterers, and real estate brokers. They were renowned tailors and shoemakers. At the end of colonial rule (1803) the city of New Orleans had 1,335 free people of color out of a total population of 8,050 (the colony of Saint-Domingue had well over 28,000). But in the year 1809, after Spain expelled Haitian refugees from Cuba, at least 9,059 French-speaking refugees arrived in New Orleans. Of these, 3,102 were free people of color, more than doubling the total free colored population of the city (to 4,950). The total city population is now 17,242. These refugees were to have a substantial impact on the culture and vernacular architecture of the city.[11]

During the 1790s and the first decade of the nineteenth century, the free colored Creole population of New Orleans settled in certain peripheral areas. Creole neighborhoods included the northern corner of the French Quarter (not completely settled before circa 1820), Faubourg Tremé and the Bayou Road (the Esplanade Ridge-Tremé-Lafitte neighborhood), and Faubourg Marigny (being laid out for residential settlement

Figure 9. Les Cayes, Saint-Domingue (Haiti), circa 1729, showing many shotgun-style houses. Detail of a watercolor painting by Pierre Caillot. Courtesy Historic New Orleans Collection (2005.11).

circa 1805). These became the natural settlement zones for French- and French Creole–speaking Haitian refugees between circa 1800 and 1812.[12]

Suddenly, pressure on the housing stock of New Orleans was enormous. In 1809–10 the city had doubled its population in a single year; there was no place to put all of the new refugees. They were crowded into attics and outbuildings. "The women did sewing, embroidery, dress-making, millinery, living or lodging, not in the new brick houses, but in the little two-room cottages opposite or alongside."[13] The refugees built a temporary fringe housing in and around the edges of the expanding city. Among the house types they constructed were small, inexpensive modules similar to those they had known in the country-side and plantations of Saint-Domingue.

While Vlach's "early genesis" hypothesis is not supported by sufficient data to permit a claim of clear proof, it *is* buttressed by growing evidence that suggests that houses with shotgun type floor plans were commonplace in the 1805–40 period. At the same time, Creole cottages were strongly preferred by French Creoles, both white and black, before circa 1840. Timing is an important factor in determining the plausibility of either of the two prevailing narratives explaining the shotgun house. Architectural historians Malcolm Heard, Sally Reeves, Ellen Weiss, and Karen

Kingsley find little hard evidence of shotgun houses at all before the Antebellum period. "The oldest shotguns are recorded in New Orleans by 1840." Weiss states, "Shotguns seem to have appeared in New Orleans by the 1840s." By the 1870s, "New Orleans builders even figured out how to shape the city's vernacular house types: the shotgun, the double shotgun, and the latter's cousin, the two-story party-wall double, and make them speak to the [Queen Anne] taste of the time." In 1997, architectural historian Malcolm Heard argued:

A handful of French Quarter cottages one room wide and several rooms deep . . . survive from the first decades of the nineteenth century. . . . These have been used to support a theory proposed by John Michael Vlach that the New Orleans shotgun house evolved from a house found among the Yoruba people of west Africa, having been transmuted and brought here by refugees from the slave uprisings in the Caribbean in the late eighteenth and early nineteenth centuries. This theory may be plausible in the case of the early cottages. It was decades later however (relatively late in the nineteenth century) when the shotgun as we know it came to be built in large numbers in New Orleans. To think that this movement took its remarkable energy from a fairly uncommon type of cottage built decades earlier seems too much of a stretch. . . . More likely, the shotgun developed as a relatively inexpensive solution to building separate houses on New Orleans' narrow lots.[14]

One difficulty with Wilson's Creole cottage–genesis theory is that *if* before 1840 there were comparatively few single-wide linear cottages to act as models for the expanded shotgun (Figure 8), there were also comparatively few single-room-wide Creole cottages, as revealed by surviving examples, contemporary poster sale images of the New Orleans Notarial Archives, and by the 1876 Sanborn maps (Figure 7). Given the roughly equal proportion of early single-story linear cottages and one-and-one-half-story gabled Creole cottages in the Creole faubourgs, the linear cottage is an obviously closer fit as a prototype.

The significance of Wilson's late-genesis theory, if valid, would be that Vlach's proposed diffusion of the shotgun from the French colony of Saint-Domingue is eviscerated. If shotguns were invented or massively reinvented in the Antebellum period, blacks and free people of color played a relatively insignificant creative role in the development of this, the overwhelmingly dominant vernacular house type in the city of New Orleans.[15]

The issue of the origins of the shotgun house has been raised in several kinds of post-Katrina public forums in New Orleans, with different groups either denying or defending the Caribbean and African connection.[16] Recent publications by anthropologists and representatives of African American shotgun preservation groups generally support Vlach's position, while the architecture historians of New Orleans remind us with increasing vigor that Vlach and his followers have offered insufficient evidence to provide a convincing argument that shotguns represent an invaluable historical resource.[17] If Vlach's early genesis theory is not supported by hard evidence, and shotguns are a contribution of Antebellum period developers, the Afro-Creole contribution to the historic cultural landscapes of New Orleans is less central to questions of historic preservation and the politics of recovery.

While New Orleans is a city where "interest groups are sharply factionalized along racial lines," members of the white preservation community have written in some detail on the architectural contributions of Africans and Afro-Creoles.[18] The preservationists are a comparatively small and close-knit subculture, sharing ideas and cooperating closely with prominent preservation-oriented associations such as the Preservation Resource Center, the Historic New Orleans Collection, local neighborhood development associations, and community-oriented projects of the Tulane University School of Architecture. Foremost among the preservationist community is the influential Friends of the Cabildo group, who are individually or jointly the authors of much of the significant literature on the architecture of New Orleans and its preservation. As such, they have provided the master narratives for popular conceptions surrounding New Orleans's unique vernacular architecture.

One measure of the preservation community's concern for the architectural significance of the shotgun house is the fact that, out of the 147 specific Historic American Buildings Survey (HABS) projects that have been completed and posted online for Orleans Parish, only *eight* woefully incomplete surveys deal with the Shotgun Family of house types. This is despite the overwhelming preponderance of this historic house type in the city. By my rough estimate approximately 60 percent of the housing stock of Orleans Parish falls within the Shotgun Family of house types. Clearly, comparatively little effort has been expended on documenting the historic shotgun houses of New Orleans by its architectural historians. There has been no census of shotgun houses, nor is there even a definition agreed upon by geographers, folklorists, anthropologists, and architectural historians. Nor is there a master plan for New Orleans that might provide guidelines and protection for the neighborhoods of the shotgun crescent.[19]

It would seem that all that is required to resolve the historical argument over this building type is to conduct surveys of shotguns in New Orleans between circa 1800 and 1840. Unfortunately, expansive and detailed surveys of New Orleans neighborhoods do not exist prior to 1876, when the first Sanborn maps were published. By that time, shotgun houses were common, though

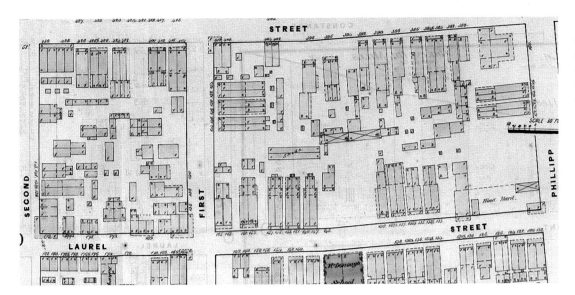

not dominant, throughout most subdivisions of the city (Figure 10). Archivist Sally K. Reeves has pointed out that the approximately sixteen hundred archived nineteenth-century *affiches* (advertising posters) of buildings and properties for sale in New Orleans, and the records of surviving building contracts held in the New Orleans Notarial Archives, do *not* support the contention that shotgun houses were numerous in the city before 1845. This would seem to end the matter, except for the fact that a broader historical assessment of the development of the shotgun has not been undertaken.

In order to demonstrate that the late-genesis hypothesis is based on incomplete evidence, one would have to show that many dozens or hundreds of shotgun houses existed in the city from at least shortly after the largest influx of Haitian émigrés in 1809. But how does one reexamine the architectural history of a historic city when the very best sources *in the entire country* for nineteenth-century architecture have proved unsupportive? Not only must we uncover sweeping new evidence, but we must also explain why the traditional sources have failed so completely to record a once popular house type.[20]

Reassessing Architectural History

To address these problems, I began a reevaluation of the architectural history of New Orleans by constructing a database of identifiable historic shotgun-like houses. Several kinds of empirical data were used as evidence that a linear cottage had existed during a specific decade. First, using style dating, architectural features, settlement history, and other information, professional architectural historians of the New Orleans Notarial Archives had provided approximate dates for a considerable number of linear cottages in their files. These dates serve as a first rough cut for the establishment of a timeline for the recorded residences. In addition, each property in the French Quarter had been subjected to chain-of-title searches. Second, a number of standing structures survive from the 1800–1840 period. These were identified by field surveys and by checking the property locations against recorded histories and chains of title as provided by the Historic New Orleans Collection, the Vieux Carré Commisison, and the Notarial Archives. A few chains of title were run specifically for this study. Third, in addition to these sources, new survey data was uncovered for the early American period, particularly from the manuscript Trudeau (Pintado) and Lafon survey books. The resulting database included 140 historic linear cottages. Of these, forty-six were dated prior to 1830 and ninety-three prior to 1840. This foundation was sufficient to provide a general overall portrait of the development of the progenitors of the shotgun house prior to 1840.[21]

I shall refer to the specific kinds of proto–shotgun houses from the early period as a linear cottages. Local architectural historians do not

Figure 11. The Cajun Swamp shop, a single *appentis* cottage 631 Bourbon Street (constructed 1801). Photograph by author, 2008; detail.

classify them as shotguns. No less than four different types of proto–shotgun houses existed in the city of New Orleans between circa 1790 and 1830. Most were a single room wide and two or more rooms in depth. Each had its roof ridge running perpendicular to the street. Its front doors were set in the narrow end of the building, opening onto the street.

Appentis Cottages

Earliest recorded are the *appentis* cottages. They can be documented prior to the Louisiana Purchase in 1803. The "Cajun Swamp" shop, an excellent surviving example dating from 1801 stands at 631 Bourbon Street, its *briquette-entre-poteaux* walls and "Norman" roof truss exposed to view from the interior (Figure 11).

The term *appentis* refers to a shed roof in French. In colonial times, shed-roofed buildings were often used as service structures set in courtyards behind the main house. They served as storage "*magazins*," as stables, as detached kitchens, as quarters for enslaved servants, and as bedroom *garçonnières* for the teenaged men of the family. As in eighteenth-century Paris, such buildings were built as if they were one-half of a complete building, each half being set against one side of the party wall that stood along the property line separating urban lots. Their roofs consisted of a single shed with its high side abutted against the brick party wall and the lower side covering the wall facing the courtyard. The doors of *appentis* buildings opened from the long side directly onto the courtyard. Their roofs were generally hipped, with their (half-) hip sheds facing the front and the rear. Curiously, in New Orleans, such "half" buildings were often built as freestanding houses, without the mirror-image structure or any other structure present or even anticipated on the opposite side of the party wall (Figures 11, 25). Many survive.[22]

For some unknown reason in the 1794–1810 period, New Orleans residents began moving their *appentis* service structures to the front of the lots and treating them as if they were shotgun houses. Often they were the only structures on the lot with the exception of a detached kitchen and a privy in the rear. Front doors opened directly onto the *banquette* or sidewalk. This building type remained popular and continued to be built in frame through the 1840s.[23]

Cabannes and Shanties
During the period of the Haitian Revolution, and particularly in the period between 1803 and 1815, temporary housing was thrown up for the thousands of refugees pouring into the city of New Orleans. Linear freestanding settlers' shacks were referred to as "*cabannes*" in New Orleans: something less substantial than a frame house or one with *murs en dur* (masonry walls). In the local English, the term "shanties" was used, while the Spanish colonial word "*brigadores*" was sometimes applied to the small residences of blacks.

Temporary vernacular architecture was ignored as huts and hovels by most record makers. Because these were not considered permanent buildings there was little official government interest, except when houses were constructed on "borrowed" property. No building contracts were drawn up and notarized, nor did surveyors often bother to record these structures. No fancy sales posters by professional artists were hung in the coffee houses, advertising property sales at public auction. Many, being cheaply and quickly constructed, did not survive a sufficient number of decades to be recorded. In short, this was a historically invisible fringe architecture. The first accurate depiction of such a shotgun building in the United States known to me was drawn in 1803 on what was at that time the edge of urban New Orleans (Figure 12). It bears a striking resemblance in size and form to the *ti kay* linear cottages that survive in abundance in Haiti today.

But if official record keepers were disinterested, who would bother to record such refugee architecture, equivalent to the FEMA trailers of their day? (We're not recording them either). Because New Orleans was expanding out of its earlier boundaries so rapidly in these years, recordation would be left to land speculators and private surveyors. It would not be unreasonable

to assume that these may have been poorly educated opportunists of low record-keeping ability. No doubt some were, but luckily others proved to be among the most well-trained and important visionaries in the history of the city. They included cartographers and land developers, some of whom would become wealthy entrepreneurs in the new American territory.[24]

Men such as Barthélémy Lafon took on both government-sponsored and private commissions. Lafon's public and private records exemplify the kinds of contemporary architectural records that were being produced. Luckily, some of Lafon's personal survey books have survived.[25] If a land surveyor happened to also be an architect particularly interested in local architecture, the building indications in his field surveys might include details such as roof ridge-lines. These permit us to differentiate between Creole cottages and linear cottages (although not in every case). The quality of the architectural indications is apparent in these sketches from the period 1806–1810 (Figures 13 and 14). It is clear from these and his other surveys in and beyond the French Quarter

Figure 12. A Single Shotgun–style building on the fringes of New Orleans. "A View of New Orleans Taken from the Plantation of Marigny," by Boqueta de Woiseri (1803). Courtesy Historic New Orleans Collection (1958.42); detail.

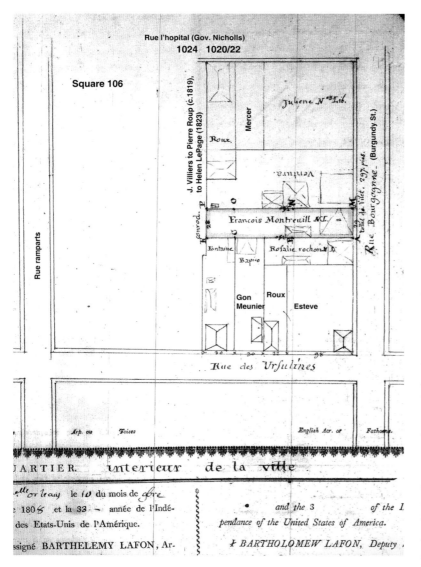

Figure 13. Plan of a portion of Square 106 in the Vieux Carré, sketch by Bethelemy Lafon, illustrating shotgun maisonette houses, including the house of Pierre Roup (spelled Roux), April 10, 1808. Courtesy Historic New Orleans Collection (Mss. 408, Bk. 2, p. 94); detail.

be forgiven for assuming that some exchange of wealth may have occurred in the interim).[26] The houses of both are clearly smaller shotgun-type houses set on open, long lots. That of Esprit is labeled a "cabane neuve"; the somewhat larger house of Boisdoré, a "maison."

Against all probability, a few surviving refugee houses in the form of small two- or three-room-deep linear cottages survived to be depicted on the 1876 Sanborn maps (Figure 15). They are almost always labeled "Old Shanties" and are shown to be frame buildings rather than brick-walled. They are found both in the Creole faubourgs and in the Vieux Carré itself.[27]

Creole Maisonettes

The third kind of linear cottage also survives from the first decade of the nineteenth century. Called the maisonette, or "small house," by New Orleans architectural historians, it closely resembles a hip-roof shotgun house (Figures 16a and 16b). These were no settlers' shacks; they were built with the very best French construction technology of the day. Our knowledge is enhanced by the fact that a few of the more solidly constructed examples survive. Sadly, Katrina dealt a last serious blow to others. The walls of early maisonettes were *briquette-entre-poteaux* or solid brick. Their pantile and slate-covered roofs were supported by heavy hewn roof beams, mortised and pegged together in the "Norman" style. Most interesting, perhaps, are the stylistic features that characterized them in the 1820s. They were built in what local historians call a generalized Federal style. Many of the earlier shotgun maisonettes share a decorative motive, an *architrave*. In French New Orleans this term also referred to a wide, flat band representing pilasters and a frieze framing the façade of the building. Above the flat frieze was a decorative cornice composed of compound cyma elements and, above that, what the local French refer to as an *abat vent*: a roof extension that projects about four feet over the *banquette* or sidewalk (Figures 6, 8, 11, 16a, 17, 18, and 21). These were required by late Spanish-period zoning laws that continued in force well into the American period.[28] *Maisons longues,* or linear cottages, of the 1820s almost always had paired double doors opening onto the street.

that many smaller shotgun-like houses existed even before 1810.

One of the more interesting examples drawn from the Lafon survey books is the case of a new landowner named Valerie Boisdoré versus a free black named Esprit. In 1808, these neighbors lived in small shotgun-style houses on the edge of the city along Bayou Metairie in what is now City Park. Lafon conducted two surveys, twelve days apart. In the first he demonstrates that Boisdoré's property extends into that of Esprit (Figure 14). In the second survey he ignores the boundary markers and "adjusts" Boisdoré's property lines so that they encompass those of Esprit, presumably rendering the boundary dispute between them in favor of Boisdoré (old New Orleans hands might

The roofs of maisonettes are inevitably hipped (Figures 16a and 17). They bear a marked similarity to the single-story townhouses (*maisons basses*) of Cap Haïtian, Haiti, in the same period.[29] Other examples, and other kinds of evidence for the popularity of this style of linear cottage, survive in the French Quarter and the Creole faubourgs. The traveling French naturalist Alexandre Lesueur made rough sketches of what is clearly a hip-roofed shotgun maisonette on the bank of Bayou St. John in May of 1830.[30]

Four-bay double-wide linear cottages appear in the decade beginning in 1810 (Figures 17 and 18). In the French Quarter today, the majority of surviving early linear cottages are "doubles"—double-wide shotgun houses—set on lots sufficiently wide to accommodate a two-room-wide Creole house if the owner had so desired. Though shotgun-like houses are not yet dominant in the Creole faubourgs in the first decades of the nineteenth century, they are sufficiently commonplace to be recognized as a recurring type.[31]

It is worth asking why dwellings such as the 1820s LePage (Figure 16a) and Baker maisonettes have not been clearly identified as shotgun prototypes by New Orleans architectural historians. They appear to have been thought of as a kind of half-width Creole cottage and are consistently identified as such in the *New Orleans Architecture* series of publications. Local architectural historians believe that early nineteenth-century houses with shotgun floor plans and hipped roofs are to be classified as two-bay Creole maisonettes (single-room wide, hip-roofed Creole cottages turned endwise), rather than as shotguns. The same assessment applies to the more popular "Doubles."[32] Historians seem to have resisted application of the term "shotgun" to what they believe to be historically inappropriate forms, believing that in roof form and in construction technology the shotgun maisonette of the 1820s participated more profoundly within the Creole cottage tradition than in the shotgun tradition. This was a time when the orientation of the roof ridge was less a diagnostic mark of ethnic or class association than it became in later decades. But by employing a designation that, if considered loosely, may have been cultur-

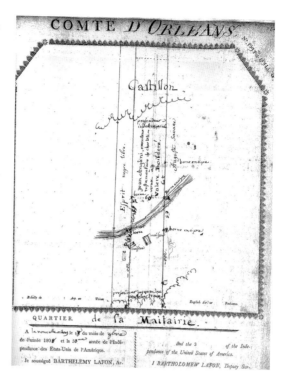

Figure 14. The first of two property surveys along Matairie Bayou (today, City Park) on the fringe of New Orleans settlement. The smaller shotgun-style house of the "negre libre, Esprit" is referred to as a "cabane" (second survey); the larger shotgun of Boisdoré is called a "maison." Survey by Bethelemy Lafon, April 15, 1808. Courtesy Historic New Orleans Collection (Mss. 408, Bk. 2. Pp. 200–202); detail.

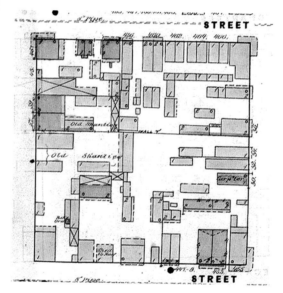

Figure 15. A square in Faubourg Marigny showing "old shanties" in wood on Mandville street. From the 1876 Sanborn map of New Orleans, vol. II, sheet 38; detail.

ally appropriate to the linear maisonette of 1825, the question of its possible parental role for the increasingly numerous framed shotguns of the 1830s and thereafter has been largely set aside. *Ti kay* "shotguns" with hip roofs are, of course, commonplace in Haiti today and have been since as early as the 1730s. How common were they in New Orleans? No reasonably complete historical survey has yet been undertaken, but the ease with which it was possible, from the

Figure 16a. The Helen LePage Maisonette, 1024 Gov. Nicholls Street, Square 106, Vieux Carré. Courtesy Hilary Irvin, New Orleans Vieux Carré Commission. The house is extant and may well be the oldest surviving shotgun-type house in New Orleans and the nation. It was constructed by the Haitian immigrant Pierre Roup in 1823, beside his own shotgun maisonette residence (Ref. NONA Felix de Armas [notary] March 17, 1836: 104:35).

Lafon survey books, to identify fifteen houses appearing to be shotguns within the architecturally conservative French Quarter prior to 1810, and indications of others in the Marigny, Tremé, and Bayou Road areas, suggests that they were not uncommon between 1805 and 1830.

Single Shotguns and North Shore Cottages
If we consider shotgun houses to be linear cottages with gabled or pedimented fronts, there is evidence that they begin to be built in relatively small numbers in the first decade of the nineteenth century. The Lafon surveys have indications of what appear to be several gable-fronted linear cottages in 1808. By the 1820s, frame, gable-fronted shotgun houses begin appearing in Faubourg Marigny.[33]

Another phase in the growing popularity of the shotgun occurs prior to the antebellum period. New Anglo residents of the Garden District begin to construct shotguns with double side galleries and with an "Ell" or "Tee" at the rear (Figure 19). None remains in its original appearance. The 1840s and 1850s witnessed severe yellow fever epidemics in New Orleans. Residents who could afford to do so deserted the city in summer and early fall for more rural places. Communities on the north shore of Lake Pontchartrain became popular. Mandeville, in St. Tammany parish, developed by Bernard de Marigny in 1834, became the site of a new variant of the shotgun: the North Shore house. Builders duplicated a style of *ti kay* (shotgun) found in Haiti, though it was probably modeled most directly on the Side-Galleried Shotguns of New Orleans. Like the Haitian houses, it often had a series of doors along its flanks. It is not known whether this represented stimulus diffusion, independent invention, or convergent evolution. Double Side Gallery Shotguns continued to be constructed in several parts of New Orleans, though in limited numbers (Figure 20).

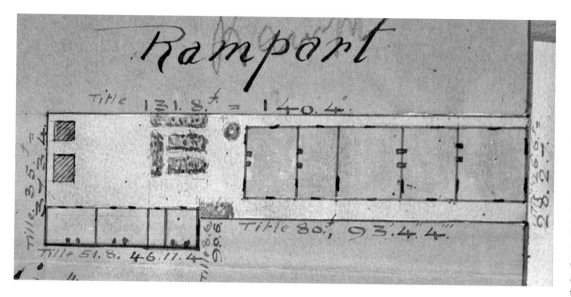

Figure 16b. Floor plan of the Helen LePage maisonette, Guy Seghers (land surveyors) Office Records. Courtesy Southeastern Architectural Archive, Special Collections, Tulane University. An undated watercolored plan (probably 1891), Box 19, folder for Dist. 2, Square 106. Pierre Roup cut a nine-foot section from the rear of his own lot so that Helen LePage could add rental rooms and/or servants' quarters to the rear of her own 28-foot-wide lot.

A Synthetic Perspective on Shotgun Origins

The "narrow lot theory" of Wilson and those who follow him is insufficient to account for the origins of the shotgun house in New Orleans. This is not to claim that it is wrong. It probably accounts for a proportion of the motivation for selection of linear-style houses, but it remains woefully incomplete. If we are to provide a satisfactory and balanced account of the rise of the shotgun in New Orleans, we must add other perspectives: social, economic, technological, and architectural.

The Landlady Effect: A Social Perspective

The rise of the linear cottage in the period following 1810 becomes more fully understandable when set against the background of racial demography and the sociology of the Early Republican period in New Orleans. Under the more liberal manumission laws and protections for the rights of enslaved workers of the previous Spanish administration (1759–1803), Louisiana had developed a society with three legally defined castes or strata: free citizens (white Creoles and Europeans), free people of color (manumitted Creoles or those born of free *mulattas*), and the enslaved (a few *mulattos* but mostly Creole *negres* and *bozales*— "salt water" slaves).[34]

The demographic patterns of free people of color in New Orleans in the first decades of the American period are worthy of note. Among the *gens de colour libres* caste in 1820, the sex ratio was only 63.88. The sex ratios were reversed on rural plantations, but in the city there were only sixty-four males for every one hundred females of marriageable age (14–45 years). This remarkable imbalance meant that many free females of color would not find a mate within their caste, even if they had wanted one, which many did not. Within French Creole society the institution of *plaçage*—formalized hypergamy—arose to fill the gap. Young quadroon ("quarter-blooded") women were described as "highly educated externally [outside of Louisiana], and probably as beautiful and accomplished a set of women as can be found."[35] In their late teens, light-skinned free women of color were introduced and, after considerable background research on the part of their mothers or family members, eventually contracted to well-to-do free white males. The institution was neither equivalent to marriage nor to concubinage. The men entailed considerable financial and other formal obligation to their *placées*. Men typically provided their mates with a small house on or near *rue de Rampart* and a stipend, and they publicly acknowledged the parentage of the children who bore the name of the father and received the sacraments of the Catholic Church. Many *placées* claimed family inheritance on the death of their "husband/lovers." For the white male there were several kinds of benefits. Contemporary observer Frederick Law Olmsted

Figure 17. Fazende cottage, 831 St. Phillip Street. Brick maisonette single, circa 1812. Photograph by author (2007).

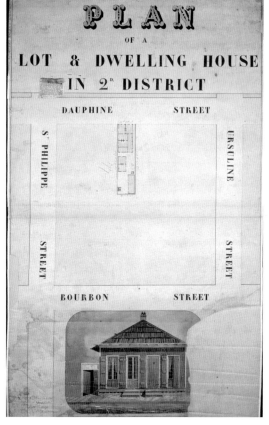

Figure 18. The (circa 1810) Phillippon cottage, 1016 Dauphine Square 77. Vieux Carré, by artist Pietro Gualdi, January 3, 1855. Courtesy New Orleans Notarial Archives (044.035).

PLAN
OF A
LOT & DWELLING HOUSE
IN 2ᵈ DISTRICT

DAUPHINE   STREET

Sᵗ PHILIPPE STREET   URSULINE STREET

BOURBON   STREET

is quoted as saying that for many young men, the life of *plaçage* was simply "much cheaper than living at hotels and boarding houses," but he clearly

underestimated the power of the attractiveness of the quadroon lady.[36]

The upside of the arrangement was that it left many young free women of color in a better financial position than they might otherwise have been. The downside was that, for most, the arrangement was impermanent. After several years many of the white men married women of their own class and, either then or later, terminated the arrangement. The result was a large number of abandoned *plaçage* divorcees who were financially comfortable and property owners. Land values were increasing almost exponentially in these decades in New Orleans. The streets of the quarter were being paved in the 1820s. Many free women of color became successful businesswomen, specializing in rental property and rooming houses in the rapidly expanding city. "Later in life these women were renowned for their successful businesses: rooming houses accommodating white gentlemen." As historian Gayarré described them, "those furnished rooms were models of Dutch cleanliness." They served hot coffee in the mornings and had a tub of hot water drawn on the tenant's return in the evening. "They were intent on guessing at your wants, on anticipating your wishes." "The female quadroons may be said to have monopolized the

Figure 19. A (circa 1836) galleried cottage at 928 Euturbe Street, Lower Garden District, by Mondelli and Reynolds, architects. Courtesy New Orleans Notarial Archives (042.015). Unsigned and undated.

Figure 20. A North Shore Duplex-style, two-story shotgun on Moss Street (west). Photograph by author, 2005.

renting, at high prices, of furnished rooms to the whites of the male sex. This they easily did, for it was difficult to equal them in attention to their tenants, and those tenants would indeed have been very hard to please if they had not been satisfied."[37]

In the Spanish slang of New Orleans, the *placée* herself was known as the *casa chica* or "little house" (presumably, the white wife lived in the *casa grande* or big house). One of the most interesting of the unresearched questions about this period concerns the relationship between the free women of color and their little houses. Many lived in what was called the "Quadroon Quarter"—the northernmost sector of the Quarter, bounded roughly by Rampart Street, Esplanade Avenue, St. Peter, and Bourbon streets. They commissioned both their own houses and rental properties on

Figure 21. The (circa 1829) Louis Maillot (h.c.l.) maisonette single, 374 Love Street (N. Rampart in Marigny) where Pierre Roup died. In 1836, by Léon J. Frémaux, September 21, 1869. Courtesy New Orleans Notarial Archives (089.024).

narrow lots in this area and created an atmosphere in which narrow houses, including particularly the linear cottage, came to be associated with a certain excellence of lifestyle. "There are, in some streets, long blocks of one-story houses, with one or two rooms built purposely to be let out to bachelors. Indeed, there are neither hotels nor boarding-houses enough to accommodate one-tenth part of this class of male"[38]

Was it perhaps this association with pampered living that was remembered by their increasingly wealthy and influential tenants in future years when shotgun houses began to be built as the primary residences of successful businessmen all over the growing city? Perhaps, a shared architectonic *jouissance* helped to turn the lowly shotgun into a favored form of New Orleans residence. It was certainly the most historically obvious mechanism by which Anglo men were introduced to the unique linear cottage of New Orleans. But who originally designed and built these houses for the quadroon landladies?

Refugee free men of color who had been carpenters, masons, plasterers, and cabinet makers

in Saint-Domingue picked up their professions once again in New Orleans. Among free men of color the profession of carpenter is listed as the most common by far. Take the example of Pierre Roup, *h.c.l.* (free man of color). Roup was a builder and contractor who arrived in New Orleans in 1805.[39] By 1808 he is listed as a property owner in the Quadroon Quarter, owning four lots (Figure 13). He appears to have been comfortable building a localized form of the *maison longue* with which he was previously familiar in Saint-Domingue, and his native Gonaïves (Figure 16). Over the next two decades, he and his wife, Coralie Lafitte (*f.c.l.* and niece of Jean Lafitte), bought and sold properties in the Quarter, Marigny, and along the Bayou Road. Roup died in 1836 in a house almost certainly of his design, a four-room-deep Single Shotgun–style house at 374 Rue d'amour (1744 North Rampart Street in Marigny) (Figure 21). He and several of his free colored contemporaries, such as Bartholemew Bacas and Jacques Tinchant, specialized in building both Creole cottages and shotgun houses.[40]

Contemporary observers make special mention of the houses of the quadroon women: "Those pretty and peculiar houses, whole rows of which may be seen in the Ramparts" and "Those peculiar little dwellings near the Ramparts."[41] Creole cottages had been commonplace in the French Quarter since early colonial times. They were found throughout the Quarter, not confined to "the Ramparts," so observations of the 1830s about the peculiarity of the local houses almost certainly refer to the then more recently popular linear cottages. Conceivably, they may also have referred to the unusual single-room-wide, two- and three-bay Creole cottages that were also fairly popular in the Ramparts area, except that other commentators refer to the new houses as "low" (see above). Creole cottages in this era are one and one-half stories tall (Figure 7).

By the 1830s and 1840s, the shotgun form was becoming accepted as a basic house type throughout the Creole faubourgs and beyond, not only among free people of color and their renters but, increasingly, among both white and black businesspeople. Many of these new linear cottages were built only two rooms deep. Each residence

Figure 22. 1031 Clouet Street in Marigny. A (circa 1840) Greek Revival–period Single Shotgun. Photograph by author, 2007.

was served with a detached kitchen, servants' quarters, and privies in the rear yard. Also during this period, the clapboard or board-and-batten-clad shotgun became increasingly popular. An example of an 1830s shotgun presumed to be prototypical is the Greek Revival–style frame house at 1031 Clouet (in Bywater) (Figure 22).[42]

An important innovation resulting from the sizable number of rental linear cottages being built was the Side-Hall and Side-Gallery Shotgun. The evolution is clearly seen in the floor plans of linear cottages, so carefully documented by the artists of the sales affiches archived in the New Orleans Notarial Archives. Whether single or double wide, they share two distinctive features. Rental rooms were always set at the rear of the main house; they are distinguished by not having direct access into the front portion of the residence where the landladies lived. Rather, the renter had to pass outside to get to and from the street. In order to further the passage of renters to their rooms, side-hall and side-gallery linear cottages provided access under a roof to the rear rental rooms (Figure 18). The same passageways permitted landladies to service the rooms in all kinds of weather when the renters were absent.

Figure 23. A (circa 1850) shotgun on Ursulines Street in Faubourg Tremé, by F. Nicolas Tourné, August 31, 1869. Courtesy NOMA (002.008).

An early approximation of the side-hall and side-gallery accommodation may be seen in certain early linear cottages that have extended roofs running down one side of the building only.

Figure 24. A Single Shotgun in Greek Revival trim, 5703 Chartres Street in Holy Cross (Lower Ninth Ward). Photograph by author, 2006.

The Economic Impact:
Creole Cottage versus Shotgun

Assuming that you are faced with the decision of building a single-family Creole cottage or a linear cottage–type house of similar square living footage, which kind of house would you wish to build? The costs of construction are clearly an important factor in the selection of a building type. Inexpensive, machine-cut framing material in standard sizes was becoming available in these decades. Most shotgun-type houses could be built without the use of heavy framing and specially fitted roof trusses. Ceiling joists did not have to support a second story as they did on the post-1820 Creole cottages.[43]

As a first and very rough approximation, I collected data on sixteen probable Creole cottages and fifteen probable linear cottages (sometimes described as "low houses") built between 1814 and 1839. The information was gleaned from the building contract database housed in the Historic New Orleans Collection. The average construction cost of the Creole cottage group was $3,058.50, while the mean cost of the linear cottage house type was $1,258.00. The mean date of construction of the Creole cottage group

was March 1832, and that of the linear group was April 1833. My tentative conclusion is that in these decades it was approximately twice as expensive to build a Creole cottage as it was to build a linear cottage of approximately the same floor space—for many, clearly a motivation for the selection of shotgun-type houses.

The Greek Revival Revolution:
An Architectural Theory

By 1834 a truly remarkable transformation was underway in New Orleans vernacular architecture. The hugely popular pattern books of Asher Benjamin (1838, 1843) and Minard Lafever (1833) were being used as guides by builders across the country. Architects formally trained in classical "Greek Revival" forms such as those depicted in these pattern books had begun to arrive in New Orleans. Two were particularly significant: James Gallier Sr. (1798–1866) arrived in New Orleans in 1834, and James Dakin (1806–1852) followed in 1835. Almost immediately they began to impact local architectural styles. Soon, Greek Revival fever was sweeping the increasingly prosperous city. Builders and contractors who labored to construct the mansions and public buildings

Figure 25. A (circa 1820) *appentis* cottage with attached two-story kitchen, by Alexander Castaing and J. A. Celles, August 4, 1866. Courtesy New Orleans Notarial Archives (045.051).

designed by these architects were soon applying similar decorative treatments to their own more modest commissions. Those who built even humble traditional dwellings began to add elegant new forms of decoration to the façades of their otherwise commonplace cottages. Dental frieze moldings outcropped immediately below the eaves of the roof. Doorways sometimes receded behind open vestibules in imitation of the Greek *prothyron,* or domestic entrance hall. Decorative treatments of doors came to include any combination of transom lights, side lights, classical columns, entablatures, and, increasingly, pediments—all considered "Greek Revival" elements. Among the more popular stylistic innovations were trapezoidal door surrounds that sprouted up on vernacular structures throughout the city, even on humble shotgun houses (Figures 22, 29). These surrounds were referred to as "mouldings with diminished architraves" in building contracts of the period. Since the 1970s they have been called "Greek Key" architraves by New Orleans architectural historians. All of these elements were, in fact, a new reworking of the Classical Revival, which had been popular in America since the 1780s.[44]

This stylistic revolution is curiously coincident with the rise of the gable-fronted shotgun house and the end of construction of new Creole cottages. They co-occur beginning in the 1835–45 decade. Could they possibly be causally linked? I believe that they are. It is difficult to Greek Revivalize a Creole cottage. The steep gable roof is unlike the massing of any classical building, so the entablature must be very tall to mask the shape of the roof. On the other hand, a linear cottage with a gabled front is simply a Greek temple form in miniature. All that is required is the addition of Classical Revival columns, pilasters, entablature, and a pediment and—oipa!—you have your own Greek temple (Figure 24). Jump ahead two decades, to 1855, and you find such a variety of Greek Revivalized shotgun houses throughout every district of the city that to term it an architectural revolution is not an exaggeration. It was Greek Revival mania in the streets.

By the end of the 1840s, the single-room-wide linear cottage had become popular with both the working class and middle-class Anglo businessmen, as well as with Germans, Irish, and other European immigrants. They began to construct larger and more elegant shotgun

Figure 26. Evolution of
the Camelback Shotgun,
footprints drawn from
1876 Sanborn maps.
Drawing by Mary Lee
Eggart for the Kniffen
Lab.

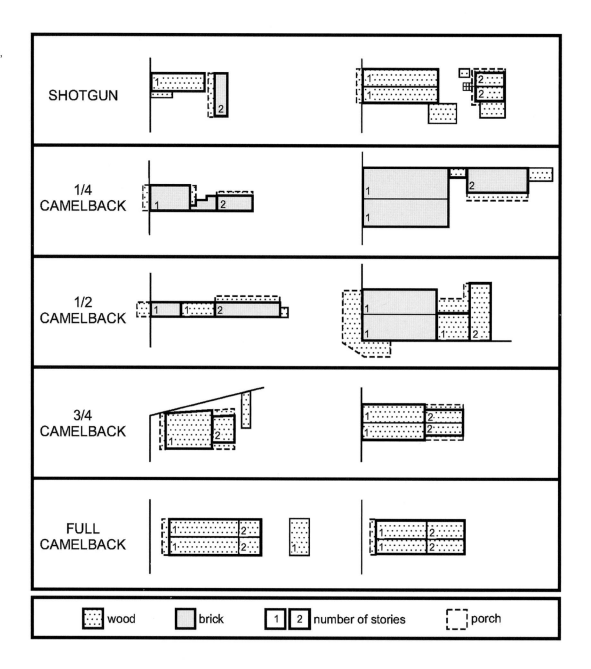

houses for themselves in the new neighborhoods of the Garden District, the Irish Channel, Faubourg Pontchartrain, Carrollton, and
elsewhere throughout the American sector.
The shotgun grew to four or more rooms deep
with rear extensions. Side-Hall and Side-Gallery
Shotguns were popular, as were Doubles. Gable
fronts replaced earlier hip roofs and *abat vents*.
Elaborate Greek Revival and Italianate entablatures were added to the façades of whole groups
shotgun houses, now being built in rows and
entire squares. Some were raised a full story

on a masonry ground floor or on pillars. Others
were built two full stories in height.[45]

The Camelback House:
A Technological Transformation
With the spectacular coincident growth of the
urban population and the cypress lumber industry in Louisiana in the 1870s and 1880s, the number of wooden houses mushroomed. Growing
prosperity among working-class people resulted
in a variety of expansions of the shotgun house—
the old linear cottage still had a few tricks up its

sleep. As early as the 1830s, and continuing through the 1870s, it was not unusual for single-story shotguns and doubles to have detached two-story *cuisine/garçonnier* service buildings at the rear (Figure 25). The kitchen was on the first floor and the second story functioned for servants' quarters, bachelor's rooms, and rental spaces. With increasingly inexpensive and convenient cast iron stoves pouring from retooled iron foundries following the Civil War, detached kitchens could be safely brought up and connected directly to the rear walls of the houses, or the two might be joined by an extension (Figure 26). When a two-story kitchen unit is attached directly to the rear of the single-story shotgun or Shotgun Double, the result is the curious and unique Camelback house.[46] Proto-Camelbacks appeared in small numbers in all stages of attachment in the 1876 Sanborn maps, and by the 1896 edition, Camelbacks, fully formed, were commonplace. During Reconstruction, the second-floor bedroom over the kitchen, once a slave quarter or rental unit, was given a new role as the secluded master bedroom. Homeowners had created a new zone of undisturbed privacy in the otherwise very public shotgun house. Soon, the rear kitchen section was fully integrated with the shotgun front, creating the familiar New Orleans Camelback.

A remarkable variety of "Victorian" shotgun forms appeared in the late nineteenth century. Double Shotguns became more popular than single-wide shotguns (Figure 27). The shotgun expanded creatively into two-story Single Shotguns (sometimes called "Duplexes") (Figure 28), and double-wide versions of these (Fourplexes). The two-story-tall shotgun merged with the East Coast style two-story townhouse so that in many cases it is not possible to tell which form is the progenitor (Figure 29). With the appearance of elaborate but inexpensive machine-manufactured wooden decoration from steam-powered sawmills and sash-and-blind companies, the shotgun was dressed up in Italianate, Eastlake, Queen Anne, and other popular styles of the day. The "bracket style" was also popular in the 1880–1900 decades (Figure 27: Single Shotgun). The last two decades of the nineteenth century witnessed a cultural florescence in which the

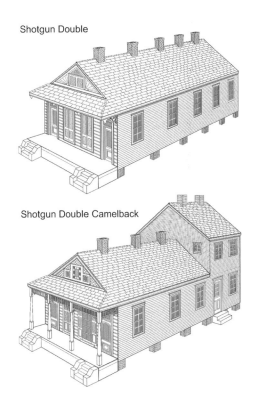

Shotgun Double

Shotgun Double Camelback

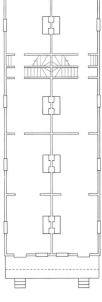

Shotgun Double Camelback Plan

Figure 27. Plan and elevations of a Double Shotgun and a Camelback Shotgun. Drawing by Mary Lee Eggart for the Kniffen Lab.

once humble shotgun enjoyed enormous expansion and decorative variation in every part of the city. It has become an architectural canvas on which every family may paint its own new distinctive autobiography of cultural identity and social success.

In the twentieth century Singles and other varieties of this architectural family continued to be built with more modern materials and techniques. The shotgun adapted easily to the "Bungalow," or craftsman style. They were built by the hundreds in the newly opened sections in the eastern portions of the city (Figures 3, 30). Singles and Doubles were elevated a full story on a brick "basement." These survived the floods of Hurricanes Betsy (1965) and Katrina (2005), but for most of New Orleans, World War II and the G.I. Bill finally rang the death knell on shotgun expansion. Beginning in the late 1940s, new national styles of suburban cottages on slabs and ranch houses were constructed by the thousands for returning G.I.s in the newly drained sections of the city, mostly lakeside of the Metairie-Gentilly Bayou ridge. Those who design and build their own houses often continued to adopt the shotgun and Camelback styles in the

Figure 28. A (circa 1839) three-bay Duplex Shotgun in the 1400 block of Villere on the Esplanade Ridge, with two-story detached kitchen, by Alexander Castaing and J. A. Celles, August 4, 1866. Courtesy New Orleans Notarial Archives (070.019).

Figure 29. A (circa 1830s) side hall Creole townhouse (or Shotgun Duplex), 1300 block of Dauphine in the Vieux Carré, by Paul C. Boudousquié, June 15, 1868. Courtesy New Orleans Notarial Archives (002.004).

rapidly expanding eastern suburbs of New Orleans: Gentilly, the Seventh Ward, the Ninth Ward, and New Orleans East. Newer national styles dominated in middle-class neighborhoods.

This process was abruptly halted by Katrina. Post-Katrina, various schemes for adapting shotgun-like replacements to imperiled low-lying areas of the city are being designed and promoted by architectural firms and by schools of architecture and engineering.

Interpretations

The history of the shotgun house reminds us that architectural histories are never neutral. They are, rather, inherently political documents that require close scrutiny. Even in those cases in which the vast majority of the scholarly community appears to agree on a single account of architectural origins, reevaluation is always essential. Indeed, conceptual unanimity amounts to a call to scholars everywhere to test the presuppositions of a master narrative against new ideas and novel perspectives. More socially responsible histories cannot help but result.

Previous attempts at writing the architectural history of New Orleans's historic neighborhoods have been too narrow to account for the rich complexity of transformation that characterizes their development. The linear cottage introduced new forms of architectural adaptation, which proved to be incredibly successful. In pre-Katrina New Orleans alone, shotgun variants survived in the order of 60,000 units, far beyond the level of any other architectural family. Single linear cottages similar to those from the earliest stages of introduction are still to be found in significant (though diminishing) numbers throughout the city and, indeed, across Louisiana and beyond. They have been built continuously from the time of their introduction about 1800 until the present, a period of more than two centuries. They are an essential ingredient of any interpretation of the development of the cultural landscapes of New Orleans. Yet, their history has been badly neglected, raising the question of how such an uneven architectural history became established.

Édouard Glissant and the *créolité* writers have described resistance strategies as one of the principal mechanisms in the development of creolized societies such as New Orleans.[47] Since forms of material culture have rarely been interpreted from the perspective of resistance, it is

Figure 30. A (circa 1910) Craftsman-style bungalow Double on Greenwood Street near Canal Boulevard. Courtesy New Orleans Notarial Archives (111.001).

appropriate that we raise the obvious question of how architectural forms might function as survival techniques under the severe economic and social limitations imposed on subjugated racial and social classes.[48]

It is useful to divide strategies of resistance into two categories: subversive and circumventional. Most scholars have focused on forms of subversion, but during the latter years of the Spanish colonial regime, as formal education became available to the children of freed persons of color, new forms of resistance arose in New Orleans. Emerging new strategies were expanded dramatically with the massive influx of Caribbean Creole *affrachis* from Saint-Domingue between 1791 and 1810. It was particularly the immigrant free people of color who redefined Afro-Creole society, providing an expanded repertoire of creative strategies.[49] Drawing heavily from their own cultural patrimony from Saint-Domingue, they struck out on their own, redefining both themselves and their architectural symbols in creative ways.[50]

The Caribbean-style linear cottage functioned as a vehicle of cultural survival and adaptation to changing forces and circumstances. It empowered the Creole population and assisted it to survive and even prosper more successfully than it might otherwise have done under the hegemony of growing social and legal constraints of the Republican and Antebellum eras, and under the institutionalized racism of Reconstruction and Jim Crow segregation.[51] Afro-Creoles and African American builders specialized in the construction of a house type well suited to both working-class and middle-class incomes and to Louisiana's cypress-rich, low-lying tropical, environments. In the process of becoming the favored house type for tens of thousands of African American residents, it also became an emblem of the Creolized vernacular neighborhoods of the city.[52]

Perhaps the most remarkable aspect of this family of houses has been their adaptability. At each stage of its development, the Creole linear cottage adapted successfully to different social, cadastral, legal, economic, and constructional exigencies, always incorporating new patterns, styles, and geometries to meet the demands of New Orleans' residents. Apart from cuisine, this writer is hard-pressed to identify a more successful form of Creole material culture in the

United States. In Louisiana, for example, far more people live in shotgun-style houses than speak a Creole language.[53]

Whether the continuous reinvention of the shotgun can be accounted for by the hegemonic forces of "brutality, domination, and violence" is another question. As Tremé, the Esplanade Ridge, and Marigny were being populated, the shotgun became a symbol of establishment and identity for an important segment of society. For the most part these residents were not slaves, though many enslaved people lived among them. Rather, they were mostly members of the middle caste of New Orleans society, struggling to carve out a successful niche for themselves in a highly competitive and increasingly racially stigmatized environment. Free Creoles of color creatively reformulated elements of their heritage in building a new urban landscape. This was at heart a circumventional form of resistance, one that succeeded by contributing successfully within the system and that profited from it instead of subversively attempting to damage it through numerous small acts of defiance. "One of the salutary elements of Creoleness is its inversive logic, that is, its ability to invert and convert the logic of the hegemonic sphere into the symbolic capital of cultural difference."[54]

In that it inserted novel, uniquely creolized, rather than locally received patterns into the existing cultural mix, Creole architectural practice remained closer to resistance than to compliance. It was a form of positive symbolic defiance that molded and reformulated earlier cultural forms in the direction of novelties more symbolic of French Caribbean colonial identity. To those with roots in the colony of Saint-Domingue, the refugees were reconstituting architectural identities of a now lost but previously self-sufficient Creole society. In Creole New Orleans, they had discovered a new and tentatively receptive environment for this endangered culture. To Louisiana residents without experience in the former colony of Saint-Domingue, the new architectures represented, perhaps, simply a curious and unsophisticated reworking of earlier local French colonial forms adjusted to the practicalities of an increasingly crowded urban environment.

Each time the shotgun was endangered by rigidity and stagnation, another set of historical events launched it on a new trajectory. It crossed racial and class boundaries with ease. As a changing form of cultural adaptation central to domestic life, it helped the people of New Orleans to undermine and redefine externally generated authoritarian preconceptions of racial identity and social place. Enlisting an entire society into the advantages of what was originally an Afro-Creole symbol of cultural identity, it became the cutting edge of a tactic far more subtle and successful than any of the multiple subversive forms of resistance that might have been adopted. As with other forms of Afro-Creole culture, the people of the Creole faubourgs enticed the entire society to imitate them and to participate with them in its sensuality and practicality. The linear cottage legacy was adopted by white French Creoles, African Americans, Anglo-Americans, and European immigrants, all of whom continued to use and to expand on it. Indeed, many of its most exuberant subsequent expressions were the creations of other ethnic groups. In the Big Easy, the shotgun played an important role in providing bridges for uniting all of its races and classes under the big tent of Creole culture identity.

The study of the history of the shotgun carries important implications for architectural theory. It shows us that the established architectural histories of the shotgun house have been both right and wrong, but mostly they have been unimaginative and incomplete. It suggests that architectural historians need to critically reexamine the implications of the strategies they adopt in the telling of their tales. They might wish to consider how circumventional processes of identity formulation and cultural resistance might be more central to the history of architectural forms. More importantly, we need to adopt a broader vision of the place of our architectural histories in the marketplace of political ideas.[55] We are compelled, for example, to dramatize the real tragedy of the loss of so much of the shotgun crescent. It is not so much the disappearance of specific shotgun houses, as numerous as those losses are, but rather the potential loss of an entire cauldron of Creole cultural creativity that is at stake.

Before Katrina, the shotgun-rich neighborhoods of New Orleans were no object for tourist veneration and commodification. They were, rather, creative, living generators of an almost infinite variety of new cultural forms. It is those cultural forms that made New Orleans world-renowned. They were the gifts of New Orleans to America. It was in and around these houses and on their front porches that a unique culture flourished. Here jazz and the blues sprang to life, local Creole French continued to be spoken, and folk Catholicism and Afro-Caribbean spirituality were practiced. Here, too, Creole percussion, dance, cuisine, and craftwork, and the public performances of Mardi Gras and second lines and jazz funerals were celebrated.[56] After the houses have disappeared, their supporting social networks and shared cultural practices may never be reestablished. When their creative base is lost, architectural history will bear some of the responsibility for that loss. Although the Road Home Program of support to homeowners affected by Katrina and Rita ended September 2008, perhaps there is still time to revalue and reinvigorate the Afro-Creole and multicultural nineteenth-century neighborhoods of New Orleans and to restore at least some of them to levels of social viability. In this, traditional vernacular architecture will function as an essential foundation for recovery. The shotgun house, although currently imperiled, has been difficult to annihilate in the past. Perhaps it should not yet be written off. Although it will change again, it may well outlive Katrina and disasters yet to come.

NOTES

This paper is expanded from a talk delivered on March 31, 2007, at the Vernacular Architecture Forum meetings in Savannah, Georgia. The author wishes to thank Mary Lee Eggart (MLE), staff artist of the Department of Geography and Anthropology, for her talented efforts in illustrating this paper. I also wish to thank John Anderson of the Louisiana State University Cartographic Information Center, Kevin Williams of the Southeastern Architectural Archive of Tulane University, Hilary Irvin of the Vieux Carré Commission of the City of New Orleans, the staff of the Historic New Orleans Collection, Sybil Boudreaux of the University of New Orleans Library, Louisiana collection, Anne Wakefield, Juliette and Isabel and the staff of the New Orleans Notarial Archives (hereafter NONA), and the staff of the Special Collections and Louisiana Collections of the LSU Library for their invaluable help in acquiring information and images for this article. The staff of the Maps Division of the Library of Congress was particularly helpful in permitting the author to gather large amounts of historic cartographic information on New Orleans. Finally, I wish to thank Sally K. Reeves for her continuing professional assistance to me and for her passion in furthering the architectural history of New Orleans.

1. Fred B. Kniffen, "Louisiana House Types," *Annals of the Association of American Geographers* 26 (1936): 179–93. "The folk-term here employed is commonly used in Louisiana to designate a long, narrow house. It is but one room in width and from one to three or more rooms deep, with frontward-facing gable." This definition has been expanded since Kniffen's time. A shotgun house may have either a hip or a gable roof. Its narrow front must face a street, path, or waterway, if one is present. The roof ridge always runs perpendicular to the front of the building. A shotgun may or may not have a front porch. If present, the porch may be either in-set under the main roof, or it may be attached to the façade of the building. A shotgun may or may not be elevated above grade on pillars, cypress blocks, or a chain wall. The shotgun is not necessarily an urban form. Many thousands of shotguns in Haiti, Cuba, and Louisiana are set in rural places. The early Single Shotgun evolved through no less than eleven distinct architectural types, each represented by dozens or hundreds of examples in New Orleans. In this paper, named types of the shotgun family are capitalized (i.e., Camelback Shotgun). The entire collection of house types genetically descended or influenced by the shotgun is referred to as the Shotgun Family.

2. Katrina hit New Orleans on August 29, 2005, with the flooding taking place the following day. See Nebla Banerlee, "In New Orleans, Rebuilding with Faith," *New York Times*, October 26, 2007. No geographical survey of the shotgun house in New Orleans has ever been undertaken, to my knowledge. Refer to City of New Orleans, *The Unified New Orleans Plan* (2007), 3–17, accessed at: http://www.willdoo-storage.com/Plans/CityWide/UNOPFINAL_3.pdf.

3. The Shotgun Crescent: a nineteenth-century zone of the city extending from historic Uptown

neighborhoods of West Riverside, Audubon, Carrollton, Broadmore, and Girt Town, into the "bowl" of Mid City, Bayou St. John, upper Tremé, and the Esplanade Ridge, and eastward through the Seventh Ward, St. Roch, St. Claude, and back to the river below the French Quarter in Bywater and Holy Cross.

4. The New Orleans Planning Initiative (Acorn Housing–University Partnership), *The People's Plan for Overcoming the Hurricane Katrina Blues* (2007), a pdf file accessed November 15, 2007, at http://www.rebuild ingtheninth.org/resources; City of New Orleans, *The Unified New Orleans Plan*. See also Rose Kalima et al., *Equity Atlas: A Long Way Home, the State of Housing Recovery in Louisiana* (2008), http://www.policylink .org/threeyearslater/index.html and Kaiser Foundation, *Giving Voice to the People of New Orleans: The Kaiser Post-Katrina Baseline Survey* (May 2007), http:// www.kff.org/kaiserpolls/upload/7631.pdf.

5. Seventy-five percent of those living in the low-lying, flood-damaged areas of the city were African Americans. John R. Logan, "The Impact of Katrina: Race and Class in Storm-Damaged Neighborhoods" (2007), accessed October 10, 2007, at http://www .s4.brown.edu/Katrina/report.pdf; Associated Press dispatch quoted in Mike Davis, "Gentrifying Disaster: In New Orleans: Ethnic Cleansing, GOP-Style" (October 25, 2005), http://www.motherjones.com/ commentary/columns/2005/10/gentrifying_disas ter.htm. Jakuna Tarhakah, interviewed in *Community Forum on Rebuilding New Orleans* (DVD; New Orleans: Acorn, 2005); The *Advocate* (Baton Rouge), September 28, 2007, 1; Peter Dreier, "Katrina and Power in America," *Urban Affairs Review* 41, no. 4 (2006): 1022; Becky Bohrer, "N.O.'s Racial Political Balance May Be Shifting," *The Advocate* (Baton Rouge), November 15, 2007, 17a.

6. Judith Browne-Dianis, "This Is My Home," part 1 (2006), documentary on New Orleans housing, accessed February 19, 2007, at http://www.advance mentproject.org/katrina/video1.html; Min. J. Kojo Livingston, "Housing: A Crisis of Courage, Compassion & Leadership," *The New Orleans Agenda* (Web newsletter), December 20, 2007, accessed at http://www .theneworleansagenda.com/.

7. Sam Wilson Jr. et al., *New Orleans Architecture: The Creole Faubourgs* (Metairie, La.: Pelican Press, 1984), 71. The argument that the shotgun form originated as the result of expansion of the Creole cottage into long, narrow lots is cast into question through historical and comparative perspective. Many hundreds of shotguns employed as quarters houses on Louisiana plantations are sufficiently widely spaced to permit the use of alternate forms. The earliest shotguns on the fringes of the Creole faubourgs in New Orleans were not confined to narrow lots (Figures 9 and 13). In both Haiti and Cuba, the free-standing, shotgun-style cottage antedates the development of densely occupied towns (Figure 10). John Michael Vlach refers to this argument in an article on the shotgun in his edited collection *The Afro-American Tradition in Decorative Arts*, chapter 8, "Architecture" (Athens: University of Georgia Press, 1990), 128–29.

8. Sally Kittridge Reeves, "Contribution of Free Persons of Color to Vernacular Architecture in New Orleans before the Civil War," talk given before the conference Raised to the Trade—Creole Building Arts of New Orleans, New Orleans Museum of Art, February 13, 2003.

9. John Michael Vlach, *Sources of the Shotgun House: African and Caribbean Antecedents*, 2 vols. (PhD diss., Indiana University–Bloomington, 1975). See also his "Shotgun Houses," *Natural History* 86:50–57, and "The Shotgun House: An African Architectural Legacy," *Pioneer America* (now *Material Culture*) 8, no. 1: 47–56, and 8, no. 2: 57–70.

10. The painter was the sailor Pierre Caillot. The French town of Les Cayes was established in 1726 on the location of a previously destroyed Spanish settlement. See Priscilla and John Lawrence et al., *Common Routes: St. Domingue—Louisiana* (New Orleans: The Historic New Orleans Collection, 2006), 94 (Acquisition No. 2005: 11).

11. Caryn Cossé Bell, *Revolution, Romanticism and the Afro-Creole Protest Tradition in Louisiana 1718–1868* (Baton Rouge: Louisiana State University Press, 1997), 11, 37; Carl Brasseaux and Glenn Conrad, *The Road to Louisiana: The Saint-Domingue Refugees, 1792–1809* (Lafayette: Center for Louisiana Studies, 1992); Nathalie Dessens, *From Saint-Domingue to New Orleans: Migration and Influences* (Gainesville: University Press of Florida, 2007), 147, 149.

12. Kimberly S. Hanger, *Bounded Lives, Bounded Places: Free Black Society in Colonial New Orleans 1769–1803* (Durham, N.C.: Duke University Press, 1997); Roulhac Toledano and Mary Louise Christovich, "The Role of Free People of Color," *New Orleans Architecture*,

vol. 6, *Faubourg Tremé and the Bayou Road* (Gretna, La.: Pelican Publishing, 2003), 85–107; Lois Virginia Meacham Gould, *In Full Enjoyment of Their Liberty: The Free Women of Color of the Gulf Ports of New Orleans, Mobile, and Pensacola, 1769–1860* (unpublished PhD diss., Department of History, Emory University, 1991).

13. Grace King, *New Orleans: The Place and the People* (New York: Macmillan, 1915), 171; Charles E. A. Gayarré, *The Quadroons of Louisiana* (Baton Rouge: Special Collections of the Louisiana State University Library, ca. 1866–95, MSS. 1558), 7.

14. Karen Kingsley. *Buildings of Louisiana* (New York: Oxford University Press, 2003), 25–26; Ellen Weiss. "City and Country, 1880–1915: Shotguns, a Louisiana Building Type," in Louisiana Buildings 1720–1940, ed. Jessie Poesch and Barbara SoRelle Bacot, 267–85 (Baton Rouge: Louisiana State University Press, 1997), esp. 276, 279–85. The quote by Malcolm Heard represents another expression of the traditional Wilson origins narrative adopted by the preservation community: *French Quarter Manual: An Architectural Guide to New Orleans' Vieux Carré* (New Orleans: Tulane School of Architecture, 1997), 48.

15. The historical research described in Vlach's dissertation does not push the origins of the shotgun much further back in time. "The earliest shotgun house appearing in these records was located on Bourbon Street near St. Philip, in the French Quarter and was sold in November, 1833" (Vlach, Sources of the Shotgun House, 1:63–64, 77). Other early shotguns discovered by Vlach in the records of New Orleans Notarial Archives date to the 1830s and 1840s. Even this research comes in for criticism by the New Orleans architectural historians. In fairness to the New Orleans architectural historians, some of Vlach's titles seem to overstate his case for African influences on the shotgun: for example, "The Shotgun House: An African Architectural Legacy."

16. This writer has attended several and was invited lecturer at one: Jay Edwards, "A History of the Shotgun House," Shotgun House Lecture Series at the Preservation Resource Center, New Orleans, March 30, 2006. The leadership personnel of most preservation organizations in New Orleans disagree rather strongly with what they interpret as Vlach's "African Origins" theory of the shotgun.

17. Karolyn Smardz Frost, *I've Got a Home in Glory Land* (Toronto: Farrar, Straus & Giroux, 2007); Greg Langley, "Remnant of African Culture Common in Neighborhoods across Louisiana," *The Sunday Advocate*, February 4, 2007, 3E; Lloyd Vogt, *Historic Buildings of the French Quarter* (Gretna, La.: Pelican Publishing, 2002), 116.

18. See, particularly, Sally Kittridge Evans, "Free Persons of Color," in Wilson et al., New Orleans Architecture, 25–36; Reeves, "Contribution of Free Persons of Color"; Toledano and Christovich, "The Role of Free People of Color," 85–107.

19. Based on a detailed examination of 1933 aerial photography of Orleans Parish. Most of the completed shotgun HABS projects are little more than a few photographs developed for salvage documentation projects. There are only two sets of plans, one from a set of photocopied blueprints. The report on the 1923 Alton Lear house at 2016 Louisiana Avenue states that 48 percent of the building stock in the Uptown Historic District's 10,716 buildings "adopt a shotgun form" (Goodwin & Associates for HABS survey LA 36, 1996). This proportion is higher in much of the shotgun crescent.

20. Through the nineteenth century, New Orleans enjoyed the peculiar combination of French inheritance law and trained artists employed by the city government to record properties for sale. In order to determine the market value of a property at the death of an owner, it was auctioned publicly and the proceeds distributed equally among the heirs. Each sale entailed drafting an attractive, watercolored advertisement poster (*affiche*), based on an onsite survey. The large-format posters included a great deal of architectural and dimensional detail. About 1,600 that include architectural "indications" are archived in the New Orleans Notarial Archives' historical section. No other American city enjoyed such an abundance of contemporary architectural surveys in the nineteenth century. Notaries' records including thousands of property-transfer records and many hundreds of building contracts are housed in the same location. Even this excellent historical record identifies only a tiny proportion of the buildings that stood in the 1800–1840 period. Numerous buildings of each specific type that never appeared in the historic record also existed, particularly smaller vernacular structures. Given the extreme loss and replacement of smaller buildings from the pre-1840 period, we can assume that for every ten linear cottages that were sufficiently fortunate to be documented in

this period, well over ten times that number remained anonymous.

21. The earliest linear cottage in the database is a service building on Bourbon Street dated 1790. It opens onto the street, but each of its three rooms functions as a separate apartment opening on the courtyard. In addition, it has a flat or "terrace" roof, conforming to the antifire zoning ordinances of the period (Database No. 107, NONA: 015:030). Recognizing that gaps exist in the legal records, at some later date information of the historic shotgun database should be augmented by more complete chain-of-title information and cross-checked with other sources such as the building contract data, wills, city directories, and legal cases.

22. *Appentis* is pronounced "apénti." See, for example, NONA 090.014 for another classic 1830s freestanding *appentis* cottage.

23. Twenty-two examples, or 15.7 percent of the shotgun database, are *appentis* cottages.

24. Notable among them are Carlos Trudeau, land surveyor (from 1793); Barthélémy Lafon, architect, surveyor, and land speculator (active 1805 to about 1815); Gilie Joseph Pilié, city surveyor of Orleans Parish (1808–1836); Jules Allou d'Hemecourt (active 1809–1832); Jacques Tanassee, architect, cartographer, and surveyor (1810–1818); Jean Mager, commission merchant and land speculator (from circa 1814), and Jaques Tinchant (with Pierre Duhart *(h.c.l.)*, Haitian carpenter turned builder and land developer, active in the 1830s. On the history of the Tinchant family, see Rebecca J. Scott, "Public Rights and Private Commerce: A Nineteenth-Century Atlantic Creole Itinerary," *Current Anthropology* 48, no. 2 (2007): 237–56.

25. Roger G. Kennedy, "Barthélémy Lafon: True Tales of the Pirate Architect of New Orleans," *Architectural Digest* 50 (1993): 102, 104, 112, 114, 115; Barthélémy Lafon, personal survey books 1 and 2 [mostly property surveys and maps for the Comté d'Orleans, Territoire d'Orleans (1803–1812)], Historic New Orleans Collection MSS 408, acquisition no. 92-51-L. So numerous and important are these property surveys that it is difficult to describe the early nineteenth-century history of New Orleans without reference to them. Yet, for some reason, they have seldom if ever been used as evidence by the New Orleans architectural historians.

26 Barthélémy Lafon, personal survey book 2 (April 24–25, 1808): 220–22. Shotgun survey database No. 7.

27. Small structures labeled "Old Shanties" and "Old" in the form of tiny shotgun houses are to be found on several of the 1876 Sanborn maps, in the French Quarter and in Faubourg Marigny: 1876 Sanborn maps courtesy Southeastern Architectural Archive, Tulane University Library. No specific mention or description of such shanties seems to survive in the legal records of the parish. Five Single shotguns: Database nos. 80, 81.

28. New Orleans *Counseil de Ville, Ordinances and Resolutions 1805–1835,* translated by the Work Projects Administration, MSS., New Orleans Municipal Library, n.d. (ca. 1835).

29. The visual similarities between the "Federal" maisonettes of the French Quarter and the hip-roofed town houses of post-1803 Cap Haïtien (Le Cap, Haiti) are closer to one another than they are to North American Federal decor, in my opinion. The early Spanish colonial domestic architecture of Saint Domingue was influenced by Italo-Spanish early Renaissance vernacularized Tuscan styling. This included simplified flat pilasters at the edges of façades, steep hip roofs covered with tile or slate, and multiple doors facing the street—features all shared with the shotgun maisonettes of 1820s New Orleans. Jay Edwards, "The Origins of Creole Architecture," *Winterthur Portfolio* 29, nos. 2/3 (1994): 155–89; Christian Goguet with Frédéric Mangones, *L'architecture de la ville historique du Cap Haïtien* (Cap Haïtien, Haiti: Schema directeur du centre historique de la ville du Cap Haïtien, 1989). In Goguet and Mangones's book, note particularly the sketches on pages 31, 40, 43, 49, 53, 72a, and 121, and the photos on pages 93, 145, 147, and 159. *Abats vents* also survive occasionally on the townhouses of *Le Cap,* as depicted on pages 44 and 47 of Goguet and Mangones.

30. Classic shotgun maisonettes from the 1820s are found at 1024 Gov. Nicholls and 819 Burgundy Street, in the French Quarter. One dated circa 1831, with a Greek Key door surround, existed at 928 Gov. Nicholls. Others were to be found in the 900 block of Tremé Street and the 800 block of St. Claude, before they were demolished to make room for Armstrong Park: Toledano and Christovich, "The Role of Free People of Color," 66, Figures 9A, 9B.

On May 16, 1830, the French sketch artist and naturalist, Alexandre Lesueur, standing near the present-day intersection of Moss Street and Grand Route St. John, looking west, made two sketches of the same location, one "with the rising sun," the other at 2:00 PM. See Historic New Orleans Collection, acquisition nos. 1974.25.26.17 and 1974.25.16.18. Both sketches show versions of the same hip-roofed maisonette. One clearly shows an *abat vent*. A series of shotgun houses have stood at the same location ever since. On Lesueur's recording of Louisiana's cultural landscapes, see E. T. Hamy, *Travels of the Naturalist Charles A. Lesueur in North America: 1815–1837* (Kent, Ohio: Kent State University Press, 1968).

In my shotgun database there are thirty-six maisonette-style linear cottages, amounting to 25.7 percent of the total sample. Of these, seven, or 5 percent of the total sample, are doubles.

31. The origins of the double shotgun may be seen in the development of the four-bay linear cottage in the 1810s. Some of the earliest examples exhibit a transitional plan halfway between a Creole cottage and a double shotgun. Houses like the Phillippon Cottage, 1016/18 St. Phillip Street (razed), consist of two square rooms facing the street, with another two- or three-room module set asymmetrically and perpendicularly behind the first, and a side hall or side gallery filling in the remainder of the cottage width (Figure 19). From the street, these houses appear exactly like four-bay maisonettes or double shotguns with hip roofs and *abat vents*. See NONA 044.039.

32. Sam Wilson believed that essentially all of the forms of "Creole" architecture in New Orleans were derived specifically from French sources and French inspiration. Most other architectural historians, and specifically the "Friends of the Cabildo" group, have followed his lead on questions of origins. In New Orleans, the term "shotgun" has carried a connotation of the gable-fronted wooden cottages of the 1840s and thereafter. In roof form and in construction technology, the maisonettes of 1810–1830 are similar to the hip-roofed, double-wide Creole cottages of that period, though they happened to be turned with their narrow ends toward the street. In the NONA database under the category "type," early linear cottages with shotgun and shotgun double plans are classified under a variety of titles, including "cottage," "single Creole cottage," "frame cottage," "maisonette," and only occasionally "proto-shotgun" or "shotgun" (including a few that are not shotgun-related house types).

For the Friends of the Cabildo perspective on classification of historic vernacular types, refer to Toledano and Christovich, "The Role of Free People of Color,"

143; Wilson et al., New Orleans Architecture, 52 (Figure 35) and 42 (Figure 8). The Creole cottage classification is based on the model of the much-reproduced two-room-wide, two-room-deep cottage with gallery or *abat vent* in front and with a cabinet-loggia range behind (ibid., 101, plate 8). On both single and double "Creole cottages" with the roof ridge perpendicular to the street, it is unclear whether they are better referred to as hip-roof shotgun bungalows or Creole cottage maisonettes. Those located on corner lots typically have doors on both the narrow side and the long side, further conflating the categories of shotgun and Creole cottage (ibid., 82–83, plates 3 and 4).

33. In all, eleven gable-fronted linear cottages predating 1840 (roughly 8 percent) appear in the database.

34. See Paul F. Lachance, "The Formation of a Three-Caste Society: Evidence from Wills in Antebellum New Orleans," *Social Science History* 18, no. 2 (1994): 211–42; Cossé Bell, *Revolution, Romanticism and the Afro-Creole Protest Tradition*; Joan M. Martin, "*Plaçage* and the Louisiana *Gens de Couleur Libre*," in *Creole: The History and Legacy of Louisiana's Free People of Color*, ed. Sybil Kein, 57–70 (Baton Rouge: Louisiana State University Press, 2000); Alfred N. Hunt, *Haiti's Influence on Antebellum America* (Baton Rouge: Louisiana State University Press, 1988), particularly 37–83; Henry A. Kmen, "The Quadroon Balls," in *Music in New Orleans*, chap. 2 (Baton Rouge: Louisiana State University Press, 1966), 42–55, reprinted in *The Louisiana Purchase Bicentennial Series in Louisiana History*, vol. 11: *The African American Experience in Louisiana, Part A*, ed. Charles Vincent, 417–27 (Lafayette: Center for Louisiana Studies, 1999).

35. "Many fine women with brunette complexions, are to be seen walking the streets with the air of donnas. They wear no bonnets, but as a substitute, fasten a veil to the head. As they move it floats gracefully around them. These are termed quadroons, one quarter of their blood being tinged with African. Some of the finest looking women in New Orleans are quadroons. . . . They certainly have large, fine eyes, good features, and magnificent forms. James Register, *New Orleans Is My Name* (written 1834–35; Shreveport, La.: Mid South Press, 1971), 28. See also La Chance, "The Formation of a Three-Caste Society," 273–78; Daniel E. Walker, *No More, No More: Slavery and Cultural Resistance in Havana and New Orleans* (Minneapolis: University of Minnesota Press, 2004), 61–63; Harriet Martineau,

Society in America (1837; repr., New Brunswick, N.J.: Transaction Books, 1981), 181–82; Martin "Plaçage and the Louisiana Gens de Couleur Libre." Perhaps the most insightful and detailed description of the quadroons of New Orleans by a contemporary observer is that of Louisiana historian Charles E. A. Gayarré in "The Quadroons of Louisiana," MSS. 1558, 17 pages typescript, Special Collections of the Louisiana State University Library, Baton Rouge, ca. 1866–95.

36. Martin, "Plaçage and the Louisiana Gens de Couleur Libre," 67; Walker, No More, No More, 82; Cossé Bell, Revolution, Romanticism and the Afro-Creole Protest Tradition, 112; Kmen, "The Quadroon Balls." According to historian Gayarré ("The Quadroons of Louisiana"), high-status free women of color knew that their best chance for family advancement lay in permanent or long-term arrangements with wealthy and socially prominent white men. Their fathers generally encouraged such relationships and devoted no little expense toward their educations. Some were sent to France for that purpose. The young women were always mindful that their plaçage liaisons could be easily dissolved and that they had no legal protection. Thus, they "exerted themselves to the utmost to please their illicit partners." They paid great attention to both beauty and character. Indeed, they were the "knock-out" women of the city. They dressed regally and from the time they were girls they were educated in the arts of entertainment, language, and social skills. They cultivated the art of making themselves pleasing to their partners and "indulged them in all of their whims and caprices." In their attractiveness as mates, white women seldom could compete. Many quadroons succeeded in binding their mates for life, and even if the white man kept two families simultaneously, the placée often acquired considerable wealth through the arrangement. Gifts on the dissolution of a partnership or on the death of the male partner sometimes saw $100,000 or more transferred to the placée, often through the use of a trusted third party who "whipped the devil around the stump." Litigation by wives and collaterals of the white male decedent sometimes went to the Supreme Court of Louisiana. The testimonies recorded in these cases are wonderfully illustrative of the lives and character of quadroon women. Often, the placée successfully defended against such suits. Creole quadroons are described as litigious and sophisticated concerning both their legal rights and extralegal protections. See, for example, Macarty et al. v. [Eulalie] Mandeville [f.c.l.]. Docket No. 626, Supreme Court of Louisiana, New Orleans 3 La. Ann. 239. 1848. La. Lexis 128. Original briefs and witness testimony held at the Louisiana Room of the University of New Orleans Library. On the changing economic standing of free people of color, see Paul F. Lachance, "The Limits of Privilege: Where Free Persons of Color Stood in the Hierarchy of Wealth in Antebellum New Orleans," in The Louisiana Purchase Bicentennial Series in Louisiana History, vol. 11, ed. Vincent, 428–46.

37. Gayarré, "The Quadroons of Louisiana," 8–9. For a similar statement, see Martineau, Society in America, 183.

38. Register, New Orleans Is My Name, 27.

39. George Washington Cable, Creoles of Louisiana (New York: Scribner's Sons, 1910), 273; Richard Campanella, Geographies of New Orleans (Lafayette: Center for Louisiana Studies, 2006), 131; William J. Nelson, The Free Negro in the Ante-Bellum New Orleans Press, PhD diss., Duke University, 1977: 114–16. In 1850, the occupations urban of free negroes as listed by Nelson are as follows: carpenters 355; masons 278; laborers 179; shoemakers 92; merchants 64; barbers 41; cabinet makers 19; architect 1; for a total of 1,029.

Pierre Roup, h.c.l., arrived in New Orleans in 1805 from Haiti (Roup is often spelled Roux in New Orleans documents and is sometimes confused with the homophonous French family of that surname—see, for example, Figure 14). The Sacramental Records of the Roman Catholic Church of the New Orleans Archdiocese state that Roux was a "native of Gonnayu Island [sic. Gonaïves City] in Santo Domingo." See Charles Nolan, Sacramental Records of the Roman Catholic Church of the Archdiocese of New Orleans, 1824–1825, vol. 16 (New Orleans: Archdiocese of New Orleans, 1991), 350. Roup became a builder and land developer in New Orleans almost immediately. On the 1808 Joseph Pilié map of property owners in the French Quarter, Roup (spelled Roux) is listed as owning properties in VC square 107 at the corner of Rampart and Hospital (Governor Nicholls Street) (presently 1031–1041 Governor Nicholls Street) and also in VC square 106 at 1011/1013 Ursulines. Joseph Pilie, Plan de la Ville de la Nouvelle Orléans, Avec les noms des propriétaires (1808: "true copy" in New Orleans Municipal Library). In a private property survey conducted by Bartholomew Lafon, Arpenteur-général dés territoires Sud du Ténnessée (4/10/1808: microfilm copy in Historic New Orleans Collection), Roup is listed as the owner of another property in Square 106 facing l'Hopital (1020–1022 Governor Nicholls Street). The building on this property appears to be a linear maisonette. In 1816, Roup bought several lots of land in Faubourg Pontchartrain (adjoining Bayou St. Jean) from Mr. Jean Blanque (NONA: Philippe Pedesclaux, notary, Vol. 73, October 15, 1816). Roup also built a house at 1035 N. Rampart (NONA: Book 40, Folio 11). In the same year, he was paid fifty dollars by the city of New Orleans for work done by two of his enslaved carpenters on the public works over the period of one month (Macarty, record of expenditures of the city government, December 2, 1816, Southeastern Architectural Archive, Tulane University). In an 1819 survey by Joseph Pilié, Roup is still listed as the owner of a house and land at 1020–1022 l'Hopital (Governor Nicholls Street, Tax Assessment Lot no. 23155). He apparently purchased the adjoining Jumonville Villiers property in Square 106 shortly thereafter, and subdivided the 70 *pieds* (foot of Paris) wide lot into two narrow lots (now 1024 and 1028 Governor Nicholls Street). Probably in 1823 he sold the 1024 side to Helen Le Page, a free woman of color, cutting a nine-foot-wide swath of his own (1022 Governor Nicholls Street) property near the rear of the lot to add to hers. The still extant maisonette-style shotgun cottage at 1024 Governor Nicholls Street "was built for Helene Le Page, a free woman of color, in 1823." "The record says this house was erected by Pierre Roup, a builder-carpenter-machinist, according to the directories, who did other structures in this square at the same time." Edith Elliott Long, "Along the Banquette: Case of Neglect: 1024 Gov. Nicholls St. New Orleans," *Vieux Carré Courier*, December 9, 1966, 2. The "record" referred to is NONA (Felix de Armas, Notary) 104:35, March 17, 1836. Although we have evidence of shotgun-style houses going back to 1803, the Helene Le Page house is now the oldest (known) surviving Single Shotgun house in the French Quarter and probably in the nation.

According to city directories, Roup and his family lived at 179 l'Hopital between 1823 and 1835. Roup eventually owned property at Esplanade and North Rampart. He became a city assessor for the Third District and, with Claude Gurlie, was coappraiser of the Jean Phillippon estate (Fazende linear four-bay cottage, built circa 1812, at 831 St. Philip [Figure 17], and J.-B Hardy linear double cottage, built circa 1812, at 1016 Dauphine [Figure 18], both owned by free men of color): inventory of the Jean Phillippon estate, October

15, 1827, copy in the Historic New Orleans Collection. Roup owned houses on the Bayou Road (Governor Nicholls Street) at Marais and a second home on St. Claude between Barracks (called *rue Quartier*) and Esplanade.

Roup rose to become one of the most respected and well-connected free persons of color in the city. For many years he was a high-ranking officer in the racially integrated Masonic Lodge Number 4, called "*Pérsévérance,*" which he and other Saint-Domingue refugees founded in Faubourg Tremé at the corner of St. Claude and Dumaine. On March 19, 1825, he married Catherine (called Coralie) Lafitte (*f.c.l.*), the daughter of Jean Laffitte's brother, Pierre and Pierre's quadroon mistress, Marie Louise Villars: Nolan, *Sacramental Records*, 16:350; Cossé Bell, *Revolution, Romanticism and the Afro-Creole Protest Tradition*, 182–83.

40. On Pierre Roup's last house (Figure 22) see NONA 089:024. The numerous commissions that these free men of color built are absent from the NONA database of building contracts. An interpretation of the family of Jacques Tinchant, *h.c.l.*, was recently published by the legal historian Rebecca J. Scott ("Public Rights and Private Commerce"). Tinchant was also born in Gonaïves, settled in New Orleans following the Haitian revolution, and began buying land and building houses on "deep, narrow lots for a variety of purchasers, many of the them men and women of color. Blaise, *dit* Blaise Léger, *nègre libre,* for example, paid four hundred dollars for a lot in Faubourg Franklin measuring 34 feet on Washington Street and 117 feet on Morales Street": Scott, "Public Rights and Private Commerce," 240. "Tinchant is a carpenter turned builder and developer, transforming white-owned rural land on the edge of the city into house lots and houses for a multiracial clientele." He is listed in the 1838 *Gibson's Directory* for New Orleans as a builder, living on Craps Street (Burgundy in Marigny, a neighbor of Pierre Roup).

41. Because the old city fortifications had been five-sided, "the Ramparts" probably extended several squares beyond the French Quarter into faubourgs Tremé and Marigny. Martineau, *Society in America*, 182; Lyle Saxon, *Lafitte the Pirate* (New York: Century Company, 1930), 57.

42. A typical statement from Roulhac Toledano, a member of the Friends of the Cabildo: "One of the earliest shotgun-type houses in the city, dating from before 1846, is at 920 Spain Street [in Faubourg

Marigny], the J. B. Bordenave [*h.c.l.*] house." It is a frame shotgun decorated in the Greek Revival style of the 1840s. *National Trust Guide to New Orleans* (New York: John Wiley & Sons, Inc, 1996), 52; Wilson et al., *New Orleans Architecture*, 173, 71.

43. The research problem is to acquire reliable comparative cost data for linear cottages and Creole cottages for the same time period, based on approximate square footage, but it has not been possible to do this with precision. Building contracts for the early nineteenth century (mostly in French) do not clearly describe houses as Creole cottages or linear cottages, and the word *shotgun* was unknown. Floor plans are generally not attached to the contracts, though cost of building is always specified.

44. Asher Benjamin, *The Builder's Guide* (circa 1838; repr., New York: Da Capo Press, 1974) and *Elements of Architecture, containing the Tuscan, Doric, Ionic, and Corinthian orders, with all their details and embellishments. Also, the theory and practice of carpentry* (circa 1843; repr., New York, Da Capo Press, 1974); Minard Lafever, *The Modern Builder's Guide* (repr., New York: Dover Publications, 1855), and *The Beauties of Modern Architecture* (New York: D. Appleton & Co. 1869). Both Gallier and Dakin had enjoyed close working relationships with Lafever. See Jay D. Edwards, "Unlocking the History of Greek Key Architrave in New Orleans," in *Louisiana Cultural Vistas* 19, no. 4 (2008): 84–91.

45. The growth of shotguns differs from place to place. Geographer Peirce Lewis described a pattern of "superblocks" in the uptown section of the city: *New Orleans: The Making of an Urban Landscape* (Cambridge, Mass.: Ballinger Publications, 1976), 44–46. Mansions were built for whites along the major boulevards separated by ten to twelve squares, while shotguns for working-class and domestic employees, both white and black, were set in the middle areas between the boulevards. However, Sanborn maps and early aerial photography reveal that entire sections of the city—the Irish Channel, Central City, Uptown, and Carrollton—are crowded with Singles, Doubles and Camelbacks to the exclusion of other types. Notarial Archive images from the 1840s and 1950s show that more elaborately decorated Greek Revival and Italianate shotguns—the dwellings of reasonably prosperous families—are being built in the American Sector. In both their inventories and their illustrations, studies by New Orleans architectural historians on these sections of the city numerically underrepresent shotguns

in favor of mansions and multistory townhouses. Twenty-five, or about 18 percent of the total shotgun database, are drawn from this area of the city.

46. "The [single-story shotgun] cottage at 819 Burgundy street has a relatively intact two-story kitchen building of masonry construction with a small patio in the rear. Originally this two-story kitchen also separated from the main house by a court which has been filled in around 1940 with a two-story wooden addition" (MS. report on the Baker Cottage, Vieux Carré Commission, 1982).

In the 1870s the process of Camelbackization of shotguns occurred simultaneously in all sections of the city, both in working-class neighborhoods and in those of the well-to-do, in both predominantly black and in white neighborhoods. This indicates that rather than cultural diffusion from a specific point of origin, the Camelback resulted from a citywide technological and economic transformation. This is revealed on the 1896 and 1908 series Sanborn maps. The Camelback was built in increasingly fewer numbers in those sections of the city developed after circa 1900, when internal kitchens had become commonplace.

47. Resistance was first viewed as a form of cultural practice common to enslaved populations on plantations, and perhaps marginally in urban environments. Sociocultural adaptations to difficult hegemonic conditions, including patterns of resistance, have been special interests of Caribbeanists. An important point about the process of creolization is that it is multidimensional, referring both to a form of "ethnogenesis specific to plantation contests" and to an adaptive reinterpretation of colonial material forms and the local products of domestication. See Charles Stewart, "Creolization: History, Ethnography, Theory," in *Creolization: History, Ethnography, Theory*, ed. Charles Stewart, 1–25 (Walnut Creek, Calif.: Left Coast Press, 2007); James A. Delle, "The Material and Cognitive Dimensions of Creolization in Nineteenth-Century Jamaica," *Historical Archaeology* 34 (no. 3: 2000): 56–72.

48. Under a developed political hegemony the dominating power structure generally cannot be attacked directly. Indirect forms of resistance are called for. Notable among these are evasion; mimicry; masking (literal and figurative); false flattery; foot dragging; reinterpretation of received forms; obfuscation and opaqueness; subversion through counterdiscourse, dissembling, sabotage, and expropriation; the abrogation of established cultural standards; and even humor.

See James C. Scott, *Weapons of the Weak: Everyday Forms of Peasant Resistance* (New Haven, Conn.: Yale University Press, 1985), xv–xviii, 290; Henry Louis Gates Jr., *The Signifying Monkey* (New York: Oxford University Press, 1988); Bill Ashcroft, Gareth Griffiths, and Helen Tiffin, *The Empire Writes Back* (New York: Routledge, 1989). On resistance in Creolizing contexts, see Jean Bernabé, Patrick Chamoiseau, and Rapheël Confiant, *Éloge de la Créolité* (Paris: Gallimard, 1989); Celia M. Britton, *Édouard Glissant and Postcolonial Theory: Strategies of Language and Resistance* (Charlottesville: University Press of Virginia, 1999); Françoise Vergès, "Kultir Kreol: Precesses and Practices of Créolité and Creolizatin," in *Créolité and Creolization, Documenta 11 Platform 3*, ed. Okwui Enwezor et al., 179–84 (Ostfildern-Ruit, Germany: Hatje Cantz Publishers, 2003); Scott, *Weapons of the Weak*, 290; Walker, *No More, No More*. On the influence of political power and literary hegemony on the writing of historical master narratives, see Michel-Rolf Trouillot, *Silencing the Past: Power and the Production of History* (Boston: Beacon Press, 1995).

49. James C. Scott, in *Weapons of the Weak*, defines resistance as: "*any* act(s) by member(s) of a subordinate class that is or are *intended* either to mitigate or deny claims . . . made on that class by superordinate classes . . . or to advance its own claims . . . vis-à-vis those superordinate classes" (290). The rejected claims may include conventional values, appropriate forms of material culture, or characterizations of relative status or legal standing.

With respect to New Orleans in the Republican period, three typical tactics of resistance are worthy of note: (1) rejection of received categories bearing heavy burdens of Gramsian conceptual hegemonies (example: rejection of the rules of racial separation in St. Louis Cathedral by Father Père Antoine Sedella; (2) rewriting of, and blurring of, the established boundaries of separation and objectification (example: intermittent use and incorrect assignments in the application of stigmatized racial categories such as *h.c.l.* and *f.c.l.* on legal documents as required by law of priests and notaries); (3) a rapid replacement of accepted but stereotyped conceptual tools and material forms associated with disadvantage and powerlessness and their replacement with entirely novel forms not bearing old social stigmas (example: the definition of a new self-identifying social class, "we Creoles" placed between blacks and whites). In this, the linear cottage played

a significant role in celebrating the identities of economically independent free people of color. These and similar strategies helped to destabilize the dominant system of racial classification prior to the establishment of the new racial hegemony in American politics (the passing of the Kansas-Nebraska Act and the reaction of the South to the rise of the Republican Party) in the Antebellum period. See Cossé Bell, *Revolution, Romanticism and the Afro-Creole Protest Tradition*, 65–97.

50. They founded self-interest societies (*la Société des artisans*, Masonic lodges). They initiated newspapers (*le Libéral, Revue de Louisiane*) and other outlets of artistic and political expression. They founded businesses and speculated successfully by taking control of land resources. They played a major role in sugar- and tobacco-related businesses, where they excelled in importing and exporting. Refer to Cossé Bell, *Revolution, Romanticism and the Afro-Creole Protest Tradition*, 89–144.

51. For example, the Caribbean-style linear cottage was a comparatively inexpensive mechanism for raising rental income. On the (losing) struggle for racial equality, see, for example, Stephen J. Ochs, *A Black Patriot and a White Priest* (Baton Rouge: Louisiana State University Press, 2000); Violet Harrington Bryan, "Marcus Christian's Treatment of *Le Gens de Couleur Libre*," in *Creole: The History and Legacy of Louisiana's Free People of Color*, ed. Sybil Kein, 42–56 (Baton Rouge: Louisiana State University Press, 2000). Although now somewhat dated, for references to essays on race, class, economics, and politics in Antebellum and Reconstruction New Orleans, see the essays referenced in Light Townsend Cummins and Glen Jeansonne, *A Guide to the History of Louisiana* (Westport Conn.: Greenwood Press, 1982), 27–49, 85–93.

52. See, for example, the New Orleans art of John Biggers, "Shotguns, Fourth Ward" (1987); reproduced in Jonn Hankins and Steven Maklansky, eds., *Raised to the Trade: Creole Building Arts of New Orleans* (New Orleans: New Orleans Museum of Art, 2002), 60. Michapoulous (www.michapoulos.com); Keith Perelli (search http://www.flickr.com for "Keith Perelli"); Terrance Osborne (http://www.galleryosborne.com/catalog/); Bruce Brice (http://www.brucebrice.com/gallery2.htm).

53. Speaking a Creole language was formerly taken as an important mark of Creoledom in Louisiana.

54. Okwui Enwezor et al, *Créolité and Creolization. Documenta11_Platform3* (Ostfildern-Ruit, Germany: Hatje Cantz Publishers, 2003), 15.

55. In a recent *Buildings & Landscapes* article ("Viewpoint: Vernacular Architecture and Public History, Buildings & Landscapes 14 [2007]), Edward A. Chappell called for an expansion of vernacular architectural studies from a previous emphasis on heritage and patrimony to one that engages cultural, social, and public policy issues. He might have paraphrased Claude Lévi-Strauss, "Buildings are good to think with" (3).

56. Roger D. Abrahams et al., *Blues for New Orleans: Mardi Gras and America's Creole Soul* (Philadelphia: University of Pennsylvania Press, 2006), particularly 7–9, 23–28. Afro-Creole builders and craftsmen were also participants in many of these other cultural institutions. See also the following articles in Hankins and Maklansky's Raised to the Trade: Nick Spitzer, "The Aesthetics of Work and Play in Creole New Orleans," 96–130; C. Ray Brassieur, "Builder's Voices: Reflections on the Fruits of Labor," 131–35; Laura Westbrook, "Articular Craftsmanship: Verbal Art of New Orleans' Master Builders," 136–58.

ERIC SANDEEN

Robert Adams and Colorado's Cultural Landscapes

Picturing Tradition and Development in the New West

Robert Adams is one of the most important photographers of the post–World War II West. His images of the developing metropolitan sprawl along the Front Range define suburbanization in Colorado during the late 1960s and 1970s. His concerned focus on the logged-over areas in the mountains and the bulldozed fields and ponds on the plains present the sacrifices made to the burgeoning consumer culture of tract homes, housing developments, and shopping malls surrounding Denver and Colorado Springs. Starting with the 1974 publication of *The New West* and the New Topographics exhibit in 1975, Adams

has built an international reputation, augmented by his eloquent writings on the aesthetics of photography and the practice of picture taking.

During his first decade as a photographer, 1965–1975, Adams took pictures in the suburbs at the same time as he amassed the images for his first two books, both of which were historically based studies of rural structures, landscapes, and ways of life. *White Churches of the Plains* and *The Architecture and Art of Early Hispanic Colorado* are often presented as journeyman work influenced by Myron Wood, a prolific photographer of the American West who lived in Colorado Springs and took photographs for Colorado College, where Adams taught literature and film. According to one critic, the books show "a relatively impassive style of picture-making" (Papageorge 2001, 84). They exist as a prelude to "the central decision of his career" (Rubenfien 1976, 111) that brought a more skilled Adams to the suburbs where he photographed "the *locus classicus* of the [New Topographics] movement" (Jeffrey 2000, 455).

This essay argues that Adams's depictions of the material culture and traditional landscapes of two distinct, rural regions complement the creation of the new West captured in his suburban photographs. First, I will discuss Adams's vision of rural Colorado. By examining Adams's treatment of these traditional cultures we can account for the lack of a vernacular in suburban shots that inventory the materials of mass production. Then I will analyze the reading of the history of settlement that grounds Adams's images in the West. *White Churches of the Plains* and *The Architecture and Art of Early Hispanic Colorado* wrap photographs into community history; the suburban shots emanate from an incomplete present. The complex relationship among artifact, landscape, and tightly knit communities constructs an environment of meaning and belief that con-

trasts sharply with the suburban developments farther to the north, where Adams searches for remnants of these relationships amid the tract houses, freshly staked saplings, and cul-de-sacs of the suburbs. Human action in these suburban tracts erases the regional past held in the landscape, rather than drawing from it. Only the spatial organization of the frame and the use of the overpowering light of the high plains insinuate the West into these pictures. Finally, I will place Adams's work in the context of other surveys of Western terrain, conducted by nineteenth-century photographers and by contract workers on the public lands of the contemporary West. Through this reading, I suture together aspects of Adams's work that have been held apart by critics who have concentrated on his attention to beauty and form. Adams is a historian and critic of contemporary culture as well as an aesthetician and an artist.

Robert Adams in Rural Colorado

Adams focuses on two expressions of the vernacular in the two early books: one is manifested in the customs of faith communities and the other is embodied in the handcrafted artifacts of a traditional culture. *White Churches of the Plains* presents the religious structure as the culmination of a vernacular process. According to his introduction, the project to erect such a building came from the community, usually after a period of housing the functions of a church in a private home or even a general store. The community literally invested in the project, making the decision to build an exercise in both capitalism and democracy. The design and construction of the building came from the congregation, drawing on the skills of the workers and existing conceptions of church style, formed without the aid of an architect. The completed building was "the center of most of the religious and social life of the members" (Adams 1970).[1]

Photographs in *White Churches* present "examples" of "subject matter [that] is typical of an extensive architecture" (Adams 1970). More than twenty Colorado communities east of the Front Range are represented, from Peetz and several communities surrounded by the Pawnee National Grasslands in the north to Avon-

Figure 2. Catholic church, Ramah, 1918. Photograph by Robert Adams. Copyright Robert Adams; courtesy Fraenkel Gallery, San Francisco, and Matthew Marks Gallery, New York.

Figure 3. St. Agnes
Catholic Church,
Matheson, 1922.
Photograph by Robert
Adams. Copyright Robert
Adams;courtesy Fraenkel
Gallery, San Francisco,
and Matthew Marks
Gallery, New York.

dale and Grenada in the south. Mapping these communities reveals clusters that suggest specific itineraries, at least at the exploratory phase. Major highways give access to towns that sprang up in the late nineteenth century because of a railroad: Genoa, Seibert, Stratton, and Bethune along the Union Pacific (and US 46); Avondale, Fowler, and Granada along the Burlington Northern (and US 50); Calhan, Ramah, and Matheson on a now-abandoned branch of the Rock Island (and US 24). Two areas break this linear pattern: the Pawnee National Grasslands east of Fort Collins surround Grover, Keota, and Stoneham, with Eaton and Peetz on its western and eastern boundaries; Calhan, Ramah, Matheson, Elbert, Elizabeth, and Fountain lie within easy driving distance of Adams's home base in Colorado Springs. Outliers like Yuma and Clarkville, the subject of the book's first images, complete the work. Images are mixed together in *White Churches* so that these itineraries are obscured by sequencing based on architectural detail or denominational affiliation rather than geo-graphic proximity or narrative connection.

The area near Colorado Springs presents a typical cluster of examples. Images of the Catholic churches in Ramah and Matheson, small communities northeast of Colorado Springs, are typical of Adams's view of the white churches of the plains. In both images the church fills the frame from top to bottom and is photographed virtually straight on, emphasizing the bilateral symmetry of the façade. "Catholic Church, Ramah 1918" gives the building the elements of permanence. A foundation lifts the floor to eye level, and the building is sheltered by leafless trees. "St. Agnes Catholic Church, Matheson 1922" offers no protection from the elements and gives the foundationless church only a toehold on the plains in a frame that is dominated by the open sky. Adams has framed both shots to exclude surrounding buildings, implying, but not showing, the communities that sustain each structure.

A more comfortably established church structure was resituated in the town of Elbert as the result of a flood. A mechanic, "ignoring

Figure 4. Mechanic's Garage, Elbert. Photograph by Robert Adams. Copyright Robert Adams; courtesy Fraenkel Gallery, San Francisco, and Matthew Marks Gallery, New York.

the incongruity of the cross" (Adams 1970), adapted the former Sacred Heart church for use as a garage. The gaping maw of the opened sliding door, the markings of the nave, and the improbable verticality of the structure contrast with the more typical garage structure to the right. "Mechanic's Garage, Elbert" shows sacred and secular readings of this vernacular form and establishes the transitory rootedness of a structure that merely came to rest in a particular location and then accrued the trappings of solidity—a fence, a concrete pad, a sign, even a basketball hoop.

Vernacular forms, expressed through the material culture of places of worship and objects of veneration, are the focus of *The Architecture and Art of Early Hispanic Colorado.* Although he did not claim to know the territory as well as the more familiar areas on the plains, Adams photographed from a respectful distance these visual representations of a culture that he thought both impressive and imperiled. His exploration of the Hispanic south differed from his survey of the churches of the Plains. Because he viewed the white churches as examples of a vernacular form that could be found between the 100th meridian and the Front Range of the Rockies, the date of construction depending on lines of settlement that moved from east to west, his book was not bound by a particular path through the Great Plains of Colorado. There is no map to help the reader locate tiny communities such as Keota or Pleasant Prairie. *The Architecture and Art of Early Hispanic Colorado,* however, is organized by the geography of the southern tier of Colorado counties. The photographs are sectioned according to the course of a river or the contours of a valley. The introduction presents the cultural geographies of these areas as individually distinctive and yet as terrain contributing to a larger ethnic landscape inhabited by traditional, Spanish-speaking communities. A map at the end of the book helps orient the reader to the region, giving both the English- and the Spanish-language names of some of the small towns.

There is a curious disorientation in the book's imaginative geography, signaling Adams's distance from the culture that he was both picturing and writing about. While the photographs are presented generally from east to west—from the areas around Trinidad to the small communities near the San Juan Mountains—the introduction makes clear that the settlement history of the region proceeded from south to north, from a cultural hearth in Mexico to peripheral regions in northern New Mexico and, finally, southern Colorado. Adams's history of inhabitation of the isolated communities of southern Colorado is sensitive and historically resonant enough to have received the Western Heritage Award from the National Cowboy Hall of Fame. It fits well with the evolving discourse of landscape history as a field of study during the 1960s and reinforces the appreciation of patterns of settlement that challenged the orientation, the assumptions, and

the ideology of the frontier story. Both Adams's photographs and his written material show his respect for the Hispanic culture of the region and acknowledge the distance from his subjects. However, the sequencing of the photographs from east to west shows how the orientation of frontier ideology had become second nature, even in the vision of such a sensitive observer.

Adams focuses on emblematic places of worship and objects of veneration that are imbued with the faith and tradition of the area's culture. He begins the collection of eighty-four images with "St. Joseph's Chapel," a church located near Gulnare, north of Trinidad. The adobe of the walls revealed under the battered stucco of the chapel's exterior anchor it to the surrounding terrain. The details of the openings of the church—the two crosses of the paneling of the main entrance and the barely visible Gothic detailing of the windows—express the ecclesiastical vocabulary of the building. The corrugated tin roof attests to the adaptability of the structure to circumstances and the availability of twentieth-century building materials. Views of the chapel are interspersed with religious iconography that elaborates the meanings of sacred space: a statue (*bulto*) carved from cottonwood and a grave marker chiseled from the native sandstone by an artisan with a traditional way of signifying the death of a child through the representation of a lamb. Only after these six images does the first photograph of a secular building appear, a farmhouse near neighboring Aguillar.

Particularly in the San Luis Valley, west of the Sangre de Cristo Mountains, Adams widens his view to portray one of the most cohesive cultural landscapes in Colorado, the oldest domain of Hispanic settlement. He pictures the chapel at Viejo San Acacio, the oldest existing church in the region, emphasizing in one interior shot the thickness of the adobe walls in the glowing light from a side window. He photographs the San Luis commons (*la vega*), the largest communal grazing area in Colorado, and the irrigation system (*acequia*) that both supports agriculture and expresses a traditional method of water allocation. He moves inside barns and outbuildings to show the beams (*vigas*) and cross members (*latias*) that constitute the weighty framework for

Figure 5. St. Joseph's
Chapel. Photograph by
Robert Adams. Copyright
Robert Adams;. courtesy
Fraenkel Gallery, San
Francisco, and Matthew
Marks Gallery, New York.

the roofs of traditional structures. In the small town of Antonito he steps back into the middle of the street to capture an imposing shot of the Society for the Mutual Protection of United Workers (*Sociedad Proteccion Mutua de Trabajadores Unidos*), an important social organization and site of resistance against Anglo incursion that was especially important in the early part of the twentieth century.

Adams uses crosses to show how the sacred and the secular inhabit the same landscape. The cross appears in traditional uses—on or near chapel altars, in the hands of saints (*santos*) or other *bultos*, or, poignantly, as grave markers. One cross is decorated with plastic flowers, another left atilt in a remote cemetery. Crosses

are also adapted for broader use in the culture. Adams shows that the cross can become a fence post, an expedient use of wood in an area with few trees. Most significantly, he depicts a large cross of the *penitentes* to represent the marking of the land as both sacred and secular. This cross would have been used as the end point of a pilgrimage or procession (*calvario*) held during Holy Week, just before Easter, to mark the passion of Christ by a folk religious practice.

Adams's depiction of the *penitentes* (the Fraternal Society of Our Father Jesus of Nazareth) and their meetinghouses, *moradas,* shows his fascination with a religion-based vernacular and his consciousness of his position as an outsider. This camera position contrasts with the photographs of Adams's mentor, Myron Wood, who depicted this system of belief throughout his long career. Wood engaged *Los Hermanos Penitentes,* composing a group shot of a *penitente* community in front of sacred objects and holy space. His photographs assume the same sort of familiarity that might be established with any of the other groups Wood photographed throughout Colorado. Adams's view of this social and religious environment is not as self-assured. He keeps his distance, not presuming to enter the *morada,* as he had self-confidently done with the white churches farther north, or to picture the *penitentes* at worship. Adams identifies *moradas* by the cross emblazoned on their weathered exteriors but otherwise photographs them as he does other vernacular structures. In doing so, he honors the privacy of the *penitentes,* who situated their meeting places at a distance from a Catholic hierarchy that had an uneasy relationship with these folk practices (Adams 1974a, 24). From Adams's position, it is easy to see the self-consciously ordinary scale and appearance of these community buildings.

"But what was the wealth of people living by undisturbed mountains and prairies?" Adams asks at the conclusion of *The Architecture and Art of Early Hispanic Colorado.* He could well have been directing this question to the entire terrain explored in his first two books. He shot all these rural photographs during the same period and may well have separated images for two projects out of one photographic excursion—for example, two structures in *White Churches of the Plains* were taken in the San Luis Valley communities of Mosca and Bowen, not far from Los Sauses and Fort Garland, sites that appear in *Early Hispanic Colorado.* More significantly, both books retrieve a redemptive history, turning the attention of the reader to the vestiges of more harmonious relationships between humans and nature— natural economies—that animated dissenting communities within the emerging cultures of the West. The religious connotations are unmistakable; the search for a transcendent valuation of wealth inhabits both Adams's writing and his photographs. With the hope that, "if we can begin accurately to assess [this wealth], we may hope, in grace, to save ourselves," Adams concludes *Early Hispanic Colorado.*

Robert Adams and the History of Settlement

Adams's early work clarifies his position among the photographers of the New Topographics and amplifies his importance as an artist who "reshaped landscape photography for this time" (Baltz 1989, 74–75). Critics of the New Topographics attacked the passivity of photographs that approached subjects straight on, from eye level, without apparent comment: this wasn't socially grounded picture taking but "art history for the cognoscenti" (Wollheim 1982, 15). From the perspective of an environmental activist, this position required no moral commitment (Campbell 1989, 13). The photographs aimed at such a styleless style that one commentator could picture them hanging on the wall of a land developer or real estate agent (Miller 2005, 19). Defenders of the New Topographics discerned social analysis, even historical references, among the disarmingly straightforward images (Bright 1984, 16; Orvell 2003, 56; Weski 2005, 10). Lewis Baltz, in defense of a movement with which he was associated, pointed to photographs that were political without being obvious (Baltz 1984, 53) This didacticism, according to John Szarkowski,

Figure 6. An adobe house near Aguillar. Photograph by Robert Adams. Copyright Robert Adams; courtesy Fraenkel Gallery, San Francisco, and Matthew Marks Gallery, New York.

Figure 7. Interior of Chapel at Viejo San Acacia. Photograph by Robert Adams. Copyright Robert Adams; courtesy Fraenkel Gallery, San Francisco, and Matthew Marks Gallery, New York

Figure 8. Antonito Union Hall. Photograph by Robert Adams. Copyright Robert Adams; courtesy Colorado Historical Society. Courtesy Fraenkel Gallery, San Francisco, and Matthew Marks Gallery, New York.

way that the photograph acknowledged historic tensions and current developments. Using similar visual styles, the photographs of the white churches make explicit what the images of the suburbs implicitly present. The photographs of Adams and the New Topographers were austere but not laconic: "The reticence of their pictures indicates passionate conviction and sometimes dread at the implications of truth" (Phillips 1996, 41). Adams's vernacular style made these photographs disarming. As J. B. Jackson commented, during this time the camera was wielded as a part of the vernacular culture it pictured, and Adams strove for an easy style that would appeal to the general viewer (Jackson 1992, 6). However, for one commentator, these masterfully simple photographs could not mask commentary through "their social content—in Adams' case a brave one" (Phillips 1996, 41). Critics pointed to the absence of Native Americans in Adams's early photographs of the West (Wollheim 1982, 15). A full reading of Adams's work during this period shows that his interpretation of Western settlement is founded on the violent dislocation of the landscape's original inhabitants, a view that moves his *New West* closer to the emerging New Western history, a revisionist interpretation attaining full voice in the 1980s that remapped the region as a multicultural territory beset with the sort of exploitative development that drew Adams's concern.

The rural pictures highlight Adams's work as a cultural historian, a photographer of place; the suburban shots engage the discussion of how documentary photographs capture a particular moment, even an epiphany. Thus, his homage to Timothy O'Sullivan explores both the clarity of his forebear's vision and the role of those authoritative expedition images in shaping views of the post–Civil War West. Adams distances himself from his contemporary, Bill Owens, who used photographs as ideological statements about conditions in Western suburbs. He differs in perspective from Emmett Goin, with whom he shared a two-man show at the Museum of Modern Art in 1971, and in presentation from David Misrach: Goin aestheticized the landscapes of the nuclear West through aerial photographs and Misrach relentlessly drew the frame down to post-

had made the documentary tradition from which the New Topographers parted seem "leaden, tired, boring, dutiful, automatic, and Pavlovian" (Grundberg 1984, 12).[2]

Adams's early work extends the argument over the New Topographers from an episode in the history of modernism to a moment in the emergence of a new view of Western landscape. The early work reveals both his formal discipline—the way that his frame holds the scene together—and his grounding in the cultural meaning of the landscape he was photographing—the

Figure 9. Los Hermanos de Nuestro Senor Jesus, 1976. Photograph by Myron Wood. Copyright Pikes Peak Library District.

military, color soaked environmental atrocities on the ground. The sweeping black-and-whites of Ansel Adams and the intense color shots of Elliott Porter, icons of the environmental movement, evinced more faith in wilderness than Adams, who focused on the persistent beauty human-altered landscapes could muster.[3] In his efforts to view the contemporary West clearly, over the obfuscations of myth and the distractions of overwhelming scenery, Robert Adams's intentions anticipate the Rephotographic Survey Project that Mark Klett (Klett et al. 1984) and others began at the end of the 1970s. The difference in procedures, though, is telling: Klett carefully updated iconic photographs by finding the precise camera position of nineteenth-century shots and making his images in the same format, at the same time of day and seasonal angle of sun, in order to show both changes in the landscape and the subtle manipulations that had created a national anthology of views of the West. Adams remained autobiographical in selecting landscapes of meaning and articulated Western history through the composition of his frame, not attempting to duplicate a particular view or, for that matter, to return to a scene he had previously pictured.

Figure 10. An adobe *morada* in Long's Canyon. Photograph by Robert Adams. Copyright Robert Adams; courtesy Fraenkel Gallery, San Francisco, and Matthew Marks Gallery, New York.

The rural and the suburban work of Adams's first decade as a photographer show that he was an artist and a critic of contemporary culture whose images presented both the beauty and the degradation of Western environments. As he commented in *The New Topographics,* "What I hope to document, though not at the expense of surface detail, is the Form that underlies this apparent chaos" (International Museum of Photography 1975, 7). This balance between transitory detail and immutable qualities such as beauty and order differentiates his depiction of the region from those who focused on the particularities of everyday life, such as his mentor,

Myron Wood. Wood's images present an eclectic anthology of West pictures—its people, landscapes, towns, and working environments—shot in a straightforward, publishable style.[4] He frequently photographed subjects against regional markers, placing foreground objects in the context of the mountainous horizon of the Front Range by foreshortening the middle distance through the use of a telephoto lens or angling the camera upward, so that the image of the Catholic church at Matheson, for example, was overpowered by the sort of threatening sky that could dominate the expanse of the High Plains. The interest in Adams's photographs lies in the foreground—his Matheson photo is dominated by the church structure—or, particularly in photographs of suburban landscapes, in an uncontrollably vast middle ground that represented for him the indomitable space of the West.

A critical historical consciousness inhabits Adams's frame, sometimes expressed overtly through the context of the shot but more often through the photographer's grounding in the history of Western settlement. During this period, Adams contributed occasional reviews to *Colorado Magazine*, articulating his view of Western his-

tory in a magazine that positioned itself between an academic and a broader, public readership. In a 1974 review of Michael Lesy's *Wisconsin Death Trip*, Adams endorsed an attack on the myth of the frontier, a revisionist reading of the frontier thesis of Frederick Jackson Turner (Adams 1974c, 350). Turner located the formation of American character along a westward-moving frontier line and assumed a linear march of progress. Lesy subverted this view through his portrayal of a postfrontier area of Wisconsin. By interspersing contemporary quotations with the work of a local photographer, Lesy pictured despair, mental illness, and stagnation. Adams did not object to this interpretation—indeed, he saw the history of settlement as a chronicle of violence and conquest. Instead, he questioned the use of manipulated period photographs in the construction of such a revisionist view. Here Adams revealed himself as both a professional photographer—defending the work of the unsuspecting commercial photographer, Charlie Schaick, from the manipulations of a cultural commentator with a thesis to hone—and as an historian concerned with the truth-telling potential of different forms of evidence (Adams 1974c, 351).

Figure 11. Matheson, Colorado, 1959. Photograph by Myron Wood. Copyright Pikes Peak Library District.

Adams's reading of Western history separates his landscapes from traditional photos. The dominant view of Western terrain, expressed most flamboyantly at this time by Ansel Adams, replicated what the art historian Albert Boime has called "the magisterial gaze" (Boime 1991, 21) of nineteenth-century paintings and photographs, representing the vast expanse of mountains and deserts as a reflection of national glory or a source of American pride. Robert Adams often used a virtually square format to discipline his frame away from this expansive awe. For him, the ineluctable conquest of the West produced bulldozed farm ponds and utility trenches in place of the traditionally managed irrigation systems of the *acequia* and the *vega*. His was more than the Westerner's age-old complaint, voiced in *Why People Photograph* (1994), that all the newcomers were ruining the tranquility of the mountains. He lamented the passing of an intimate connection to nature that placed human history in the humbling context of a larger, natural order. Subverting the perspective of the magisterial gaze, he viewed the panoramic dichotomies of contemporary life in the West from a promontory in the foothills that he discovered with his father soon after the family's move from Wisconsin when he was fourteen years old, making from this "commanding view of the grasslands eastward" a single, problematic landscape encompassing both a preserve of Western space to which he returned often during his career's first two decades and the low buildings of the contaminated, fenced-in compound of Rocky Flats Nuclear Weapons Plant, epicenter of Cold War bellicosity. "Though not many landscapes are at once as beautiful and as damaged as is this one, most are, as we have invaded them, similarly discordant" (Adams 1994, 180).

Adams's lens relies on this broad reading of historical change and less frequently picks out moments that can be traced to a particular time in the chronicle of the West. His two photographs of downtown Denver in *The New West* (Adams 1974b) stand as anomalies, both for their overtly urban subject matter and for their capturing of Denver at an identifiable moment in its development. A reading of the buildings in "Curtis Street, Denver," for example, reveals the orientation of the photograph (we are facing north), the

Figure 12. Curtis Street, Denver. Photograph by Robert Adams. Copyright Robert Adams; courtesy Fraenkel Gallery, San Francisco, and Matthew Marks Gallery, New York.

moment of its taking (it is 1971), and the significance of the parking lot (it is a development site). Further, we can place this view in the history of the larger Skyline redevelopment project—the emerging vista that will unfold before us—and the evolving history of historic preservation that the largest of the federally sponsored Denver urban-renewal schemes fostered in opposition.[5] More characteristically, Adams photographs around the edges of a specific phenomenon, looking at the ways a particular moment affects the inhabitants and the materials that surround them day to day.

Thus, when Adams ventures into the suburbs, he carries with him both an interpretive framework for these emerging landscapes and the latent image of the traditional ways that are being supplanted. For him, the suburbs represent an antivernacular of mass-produced, interchangeable parts placed in terrain where elements of natural history have been erased. This is a world as incomplete as the traditional landscape of the Hispanic south was fulfilling. His few photographs of suburbanites show their social isolation; a woman hanging out her laundry, her yard surrounded by scrub brush and open plain; a lone man seeking refuge from the sun in the shadow of a trailer. Shots of houses establish their incompleteness, from their exposed framing to the saplings speared in the newly rolled-out sod of their front yards. Adams is not interested in what brought these people to the suburbs. He could, for example, have investigated the linkage between the militarization of the West, a subject of his intense social concern, and the Cold War landscapes nearby—Air Force bases, weapons assembly sites, and missile ranges. He could have rephotographed these new suburbs in a more presentable state or sought out more established locations for pleasing views of middle-class life. His intent, however, was to catch, in effect, the beginning of a new, all-too-predictable history that did not warrant his further attention.[6]

Henry Glassie's contemporaneous remark that vernacular structures vary from place to place but that mass-produced structures vary from time to time (Glassie 1968, 33) can be used as a way of interpreting Adams's photographs. The rural photographs show this emphasis on rootedness—particularly in the highly articulated geography of the Hispanic south, where variations in the color of the adobe signaled the differences among locations. The suburban photos dwell in a sustained moment of incompleteness—from the clearing of the housing site to the initial years of inhabitation—before the efforts of individual owners or the green veneer of irrigated lawns and trees could simulate permanence. In his photographs, the box-like tract homes of early postwar development are supplanted by larger, late 1960s boxes and the early 1970s split-level ranches of more distant suburbs. A skilled reader of suburban housing could date these photographs. It would be much harder to map them; a chronicle of displacement fills the frame. Adams overlooks the histories of these developments in favor of metaphors that carry loss and persistence, the mirror image of the rural photographs that portray the "wealth"—one could substitute "value"—of the Hispanic settlements or the constancy of the communities surrounding the white churches.

"Landscape pictures can offer us," Adams commented in a 1981 essay, "three verities—geography, autobiography, and metaphor" (Adams 1981, 14). Adams's sense of geography springs from his visual encounters with Western space, informed, as I have pointed out, by an understanding of how humans inhabited that land. His writings do not establish any direct connection with the field of landscape studies—there are no references to J. B. Jackson, for example—or any allusions to cultural geographies of the High Plains. His *White Churches of the Plains* introduction contains neither bibliography nor footnotes, so, if he ventured into the library to read about the importance of church building in Plains community formation, the information he gleaned remained in the background. Similarly, he could well have read books about the emerging Hispanic consciousness in southern Colorado, but his text in *The Architecture and Art of Early Hispanic Colorado* refers to local histories and primary records. He makes no reference to the contemporaneous nurturing of a Hispanic past for Colorado Springs on the part of the Taylor Museum and the Fine Arts Center—an effort that tapped the energies of John Gaw Meem, the architect who had created a Southwestern look for Santa Fe, New Mexico[7]—but, instead, locates his interest in Trinidad, a smaller city much farther to the south. The metaphors and autobiographical allusions in his writing draw his prose toward poetry and evoke comparisons to other great nature writers in the American green tradition. It is the mixture of the three verities that makes his view of the contemporary landscape so compelling: "the three kinds of information strengthen each other and reinforce what we all work to keep intact—an affection for life" (Adams 1981, 14).

"In the Nineteenth-Century West," an Adams essay from the early 1990s, shows how his reading, writing, and photographing fit together. In this introduction to an anthology of nineteenth-century Western photographs, he articulates the three attributes of space in the region—"its silence, its resistance to speed, and its revelation by light" (Adams 1994, 138)—and laments their passing in the contemporary West. The experience of photographing in the West led his nineteenth-century predecessors to a larger truth that subverted the patriotic excesses of the magisterial gaze. Photographers like O'Sullivan photographed what they saw. The clutter in the foreground, the factory in the distance, and, most importantly, the unmanageable space separating the two could not be edited out because of the painstaking technology that forced the photographer out into the scene for extended periods of time. A painter could omit messy elements and insert details, as Albert Bierstadt and Thomas Moran did. Further, they did not have to spend their time in the West and could work from sketches or notes in the comfort of a studio. This experiencing of place was important to Adams. William Henry Jackson, he points out, did not think of leaving the West when his commissions ran dry. Adams, too, stood his ground. Of all the *New Topographics* photographers, many of whom have had distinguished careers, only Adams has continuously lived in and photographed the West.[8] His own experience of this Western expanse is destroyed by modern intrusions: while photographing a white church the stillness of the early morning is broken by a fighter plane, out on maneuvers, roaring overhead (Adams 1994, 135). Despite the sensory fracturing of this overwhelming space—the light is degraded by pollution and the air is filled with the noise of dirt bikes and automobiles—he finds reconciliation and even reconstruction: "To love the old views is not entirely pointless nostalgia, but rather an understandable and fitting passion for what could in some measure be ours again" (Adams 1994, 139). For him, hope and reconstruction are more active activities than nostalgia or preservation.

Robert Adams and the Contemporary Western Landscape

Adams began photographing rural communities during a period of heightened concern for historic structures. His photographs of "examples" of white churches and his explorations of the valleys of the Hispanic south stand alongside other surveys of buildings and landscapes that both anticipate and follow the 1966 National Historic Preservation Act. As *The Architecture and Art of Hispanic Colorado* makes plain, he is more interested in how a particular culture inhabits its structures than in the buildings themselves. Vernacular adaptations are allowed into the frame—plastic flowers, tin roofs, and power lines—drawing the buildings into the present moment. Situating historic structures in contemporary culture is both a photographic style and a critique of the connoisseurship of historic preservation, as his contribution to Colorado Spring Landmarks, a late 1960s exhibition, points out. His photograph stands out among the twenty-nine images. Able local photographers, including Myron Wood, skillfully framed individual structures to call attention to historic qualities and architecture details. Adams photographed the First Baptist Church from across the intersection of Kiowa and Weber, approaching the church along a diagonal that balanced the church steeple with a microwave tower, looming behind.[9]

More broadly, Adams's work in the late 1960s and 1970s continues the survey work that photographers have performed in the American West since the Civil War. His early rural projects begin these explorations and delineate the two techniques for doing this—sorting by type or by territory—that continue into the suburban work. *The New West* proceeds from the Plains westward, through the city to the mountains beyond. *Denver,* subtitled *A Photographic Survey of the Metropolitan Area,* groups images into types of metropolitan land use: "Land Surrounded; To Be Developed" and "Shopping Centers; Commercial Land," for example (Adams 1977). *From the Missouri West,* a later project Adams undertook because "I had lost my way in the suburbs," reveals an autobiographical intent and shows his deep relationship with Western terrain (Adams 1980). He starts his exploration, as his ancestors had, at the Missouri River, because the pioneers "understood themselves to be at the edge of a sublime landscape, one that they believed would be redemptive." Adams recognized the idiosyncrasy of this exercise, putting "survey" in quotation marks. His selections were systematic only in that the places represented happened to be near where he or his ancestors had lived. Other than that, he set only one ground rule: "to include in the photographs evidence of man; it was a precaution in favor of truth that was easy to follow

since our violence against the earth has extended
even to anonymous arroyos and undifferentiated
stands of scrub brush." This approach put him
in conversation with contemporary wilderness
advocates, who were at that time marking off territory to be set aside as a result of the Wilderness
Act and other environmental measures of the late
1960s, but separates him from those who wished
to recreate pristine nature. He was compelled to
present scenes depicting nature and evoking
the history of exploration that showed both the
enduring beauty of the West and the violence
that human beings had committed out of sight
of most viewers.

Surveying requires physical exploration, and
Adams's journals, as excerpted in his mid-career
retrospective *To Make It Home* (1989), recount
episodes of revelation (the beauty of a country
road), frustration (mishandling film in the cold
along the Missouri), and danger (twice nearly
being run over near Hygiene, Colorado) in the
field. Adams's close attention reveals the landscape as palimpsest, as though the scene could

be read as a parchment, written, scrubbed, and
reinscribed with the markings of human inhabitation. Suburban shots show this erasure in
action, for example in the imminent demise of a
pond in *Denver*'s "Agricultural Land in the Path
of Development." Adobe ruins represent a different script that can still be read in the valleys
of the southern tier of counties. Walking on this
topography leads down paths that intersect with
other narrative lines exposed on the land. The *calvario* of the *penitentes* is the clearest recognition
of this inscription. The cross is the symbol of an
alternative way, but, more generally, in the crossing of paths lies a moment in a unique, Carte-
sian space, to explore the intersection of different
narratives. Crossing Colfax Avenue presents the
same opportunity.

Finally, a survey is both a personal exercise
and a report. In this regard Adams resembles
a photographer he admired and to whom he is
compared, Timothy O'Sullivan. Beyond the stylistic similarities in their images, it is worth noting
that O'Sullivan encountered the West through the

expedition in which he participated—Clarence King's mapping of the 40th parallel and George Wheeler's Army Corps of Engineers foray into the Southwest. Like O'Sullivan, Adams assumed a public viewership for his results. Several of his early projects were funded by public agencies—including state arts and humanities councils that had just come into existence and the Colorado Historical Society—and the photographs for *From the Missouri West* were subsidized by a bicentennial project funded by AT&T.

Examining other efforts at surveying Colorado terrain helps bring Adams's photographs into higher contrast. Because of environmental and historic preservation legislation enacted during the late 1960s, most projects supported by public funds, crossing public lands, or regulated by governmental entities required some form of inventory of historic or archeological features in the path of development. Many of these surveys were prompted by Section 106 of the Historic Preservation Act, a provision that mandated documentation of historic resources and a plan for mitigation of their disturbance, but others were the product of highway-widening projects of the Colorado Department of Transportation or the beginnings of what would later be christened heritage tourism.

Robert Adams's photographs of the rural landscapes of Colorado are, in effect, baseline information for the later, development-driven surveys. The photographer's work identified individual sites and set a narrative path through these areas, documenting artifacts, structures, and landscapes, not with the idea of preserving them but with the intention of learning from what had sustained them. For many subsequent surveys, conducted by public historians, ethnographers, and archeologists, Adams's books became part of the record to be consulted in preparation for field work, thus projecting onto Adams the role of the historian and, increasingly, as the producer of data that was in itself historic. Thus, Adams's interpretation of Hispanic settlement near Trinidad became part of the interpretive framework for a public historian's project identifying historic structures along State Highway 12 for the Colorado Department of Transportation (1988). His photographs of buildings in Elbert, farther to the north, were submitted as historic documentation supporting state and federal nominations to the register of historic places.

Because Adams's view of these landscapes is expressed in both written and visual forms, his work stands as a useful counterpoint to these later surveys, contesting development schemes and elevating seemingly ordinary buildings in their cultural importance. That is, Adams creates the opportunity to see crossings and palimpsests in landscapes that have been the site of intense development pressure over the past fifty years. For example, several of the sites Adams photographed east of Trinidad were surveyed as a part of the "Management Plan for the Fort Carson–Pinon Canyon Maneuver Site" (Department of Defense 1985), highlighting a military landscape in the West. The Tijeras *morada* appears as a part of a survey for the expansion of a dam west of Trinidad, a sign of the residential development of this area during the 1980s. While none of Adams's sites were inundated, his close attention to adobe ruins calls to mind the salvage archeology that preceded the rising waters. His photographs in this section of Colorado are connected by the Santa Fe Trail. Development projects received close scrutiny as they crossed that linear path of the narrative of Western expansion. Thus the construction of an intersecting transmission line or the digging of a twelve-inch natural gas pipeline near the trail revealed structures that Adams photographed, even as they wrote their own history of development and resource extraction on the land.

Heritage tourism and interpretations of cultural landscapes also rely on Adams's photographs. The recent *Context Study of the Hispanic Cultural Landscape of the Purgatoire/Apishapa* catalogs many of Adams's sites east of the Sangre de Cristo Mountains (Carrillo et al. 1999). West of the range, in the San Luis Valley, the history of the area has been aggressively asserted through analyses of adobe buildings, *moradas,* and cultural landscapes. Here the core of San Luis, including the Church of the Most Precious Blood, was listed as the Plaza de San Luis de le Culebra National Historic District in 1978 (National Park Service 1978). Heritage tourism brought attention to Colorado's oldest town, acknowledging

the attraction of the past and presenting historic preservation as a compensation for development. For Adams, the power of the traditional culture inhabiting this landscape must inevitably conflict with development pressures, and, in that battle, "There is no saving this landscape." His photographs of the *acequias* and the *vega,* along with the sweeping shots of the Culebra Range, challenge the concept of heritage being interpreted here. Without a living culture to inhabit them, he suggests in resignation, the structures in the valley could be reinhabitied: "assuming the growth of tourism in the San Luis Valley, there seems no reason why an adobe village outside of San Luis could not be restored and developed profitably as an art colony" (Adams 1974a, 225). This would not, however, substitute for a wider need to understand the values that brought nineteenth-century settlers north to this land.

Two examples from the town of Elbert, farther to the north, illustrate how Adams's photographs have become historic documents, to be included in nominations to state and federal registers of historic places. The more traditional nomination, St. Mark's United Presbyterian Church (National Park Service 1980), positions the property in relation to the small town in the same way that Adams had pictured it: from a hillside vantage point behind the structure. A second Adams shot focused on the most historic part of the church—the steps leading to the narthex, an emphasis of the nomination and now the site of the first restoration project, sponsored by the State Historical Fund. Adams's photograph of the mechanic's garage was particularly important in saving the former Sacred Heart church (State of Colorado 1994), for he pictured it just before almost thirty years of dereliction produced a virtual ruin. The 1994 nomination leveraged funds for its rehabilitation as a short-lived antique store. By 2008 it was a private residence, presented as a well-maintained historic jewel on manicured grounds, separated from the county road by a white, plastic fence.

All the landscapes that Adams photographed are enmeshed in their own histories, the particularities of which offer a review of Adams's critical vision and a conclusion to this essay. Adams photographed in each of these landscapes at a partic-

Figure 14. The former Sacred Heart Church, Ramah, Colorado, April 2008. Photograph by the author.

Figure 15. Frame for a tract house. Colorado Springs. Copyright Robert Adams; courtesy Fraenkel Gallery, San Francisco, and Matthew Marks Gallery, New York.

ular moment and then moved on. In this respect, he was an artist more than a historian, investing his attention to the inspiration of the moment and not in a sustained curiosity about the particularities of place or built environment that would have led him to rephotograph sites. Bringing the subjects of two of his images up to date reveals his sensitive reading of the contemporary scene and his willingness to leave the inevitable development of these landscapes beyond his frame.

Shortly after Adams photographed the Catholic church in Ramah, the parish was disestablished and the bell removed from the steeple, the kind of deprivation of community institutions that sent parishioners to a newly constructed church in Calhan and school children in the opposite direction, to consolidated facilities in nearby Simla. The structure went immediately into private hands, but, unlike the Catholic church in Elbert, this transfer did not wait until the historic nature of the property could be officially declared. The Ramah property was simply adapted for use as a dwelling, thus attaining stature as a new form of vernacular. In Elbert, the owners restored

the building to retain its original, ecclesiastical form. In Ramah, decades of living have overtaken the clean lines of the façade. Bicycles are stored under the porch, as they could be at any other house. The gothic windows remain but are covered with plastic sheeting to keep out the cold of the winter wind. The white church of a distinctive community had become a domestic structure in a community now marketed as a part of the Colorado Springs metropolitan area.[10]

One of the few suburban photographs of *The New West* that can be specifically located is an image of a tract house under construction on Darwin Place in Colorado Springs. Like so many of Adams photographs in this terrain, the image captures the provisional, almost ethereal structure of the house in the foreground and the vacant middle ground that symbolized for him the enduring quality of the Western landscape. Aside from another structure in the distance, hinting at recent development, the house in the foreground exists without reference to a specific time, the particularities of place (the "Darwin Place" sign, without a cross street reference, hinting at irony),

Figure 16. Darwin Court, August 2006. Photograph by the author.

Figure 17. Clear-cut and burned, east of Arch Cape, Oregon. Photograph by Robert Adams. Copyright Robert Adams; courtesy Fraenkel Gallery, San Francisco, and Matthew Marks Gallery, New York.

or even a familiar topography. From the evidence of the world within the frame, the house does not use local materials—there are no trees visible. It is not built according to a vernacular tradition but is assembled as balloon-framed houses have been all over the United States. Adams seeks out the structure at this exposed moment as part of a progression from subdivided and graded land to a finished product within a suburban development identical to countless others. Pairing his photograph with a contemporary shot brackets a disarmingly ordinary but transformative appropriation of natural resources to create pleasing verdure where once only the vegetation of the Great Plains had existed. This is an environmental history—and, ironically, a cultural forgetfulness—that Adams pictures directly elsewhere in the West in images of clear cuts and gnarled or deformed trees.

Adams's images have a disarming clarity that leads to a savoring of the present moment and an understanding of the historic forces that have shaped the subject. Art and history, form and culture, are contained within his frame, enriching the epiphanies that punctuate Adams's account of his photographic practice. Such a moment of revelation inhabits the picture of a logged-over hillside in Oregon, part of his autobiographical exploration of the path of the Lewis and Clark

Expedition, *From the Missouri West.* "Clouds had obscured the mountains east of Arch Cape on the Oregon coast all day," he begins, "but in the late afternoon they opened up and I drove far up a logging road to a point where I was able, before night fell, to use the one film holder I had remaining" (Adams 1980). This moment of clarity resonates with Ansel Adams's description of the taking of "Moonrise over Hernandez, New Mexico," the first photograph that Robert Adams bought in 1966, at the beginning of his career (Adams 1989, 167). Both accounts contribute to the trope of the last shot of the day that runs through the history of photography. The elder Adams focuses on quickly maneuvering his photographic apparatus to capture the serendipitous alignment of subject, light source, and camera position that only an artist could perceive. Robert Adams ends his account by assessing the value of the photograph and the quality of the landscape it uniquely represents: "I value the picture because it reminds me of a time when I was allowed to be still—as we all are—and to see again, despite our follies, that the landscape retains its own stillness."

NOTES

My thanks to my colleague Frieda Knobloch and workshop participants at the 2008 meeting of the European Association for American Studies for commenting on earlier versions of this essay. The Yale University Art Museum (Joshua Chuang) and the Colorado Historical Society (Jennifer Vega) supplied exhibit-quality copies of some of the images.

1. This work is unpaginated.

2. Szarkowski's reading places Adams in the tradition of Walker Evans, the master of a deceptively simple yet revelatory documentary style. Later, Szarkowski (1978) would situate Adams among photographers whose work explored the visible world rather than centering on self-expression.

3. For a fuller exploration of this subject, see Poole 1999.

4. Wood was, in many ways, the epitome of a nationally noted local photographer. He photographed in every region of Colorado, with his wife, Mary, published literate surveys of particular terrain, and achieved enough national stature to rate encomiums from the noted photographic historian and fellow

Westerner Beaumont Newhall.

5. My reading of Adams's photograph is informed by correspondence with Denver architectural historian Rodd Wheaton (February 2008). For the history of historic preservation and the Skyline urban-development project, see Morley 2004.

6. His view of the suburbs thus differs from Bill Owens's collection of photographs, *Suburbia* (1973), that appeared during this period. Owens's approach was ethnographic, picturing people in their elaborately decorated homes and quoting from interviews with them. His juxtaposition between photographs and quotation and his use of visual irony revealed his political intent: he was conscious of exposing the strange customs of Nixon's silent majority. The 1999 reissue of the book contains later photographs, some in color, of a more mature, postresignation suburban landscape.

7. For a full account of the Santa Fe phenomenon, see Wilson 1997.

8. For example, Lewis Baltz, whose pictures of Park City, Utah, resembled Adams's photos, moved to Europe in the 1980s. Joe Deal, who photographed suburban development in Albuquerque, became an administrator at the Rhode Island School of Design. Nicholas Nixon remained in New England and turned to portraiture, most notably of his wife and her three sisters. Berndt and Hilla Becher were famous for exhaustive series of photographs of industrial buildings, worker housing, and landscapes in a number of countries in Western Europe and North America. Frank Gohlke, now a fellow at the Center for Creative Photography in Tucson, continued a focus on landscapes but on a national scale.

9. Records of the exhibit are housed at the Colorado Historical Society.

10. The Web site http://www.epodunk.com/dgi-bin/genInfo.php?locIndex=9659 (accessed July 23, 2008) is representative of a larger array of tourist and real estate sites.

WORKS CITED

Adams, Robert. 1970. *White Churches of the Plains.* Boulder: Colorado Associated University Press.

———. 1974a. *The Architecture and Art of Early Hispanic Colorado.* Boulder: Colorado Associated University Press.

———. 1974b. *The New West: Landscapes along the Colorado Front Range.* Boulder: Colorado Associated University Press.

———. 1974c. "Review of *Wisconsin Death Trip* by Michael Lesy." *Colorado Magazine* 51 (Fall): 349–51

———. 1977. *Denver: A Photographic Survey of the Metropolitan Area.* Boulder: Colorado Associated University Press.

———. 1980. *From the Missouri West.* New York: Aperture.

———. 1981. *Beauty in Photography: Essays in Defense of Traditional Values.* New York: Aperture.

———. 1989. *To Make It Home: Photographs of the American West.* New York: Aperture.

———. 1994. *Why People Photograph: Selected Essays and Reviews.* New York: Aperture.

Baltz, Louis. 1984. "Robert Adams: *Our Lives and Our Children*," *Artspace* 8 (Fall): 52–53.

———. 1989. "The Raft of the Medusa: American Photography in the 1980s," *Revu francaise d'etudes americaines* 39 (February): 71–83.

Boime, Albert. 1991. *The Magisterial Gaze: Manifest Destiny and American Landscape Painting, c. 1830–1865.* Washington, D.C.: Smithsonian Institution Press.

Bright, Deborah. 1984. "Once Upon a Time in the West: New Landscapes by Terry Husebye and Mark Klett," *Afterimage* 12 (December): 16–17.

Campbell, Kathleen. 1989. "The Landscape Photograph in the Postmodern Age," *SF Camerawork Quarterly* 16 (Summer-Fall): 11–15.

Carrillo, Richard, et al. 1999. *Context Study of the Hispanic Cultural Landscape of the Purgatoire/Apishapa: An Interdisciplinary Approach to the History, Architecture, Oral History, and Historical Archeology.* Trinidad, Colo.: Trinidad Historical Society.

Colorado Department of Transportation (CDOT). 1988. *Cultural Resource Survey of State Highway 12.*

Department of Defense (DoD). 1985. *Management Plan for the Fort Carson–Pinon Canyon Maneuver Site.*

Glassie, Henry. 1968. *Pattern in the Material Folk Culture of the Eastern United States.* Philadelphia: University of Pennsylvania Press.

Grundberg, Andy. 1984. "An Interview with John Szarkowski," Afterimage 12 (October): 12–13.

International Museum of Photography. 1975. The New Topographics: Photographs of a Man-altered Landscape. Rochester, N.Y.: International Museum of Photography.

Jackson, John B. 1992. "Foreword: Joe Deal and the Vernacular." In Joe Deal, Southern California Photographs, 1976–86. Albuquerque: University of New Mexico Press, 3–7.

Jeffrey, Ian. 2000. "Modernism and After 1914–2000: Photography." In Martin Kemp et al., The Oxford History of Western Art. New York: Oxford University Press.

Klett, Mark et al. 1984. Second View: The Rephotographic Survey Project. Albuquerque: University of New Mexico Press.

Miller, Alicia. 2005. "Making Land," Camerawork 32: 14–19.

Morley, Judy. 2004. "Making History: Historic Preservation and Civic Identity in Denver." In Giving Preservation a History: Histories of Historic Preservation in the United States, ed. Max Page and Randall Mason. New York: Routledge.

National Park Service (NPS). 1978. Plaza de San Luis de la Culebra National Historic District Nomination.

———. 1980. St. Mark's United Presbyterian Church of Elbert Nomination, 1980.

Orvell, Miles. 2003. American Photography. New York: Oxford University Press.

Owens, Bill. 1973. Suburbia. San Francisco: Straight Arrow Books.

Papageorge, Tod. 2001. "What We Bought." Yale University Art Gallery Bulletin, 83–111.

Phillips, Sarah. 1996. "To Subdue the Continent: Photographs of the Developing West." In Sarah Phillips et al., Crossing the Frontier: Photographs of the Developing West 1849 to the Present, 12–49. San Francisco: Chronicle Books.

Poole, Peter, ed. 1999. The Altered Landscape. Reno: Nevada Museum of Art in association with University of Nevada Press.

Rubenfien, Leo. 1976. "Recent American Photography," Creative Camera 147 (September): 294–95.

State of Colorado. 1994. Sacred Heart Parish Nomination. State Register of Historic Properties.

Szarkowski, John. 1978. Mirrors and Windows: American Photography since 1960. New York: Museum of Modern Art.

Weski, Thomas. 2005. "Robert Adams," Camera Austria 89: 9–21.

Wilson, Chris. 1997. The Myth of Santa Fe: Creating a Modern Regional Tradition. Albuquerque: University of New Mexico Press.

Wollheim, Peter. 1982. "The Aesthetics of Accommodation: Robert Adams," Vanguard 11 (September): 14–17.

Book Reviews

Abigail Van Slyck
A Manufactured Wilderness:
Summer Camps and the Shaping of
American Youth, 1890-1960

Minneapolis: University of Minnesota Press, 2006.
296 pages. Black-and-white photographs, plans,
appendix. ISBN 0-8166-4876-X, HB, $34.95

Review by Nora Pat Small

Do not look here for a nostalgic view of summer idylls by the lake and the campfire, weaving lanyards and telling ghost stories. Abigail Van Slyck has written another penetrating investigation of modern American society and culture, deftly combining the evidence afforded by the camps themselves with camp marketing materials, contemporary publications by childhood and camp professionals, and photographic evidence, and looking at it all through the lens of current studies of childhood, and the theories of play, race, and gender. Her specific goal was to discern "the role of summer camps in the social construction of modern childhood" (xxxii), but more broadly, Van Slyck sought in this work to ascertain the process by which "institutional priorities are translated into material form" (xxxi). Summer camps, then, are here examined both in their role as shapers of modern youth culture and as the repositories of cultural precepts of youth. Intertwined in this story of changing definitions of youth are changing perceptions of gender roles and whiteness. *A Manufactured Wilderness* offers an illuminating look at childhood and at landscapes that many of us probably thought we knew.

In six chapters, an introduction, and an epilogue, Van Slyck examines "major trends in camp planning practices between 1890 and 1960" and "their impact on the construction of childhood" (xxxvi). As she states explicitly in her introduction, this is not a chronological narrative. Rather, she moves from camp layout to program activities to physical and psychological health (and the sleeping quarters crucial to that health), from cooking and eating to gendered camp spaces and personal hygiene, and finally to Native American motifs and the complexities of race. Nevertheless, we clearly see the transformation from summer camps of the 1890–1920 era, which were quite consciously antimodernist (and hence reflective of their own modern, cultural milieu), and which saw and sought authenticity in the past, to an era of professional camp design and management that consciously assayed, through modern psychology, health programs, planning, and technology, to shape campers into certain types of people and to prepare them for modern, white, middle-class life. In her epilogue, Van Slyck briefly examines architectural modernism at camps, and reiterates her point that architectural aesthetics are not an indicator of the presence or absence of modern attitudes. The most rustic youth camps of the mid-twentieth century still embodied and promoted "modern conceptions of children and childhood, which emphasized reforming gender roles while reinforcing racial hierarchies" (224), and the most modern camp architects "embraced the 'primitive builder' as their paragon" (220).

In the last quarter of the nineteenth century, North Americans dwelled in ever increasing numbers in urban, industrial communities. Wilderness, now safely enclosed in designated parks and no longer a threat to civilized society, came to be ever more revered. The problem was that modern culture threatened to emasculate young men, rob them of their health, and turn them into a generation of consumers, if not ne'er-do-wells, no matter if they lived in the city or the suburbs. The solution was to find, or create, some semblance of wilderness close to urban areas where these youths could clear their lungs and their heads, and learn to do for themselves what modern life had robbed them of doing. The question of how that "wilderness," usually some patch of formerly cultivated land, was created, shaped, and reimagined is a central part of Van Slyck's study. As the definitions of childhood changed over the decades, so too did the threats to it, and the camp environment had to respond. Over the period covered here, camps evolved from simple clearings where campers could put up tents and perhaps swim in a nearby lake to carefully engineered spaces that protected children, now boys and girls, while trying to give them a sense of freedom from certain modern constraints. The balance between leaving civilization behind and adhering to civilized behavior was a tricky one to strike, and camp designers, directors, proponents, and participants were all involved in searching for it.

Van Slyck's illustrations, particularly the historic photographs, are central to her analysis, and they are carefully and clearly reproduced here. Although she visited many camps in the course of her research, those environments, for reasons made clear in this book, are subject to considerable change. The photographs, camp brochures, and period camp maps that she unearthed serve both as historical record and as material culture. As material culture, the illustrations are subject to all of the analytical tools at the disposal of cultural historians, and Van Slyck wields those tools expertly. As she points out, the photos and brochures "communicate a great deal about how camps constructed a version of childhood that was inevitably complicated by interrelated ideas about gender, class, and race" (xxxiii). The photos are both formal and informal. In some instances they catch the campers in action in spaces that no longer exist; in others they and the brochures capture the hopes and aspirations of the camp promoters and of the parents who responded by sending their children to camp.

Summer camps are one of those richly layered arenas of cultural activity that are easily overlooked because of their ubiquity and apparent simplicity. Scholars of vernacular architecture and material culture are well aware of the wealth of knowledge we can glean from seemingly mute ordinary landscapes and artifacts. When examined within the context of contemporary documents—that is, within the carefully or haphazardly archived landscape of photographic image and marketing materials—even ephemeral landscapes such as summer camps can be mined for cultural insights. Van Slyck reminds us how ephemeral meaning can be, too—shifting or being lost with changes in perspective or the passage of time. In recent years, scholars increasingly have turned their attention to the more recent past, shedding light on our current cultural assumptions or blind spots in the process. Race, gender, and childhood are certainly still flashpoints for modern society. Cultural historians, architectural historians, historic preservationists, and others, former campers or not, will find their understanding of those issues in modern America considerably enriched. *A Manufactured Wilderness* was rightly honored with the 2008 Abbott Lowell Cummings Award from the Vernacular Architecture Forum.

J. Myrick Howard

Buying Time for Heritage: How to Save an Endangered Historic Property

Preservation North Carolina
Chapel Hill: University of North Carolina Press, 2007.
160 pages. 64 color and 35 black-and-white illustrations, notes, index.
ISBN 978-0-8078-5868-4. $25.00

Review by Robbie D. Jones

North Carolina is well known for its vernacular architecture, from rural farmhouses and tobacco barns to small town schools and industrial mill villages. Since 1939, preserving these historic places has been the mission of Preservation North Carolina (PNC), which established the nation's first statewide revolving fund for endangered properties in the late 1970s. Since then, PNC has become perhaps the nation's premiere statewide nonprofit for historic preservation advocacy and leadership.

Buying Time for Heritage explores PNC's experience in preserving endangered properties. Written by J. Myrick Howard, the nonprofit's president since 1978, the book provides a broad overview of PNC's work with nearly five hundred historic properties across the Tarheel State. Howard shares the organization's remarkable story in an engaging writing style that is easy to read and compelling. He gives detailed examples of particular case studies that elaborate his points and show how the group's strategy worked (or didn't work in some cases).

Howard shares how PNC has been so successful in accomplishing its mission, resulting in more than $200 million in private investment across the state thus far. Far more importantly, Howard provides the reader with an in-depth look at how other organizations can learn from PNC and what they can do to preserve endangered historic properties in their own areas. He lists inventive solutions,

what pitfalls to avoid, and precisely how to go about saving endangered properties.

Howard notes that "fundamentally successful historic preservation is an exercise in dealing with real estate" (9). Moreover, successful preservation organizations, such as PNC, have developed considerable expertise in real estate. Creating museums is no longer the preservation solution of choice, although sometimes it is a viable option; PNC owns four museums itself, including the Bellamy Mansion in Wilmington. Today's preservationists, however, are more likely to talk of economic impact, community revitalization, revolving funds, tax laws, heritage tourism, and zoning, rather than how to open a museum.

Succeeding chapters detail strategies for dealing with real estate, from criteria for selecting properties to how to protect the property legally with covenants, easements, and so forth. As Howard explains, buying time is the most important thing that a preservation organization can do to save an endangered property. This seasoned guide provides insight into methods to maximize efforts to secure time in order for creative preservation solutions to be developed, for deals to be brokered, and for partnerships to be created.

However, one of the biggest problems for most preservation organizations is lack of capital. Lack of funding and risk aversion typically prevents organizations from getting involved in real estate and "buying time." This fear is unfounded, according to Howard. To answer the doubters, he provides a comprehensive listing of creative alternatives for acquiring historic property, without having much, if any, capital. These include options, donations, bargain sales, transfers, leases, loans, life estates, preservation easements, contract provisions, as well as feasibility studies and fundraising. He also gives examples of how each alternative has been implemented in North Carolina.

Howard then discusses the pros and cons of buying historic properties, typically the last resort after considering the other alternatives. PNC asks two simple questions before buying property: Is the property truly significant? And will its preservation spur additional renovations? If the answers are yes, then they move forward. If the answers are no, then it is probably wise to let the property go and concentrate on another, more viable project.

One of the most compelling parts of the book is Howard's advice on marketing endangered properties, particularly unusual properties such as historic schools and industrial mill villages. PNC has become especially savvy at marketing its properties and with more than thirty years practice the organization has much experience to offer other groups. From how to use the media to how to choose a spokesperson, Howard gives detailed pointers on how to go about not only marketing historic properties, but marketing historic preservation in general.

Architectural historians may cringe to learn that the general public would rather hear about ghost stories than original Federal-style mantels, but telling a building's story requires drama and creativity, while still conveying the facts accurately. Who lived here? What happened here? Why is this building significant? Why does saving it matter? Of course, architectural significance is important to preserving historic places, but "the challenge is to get human interest out of an inanimate object" (51).

The book also contains much technical information, including sample documents like purchase contracts, covenants, rehabilitation agreements, and preservation easements. These documents are also available on the PNC Web site (www.presnc.org), which serves as undoubtedly the organization's most important marketing and media tool for accomplishing its mission. The Internet has taken local preservation advocacy and real estate marketing to a national level. While PNC's 4,100 members are primarily from North Carolina, buyers of its properties come from all over the country. Other marketing tools include postcards, brochures, posters, magazines, and traditional realtors.

As described in the book, successful his-toric preservation depends on people, relationships, and partnerships. Howard spends substantial time on these topics, particularly on relationships between board and staff members since these people are what make a nonprofit organization successful. Board and staff must work as a team or risk failure. Successful organizations also have long-term leadership, especially professional staff; without continuity of leadership, donors lose faith and without donors, an organization suffers financial instability. But board and staff cannot do this work alone; they must engage partnerships with city and state agencies, land trusts, other historic preservation organizations, community groups, foundations, and so on.

Howard closes by stressing how important people and strong leadership are to the success of PNC. As he explains, people are the "social capital" of the organization and its mission. Howard suggests that to be an effective preservation leader, one must have the ability to communicate a vision, connect long-term goals of preservation with immediate community needs, to work with real estate, and to persevere after defeat. Finding and retaining these types of people is vital to the success of the organization.

Buying Time for Heritage is extremely well written, practical, and readable. Howard has a knack for explaining the complicated world of real estate in a way that even a novice can comprehend. A North Carolina native, he also provides a succinct historical context for the properties that he uses as case studies, which helps explain why these unique and "difficult properties" truly are significant and worth saving.

The book features nearly one hundred illustrations, which show how "far gone" some buildings were before being saved by PNC. There are many before-and-after photographs of rehabbed properties. However, I would have preferred even more images and illustrations, particularly architectural drawings of how to renovate historic floor plans for modern uses, how to create proper modern additions for kitchens and baths, and master plans for industrial mill villages. These would have been useful additions to the otherwise masterfully written text. (Perhaps these could be added to the PNC Web site to accompany existing documents on replacing historic windows, etc.) This was the book's only shortcoming.

In conclusion, many states are in desperate need of more preservation leaders like J. Myrick Howard and preservation organizations like PNC. We stand by and lament the loss of countless endangered historic properties by throwing up our hands and exclaiming, "what can we do?" Too often, our half-measures are too little, too late, and our beloved endangered properties—whether the once grand plantation or the vacant factory on the wrong side of the tracks—fall prey to the wrecking ball. Thankfully, Howard and PNC have provided this extraordinary how-to book that shows us exactly what we can do. For that we are truly grateful. Hopefully, this book and PNC's success will inspire more of us to use these innovative and proven solutions to achieve our common goals.

Annmarie Adams
Medicine by Design, The Architect and the Modern Hospital, 1893–1943

Minneapolis: University of Minnesota Press, 2008. 240 pages. 90 black-and-white photographs, notes, bibliography, illustrations, credits, index. ISBN 978-0-8166-5113-9, $82.50

Review by Jenny Young

Medicine by Design focuses on the building and development of the Royal Victoria Hospital in Montreal from 1893 to 1943, a period that includes World War I and the interwar years. To this specific context of a single place over time, Professor Annmarie Adams brings a synthetic methodology, investigating the broadest set of cultural artifacts (including the buildings themselves, their plans, historic postcards and photographs, and popular press advertisements) as well as written texts. The book is not a chronology but a set of five linked essays that use the evidence of material culture to uncover the influence on hospital design of "Patients," "Nurses," and "Architects and Doctors" (the titles of three of the chapters).

Eighteen ninety-three was the year the much-acclaimed Royal Victoria Hospital (designed by Henry Saxon Snell) opened on the slopes of Mount Royal overlooking Montreal. Fifty years later, in 1943, Edward F. Stevens, partner of the firm of Stevens and Lee (experts in hospital design and architects of two additional buildings to the same hospital complex, the Ross Memorial Pavilion [1916] and the Maternity Hospital [1926]) retired. Within these fifty years, significant shifts happened in hospital architecture. These changes have been typically attributed to developments in medical technology, but in *Medicine by Design*, Professor Adams challenges that assumption and examines the influence on hospital design by architects with expertise, factors of social class, and cultural attitudes about gender.

During these fifty years, hospital architecture became a specialty. Hospitals went from being designed like other large civic institutions, such as prisons and schools, where plan and exterior were equally important, to being designed specifically as hospitals, where the organization of the floor plan became the primary focus. Architects went from being generalists for civic institutions to being hospital specialists who worked with medical experts and traveled in Canada, the United States, and Europe to gain additional exposure to contemporary hospital design. The two generations of architects featured in this book, Henry Saxon Snell and Edward Fletcher Stevens, built their reputations on hospital work. They increased their expertise by traveling in North America as well as in Europe, studying contemporary hospitals there. Snell began his career in Europe, and Stevens traveled there and brought back lantern slides

to use in both winning commissions and in developing designs. They worked with physicians and medical experts as coauthors and consultants to understand what was needed in a modern hospital. Stevens developed his expertise from decades of close observation, writing of the value of "a long series of visits, oft repeated, to institutions known to be satisfactory" (Adams, quoting Stevens, 102). Both architects wrote books and articles, gave conference presentations on "best practices" for hospital design, and often featured their own designs. Their interest and focus on hospitals increased their expertise and snowballed into winning more commissions, further augmenting their knowledge. This kind of reflective practice remains a model today for architecture specialization.

Over this period, hospital plans changed from pavilion plans with rectangular open wards to "block plans" with double-loaded corridors and isolated patient rooms on each side. The medical explanation for this shift lies with the acceptance of the theory that disease is transmitted by germs, so isolating patients is better than having them housed in the same space. The pavilion plan had developed at the time of the miasma theory of disease, where disease was believed to exist in putrid air, so easily supervised, open, narrow wards with high ceilings were carefully spaced to maximize light and air. Professor Adams contributes to scholarship that is debunking this simplistic interpretation. She shows evidence that the pavilion plan persisted well after germ theory was accepted and develops arguments that as hospitals changed from places to care for the indigent to places to cure the sick, they needed to reach out to the rich and middle classes. These new clients would benefit from new medical technologies and improved methods, and could pay for them, but they would only come if facilities were home-like or similar to luxurious hotels. Adams argues that being able to provide single, luxurious patient rooms, separate from the movement sequences for the poor, was a primary motivation in developing the block plan.

Reaching out to the public included designing places for women to have babies and for children. Hospital designs also developed to include outpatient services for people to access the new technologies without needing to spend the night. Other new buildings made places to house and educate nurses on the hospital campuses. These design innovations encouraged middle-class women to enter the nursing profession while at the same time "protecting" them from independent living, offering evidence of cultural attitudes about gender at the time.

Professor Adams explains that while hospitals over this period introduced all kinds of modern elements, their exterior forms did not reflect this. As modern buildings, their construction was cost-efficient and practical and included centralized heating and cooling plants (versus chimneys for each room), ventilating shafts, microleveling elevators, fireproof construction, acoustic insulation from the noise of the new urban context, factory-efficient kitchens and laundries, car drop-offs and parking, nurse call systems, antiseptic materials and equipment, daylighting and electric lighting, built-in instrument cabinets, refrigerators, blanket warmers, and drying closets. At the same time, their exteriors continued to evoke historical styles and traditional materials. The 1893 Royal Victoria Hospital looked like a Scottish castle, linked to the vernacular buildings of nearby McGill University and in deference to the historical roots of its donors. The new buildings by Stevens followed in the tradition of historic styles, although their inspiration included mansions and luxury hotels. Professor Adams points out that with some exceptions (notably Aalto's Paimio Sanitarium in Finland), the International Style did not dominate the exteriors of hospitals until after World War II. She suggests this conservatism reflects concerns that the hospital's image be familiar and comfortable for the patient and visitor, a counterpoint to antiseptic environments and medical technologies, an attitude that has recurred in today's hospital design.

One example from the book—the transformation of the places for surgery—illustrates the complexities of institutional development over time. The first surgery settings were designed as day-lit theaters, where medical students could observe the exciting new procedures and technologies in use. Large in size, prominently located and accessed directly from outside the building, these theaters welcomed the public as well as the professionals. As the drama of surgery as a spectacle diminished and the numbers of surgeries increased, more rooms were built of a smaller and standard size, and their location was internal to the hospital, with access to support facilities. Over these fifty years, daylighting operating rooms became a point of conflict between architects and medical practitioners. Architects wanted to provide daylight and windows, while practitioners wanted to eliminate glare and the difficulties of uneven lighting. Professor Adams includes a photograph showing the windows of an operating room covered with whitewash to diffuse or eliminate the sunlight. After this period and post–World War II, hospitals developed sophisticated air conditioning systems and electric lighting, and windows disappeared from operating rooms. Only today is the pendulum swinging back. Windows are again recurring in operating rooms because of biophilic arguments for staff well-being and effectiveness, and made possible because of multiple contemporary mechanisms to control daylighting.

One of the wonderful things about this well-designed book is its rich set of illustrations. To the reader's delight, architectural drawings (plans, sections, elevations, and even details), historic photographs of exterior views and interior rooms, historic postcards and advertisements from the popular press, as well as contemporary photographs are integrated into the stories of the text. For those unfamiliar with Montreal, a map locating the Royal Vic and the other hospitals would be useful. Although Professor Adams explains this book is not a chronology of hospital design, a timeline of the hospital projects cited correlated with the writings and travels of the architects Snell and Stevens would contribute that perspective.

Medicine by Design is an impeccably researched book. With a narrow focus that is investigated with great breadth, Professor Adams's hospital study examines how change in hospital design is not simply the result of medical advancements but of complex and dynamic social and cultural factors. It contributes to reassessments of the value of interwar buildings to our civic heritage. Professor Adams tantalizes us at the end with a big question about the historic preservation of these hospital buildings. Civic monuments on significant urban sites, these buildings are often at the core of medical complexes that are constantly renovating and expanding to meet current and future health-care standards. Obsolete for medical functions, can they still be saved, restored, or rehabilitated for appropriate uses? She makes the case that they should be.

Contributors

Dr. Iain Bruce is an architect with a career-long interest in the flexibility of timber-frame construction and is recently a coauthor of a patent for a stressed-skin duocoque construction appropriate to the affordable housing market. Whilst teaching at the Robert Gordon University in Aberdeen (Scotland), he set out on an ironic quest for a lost tradition of timber-frame construction in an attempt to understand the phenomenon of a variety of Victorian timber buildings in the local area. In view of the richness of the material he converted his early studies into a PhD, which produced unexpected results. Iain has been an occasional contributor to the *Sunday Times Scotland* and Radio Scotland on architecture and its context in contemporary Scottish culture.

Howard Davis is professor of architecture at the University of Oregon and coeditor of *Buildings & Landscapes*. His professional work and research are concerned with housing, the social frameworks of building production, and urban districts. He is the author of *The Culture of Building*, coauthor of *The Production of Houses*, and is completing a manuscript on urban buildings that combine commercial and residential uses. He serves on the editorial boards of the *Journal of Architectural Education*, *Urban Morphology*, and *Traditional Dwellings and Settlements Review*.

Jay D. Edwards is professor of anthropology and director of the Fred B. Kniffen Cultural Resources Laboratory at Louisiana State University. His recent coauthored books include *A Creole Lexicon: Architecture, Landscape, People* (with Nicolas Kariouk, 2004) and *Old South Baton Rouge: A Community Portrait* (with Petra Munro Hendry, 2009).

Robbie D. Jones holds a professional degree in architecture from the University of Tennessee at Knoxville and a master's in historic preservation from Middle Tennessee State University. He has published and contributed to several architectural history books and is editor of the *SESAH Newsletter* for the Southeast Chapter of the Society of Architectural Historians. He works as a senior architectural historian in the Nashville, Tennessee, office of Parsons Brinckerhoff, an international consulting firm based in New York City.

Whitney A. Martinko is a graduate student in the Department of History at the University of Virginia. She is working on a dissertation about the relationship between history and progress on the early American landscape.

Sally McMurry is professor of history at Penn State University. She is author of *From Sugar Camps to Star Barns* (2001), *Transforming Rural Life* (1995), and *Families and Farmhouses in Nineteenth-century America* (1988).

Louis P. Nelson is associate professor of architectural history at the University of Virginia and coeditor of *Buildings & Landscapes*. His research focuses on the everyday architecture of early

America, specifically the architecture of the early American South and its relationship to the Caribbean. He also writes on questions of the sacred in space and is the editor of a volume of essays entitled *American Sanctuary: Understanding Sacred Spaces*.

Eric Sandeen is professor of American studies at the University of Wyoming, where he has directed the program since 1982. He is the author of *Picturing an Exhibition: The Family of Man and 1950s America* (1995) and numerous articles on photography and American culture. He is working on a project, tentatively entitled "The Ruins of Modernity," that relates the work of contemporary photographers to ruined landscapes in American metropolitan areas.

Nora Pat Small is professor of history and coordinator of the MA program in Historical Administration at Eastern Illinois University in Charleston. She holds a PhD from Boston University and a Master of Architectural History from the University of Virginia. She is the author of *Beauty and Convenience: Architecture and Order in the New Republic* and is currently researching lighthouses of the early American republic.

Jenny Young is professor of architecture at the University of Oregon. She teaches the history and evolving design of buildings for health care. Her creative practice includes programming and design of health care facilities in rural communities in Oregon.

Join the Vernacular Architecture Forum

Please enroll me as a member of the Vernacular Architecture Forum. I understand that membership entitles me to one issue of the annual fall journal *Buildings & Landscapes,* and four issues of the *Vernacular Architecture Newsletter,* and that my newsletter subscription will begin with the next issue after the receipt of my dues. Membership also includes enrollment in our online listserv and members receive priority mailing for conferences (since field tours fill quickly).

*All receipts above the basic membership levels will be applied toward the giving category of your choice (please check one):

☐ Student and Professional Support Fund (including grants, fellowships, and awards)
☐ Publications Fund (including *B&L, VAN,* and special publications)
☐ VAF Endowment Fund

☐ Active, $45   ☐ Household, $65   ☐ Institution, $75   ☐ Contributing, $75

☐ Patron, $150   ☐ Lifetime, $2,000   ☐ Multiple Year _____ years x $45

☐ Student, $25 I am currently enrolled at _____

_____
NAME

_____
ADDRESS

_____
CITY   STATE/PROVINCE   ZIP

_____
COUNTRY

_____
EMAIL

☐ Check here if you do not wish to take part in our online listserv

Note: Memberships must be paid by check or money order in U.S. funds. VAF does not currently accept credit cards.

Please consider an additional gift in support of VAF programs.
$ _____ Student and Professional Support Fund
$ _____ Publications Fund
$ _____ VAF Endowment Fund

Please fill out this form and mail with payment to: Gabrielle M. Lanier, Secretary
                                                           Vernacular Architecture Forum
                                                           P.O. Box 1511
                                                           Harrisonburg, VA 22803-1511

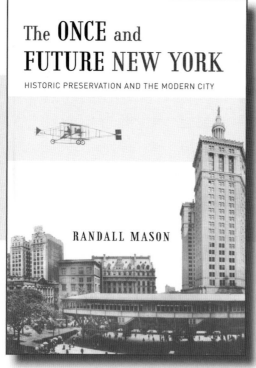

The ONCE and FUTURE NEW YORK

HISTORIC PRESERVATION AND THE MODERN CITY

RANDALL MASON

$27.95 paper · $84.00 cloth · 344 pages

Uncovering the roots of America's historic preservation movement.

"Recognizing that their city is a very special historic place, New Yorkers have long fought to keep their heritage intact and alive. In fact, as this eye-opening book points out, dedicated preservationists were leaving their mark on the nation's largest city long before the wrecking-balls and bulldozers smashed into Penn Station. Chronicling the challenges that these visionaries confronted between 1890 and 1920, Randall Mason details their insistence that they were not enemies of 'progress'—and their important role in shaping today's dynamic preservation movement. It's a story well worth hearing."

—Richard Moe

Also of interest:

"Andrew Shanken offers a fascinating, compelling, and altogether convincing new lens for understanding the burst of creative and visionary design that accompanied America's engagement in the Second World War." —**Barry Bergdoll**

"By making resourceful use of oral testimony as that period recedes from living memory, Shanken demonstrates the historical imagination at its best. In every respect, this is an original and splendidly written contribution by one of the field's most promising young scholars." —**Michael J. Lewis**

$24.95 paper · $75.00 cloth · 264 pages
Architecture, Landscape, and American Culture Series

University of Minnesota Press · www.upress.umn.edu · 800-621-2736

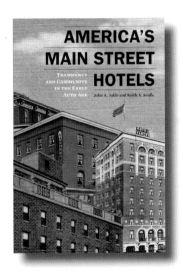
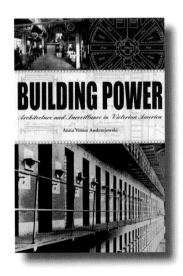